Beginning Rust

From Novice to Professional

Carlo Milanesi

Apress®

Beginning Rust: From Novice to Professional

Carlo Milanesi
Bergamo, Italy

ISBN-13 (pbk): 978-1-4842-3467-9
https://doi.org/10.1007/978-1-4842-3468-6

ISBN-13 (electronic): 978-1-4842-3468-6

Library of Congress Control Number: 2018935885

Managing Director, Apress Media LLC: Welmoed Spahr
Acquisitions Editor: Steve Anglin
Development Editor: Matthew Moodie
Coordinating Editor: Mark Powers

Cover designed by eStudioCalamar

Cover image designed by Freepik (www.freepik.com)

Distributed to the book trade worldwide by Springer Science+Business Media New York, 233 Spring Street, 6th Floor, New York, NY 10013. Phone 1-800-SPRINGER, fax (201) 348-4505, e-mail orders-ny@springer-sbm.com, or visit www.springeronline.com. Apress Media, LLC is a California LLC and the sole member (owner) is Springer Science + Business Media Finance Inc (SSBM Finance Inc). SSBM Finance Inc is a **Delaware** corporation.

For information on translations, please e-mail editorial@apress.com; for reprint, paperback, or audio rights, please email bookpermissions@springernature.com.

Apress titles may be purchased in bulk for academic, corporate, or promotional use. eBook versions and licenses are also available for most titles. For more information, reference our Print and eBook Bulk Sales web page at http://www.apress.com/bulk-sales.

Any source code or other supplementary material referenced by the author in this book is available to readers on GitHub via the book's product page, located at www.apress.com/9781484234679. For more detailed information, please visit http://www.apress.com/source-code.

Printed on acid-free paper

Table of Contents

About the Author

Carlo Milanesi is a professional software developer and expert in C++, graphics programming, and GUI design. He graduated from the State University of Milan and worked in the financial and CAD/CAM software industries. He enjoys writing software in Smalltalk and Rust.

About the Technical Reviewer

 **Massimo Nardone** has more than 24 years of experience in Security, Web/Mobile development, Cloud, and IT Architecture. His true IT passions are Security and Android.

He has been programming and teaching how to program with Android, Perl, PHP, Java, VB, Python, C/C++, and MySQL for more than 20 years.

He holds a Master of Science degree in Computing Science from the University of Salerno, Italy.

He has worked as a Project Manager, Software Engineer, Research Engineer, Chief Security Architect, Information Security Manager, PCI/SCADA Auditor, and Senior Lead IT Security/Cloud/SCADA Architect for many years.

Technical skills include Security, Android, Cloud, Java, MySQL, Drupal, Cobol, Perl, Web and Mobile development, MongoDB, D3, Joomla, Couchbase, C/C++, WebGL, Python, Pro Rails, Django CMS, Jekyll, Scratch, etc.

He has worked as a visiting lecturer and supervisor for exercises at the Networking Laboratory of the Helsinki University of Technology (Aalto University). He holds four international patents (PKI, SIP, SAML, and Proxy areas).

He currently works as the Chief Information Security Officer (CISO) for Cargotec Oyj and is a member of the ISACA Finland chapter board.

Preface

This book teaches a beginner how to program with the Rust programming language in an easy, step-by-step manner.

Only a basic knowledge of programming is required, preferably in the C or C++ languages. Let's say that to understand this text it's enough to know what an integer is and what a floating-point number is, and to distinguish identifiers from string literals.

A command-line environment is assumed, like a Unix or Linux shell, Mac OS Terminal, or Windows Command Prompt.

Please note that this book does not cover everything needed to develop professional programs in Rust. It just teaches the difficult concepts needed to understand more advanced texts, like the official tutorial of the language.

CHAPTER 1

Printing on the Terminal

In this chapter, you will learn:

- How to write and run your first program in the Rust Language

- How to output texts and numbers on the terminal

- How to write a small script that makes more readable the output of the compiler

- How to write comments in your code

How to Start

The smallest valid Rust program is:

```rust
fn main(){}
```

Of course, it does nothing. It just defines an empty function named "main". By "function" we mean a set of instructions that does something and that has been given a name.

The "fn" word is shorthand for "function". The "main" word is the name of the function. The round parentheses contain the possible arguments of the function; in this case there are no arguments. To close, the braces contain the possible statements that comprise the body of the function; in this case there is no statement.

When a program written in Rust is run, its "main" function is executed. If there is no "main" function, then it isn't a complete program; it may be a library, though.

© Carlo Milanesi 2018
C. Milanesi, *Beginning Rust*, https://doi.org/10.1007/978-1-4842-3468-6_1

To run this program, complete the following actions:

- Install the package containing the Rust compiler and its utilities. A compiler can be downloaded for free from the website `https://www.rust-lang.org`. Linux, Windows, or macOS platforms, with processor architecture x86 (32-bit) or x86-64 (64-bit), are available. For each platform, there are three versions: "stable", "beta", and "nightly". The "stable" version is recommended; it is the oldest, but also the most tested and the one less likely to change. All of these program versions should be used from the command line of a console. After installation, to check which version is installed, type at a command line (with uppercase V): `rustc -V`.

- Create or choose a folder where your Rust exercises will be stored and, using any text editor, create in that folder a file named `"main.rs"`, having the above contents.

- At a command line, in the folder, type: `rustc main.rs`. The prompt should be printed almost immediately, after having created a file named `"main"` (in a Windows environment, it will be named `"main.exe"`). Actually, the `"rustc"` command has correctly compiled the specified file. That is, it has read it and generated the corresponding machine code, and it has stored this machine code in a file in the same folder.

- At the command line, if in a Windows environment, type: `main` For other operating systems, type: `./main`. You just run the program generated before, but the prompt should be printed immediately, as this program does nothing.

Hello, World!

Let's see how to print some text on the terminal. Change the program of the previous section to the following:

```
fn main() {
    print!("Hello, world!");
}
```

If it is compiled and run as before, it prints: `"Hello, world!"`

Notice that the newly added line contains eight syntax items, aka "tokens". Let's examine them:

- `print`: It is the name of a macro defined in the Rust standard library.

- `!`: It specifies that the preceding name indicates a macro. Without such a symbol, `print` would instead indicate a function. There is no such function in the Rust standard library, and so you would get a compilation error. A macro is a thing similar to a function - it's some Rust code to which a name is associated. By using this name, you ask to insert such code in this point.

- `(`: It starts the list of arguments of the macro.

- `"`: it starts the literal string.

- `Hello, world!`: It is the content of the literal string.

- `"`: It ends the literal string.

- `)`: It ends the list of the arguments of the macro.

- `;`: It ends the statement.

Let's examine the meaning of the "literal string" phrase. The word "string" means "finite sequence of characters, possibly including spaces and punctuation". The word "literal" means "with a value specified directly in source code." Therefore a "literal string" is a "finite sequence of characters (possibly including spaces and punctuation) specified directly in source code".

The `print` macro simply inserts some code that prints on the terminal the text that is received as an argument.

Rust always distinguishes between uppercase and lowercase letters - it's "case sensitive". For all characters that are outside literal strings and comments, if you replace some uppercase letter with a lowercase one or conversely, typically you get a compilation error, or anyway a program with a different behavior. Instead, making such errors inside literal strings always allows a successful compilation, but it's likely the behavior of the program will be different.

For example:

```
fn Main() {}
```

If you compile this program, you get the compilation error "main function not found", as no main function (with a lowercase m) is defined in the program.

From now on, except when specified, we will assume the example code will be inside the braces of the "main" function, and so the braces and the text preceding them will be omitted.

Printing Combinations of Literal Strings

Instead of using a single literal string, you can print several of them, even in a single statement. In this way:

```
print!("{}, {}!", "Hello", "world");
```

This statement, put inside the braces of the "main" function, will print again: "Hello, world!".

In this case, the print macro receives three arguments, separated by commas. All three arguments are literal strings. The first string, though, contains two pairs of braces ({}). They are placeholders, indicating the positions in which to insert the other two strings.

So, the macro scans the arguments after the first one, and for each of them it looks inside the first argument for a pair of braces, and replaces them with the current argument.

This resembles the following C language statement:

```
printf("%s, %s!", "Hello", "world");
```

But there is an important difference. If you try to compile

```
print!("{}, !", "Hello", "world");
```

you get the compilation error "argument never used", as the arguments of the macro after the first one are more numerous than the placeholders inside the first argument; that is, there is some argument that doesn't have any corresponding placeholder.

And if you try to compile

```
print!("{}, {}!", "Hello");
```

4

you get a compilation error too, as the placeholders inside the first argument are more numerous than the arguments after the first argument; that is, there is a placeholder that doesn't have any corresponding argument.

Instead, the corresponding statements in the C language do not raise compilation errors, but instead cause the compiled program to crash or misbehave.

Printing Several Lines of Text

So far, we wrote programs that print only one line. But a single statement can print several lines; in this way:

```
print!("First line\nSecond line\nThird line\n");
```

This will print:

```
First line
Second line
Third line
```

The sequence of characters \n, where n stands for "new line", is transformed by the compiler into the character sequence that represents the line terminator for the currently used operating system.

Given that it is very common to go to a new line only once for every printing statement, and just at the end of the statement, another macro, "println", has been added to the Rust standard library. It's used in this way:

```
println!("text of the line");
```

This statement is equivalent to:

```
print!("text of the line\n");
```

Calling this println macro (whose name is to be read "print line") is equivalent to calling print with the same arguments, and then outputting a line terminator.

Printing Integer Numbers

If we want to print an integer number, we can type:

```
print!("My number: 140");
```

or, using a placeholder and an additional argument:

```
print!("My number: {}", "140");
```

or, removing the quotes around the second argument:

```
print!("My number: {}", 140);
```

All these statements will print: "My number: 140".

In the last statement, the second argument is not a literal string, but it is a "literal integer number", or, for short, a "literal integer".

The integers are another data type, with respect to strings.

Even for integers, the print macro is able to use them to replace the corresponding placeholder inside its first argument.

In fact, the compiler interprets the string 140 contained in the source code as a number expressed in decimal format, it generates the equivalent number in binary format, and then it saves it into the executable program.

At runtime, the program takes such number in binary format, it transforms it into the string "140", using the decimal notation, then it replaces the placeholder with that string, so generating the string to print, and finally it sends the string to the terminal.

This procedure explains, for example, why if the following program is written:

```
print!("My number: {}", 000140);
```

the compiler generates exactly the same executable program generated before. Actually, when the source string 000140 is converted to the binary format, the leading zeros are ignored.

The argument types may be mixed too. This statement

```
print!("{}: {}", "My number", 140);
```

will print the same line as before. Here the first placeholder corresponds to a literal string, while the second one to a literal integer.

Command-Line Script

The rustc command shown above has a drawback: it prints all the errors it finds in your code in the order in which it finds them. Well, often your code will contain many syntax errors, and you should process them from the first one to the last one. But after the compiler has finished printing the errors, you are faced with the new prompt preceded by the last error found. So, you have to scroll back to the first error.

A way to improve this situation is to use a command-line script, whose syntax depends on the operating system.

In a Linux system, you can put the following lines in a new script file:

```
clear
rustc $* --color always 2>&1 | more
```

In a Windows system, you can put the following three lines in a .BAT file:

```
@echo off
cls
rustc %* --color always 2>&1 | more
```

If the script file is named, say, rs (rs.bat on Windows), to compile a file named main.rs you can type:

```
rs main.rs
```

This script first clears the screen, then runs the rustc compiler with all the arguments you give to it. If the compilation is successful, or if it generates less than a screenful of error messages, it behaves like a normal run of rustc.

Otherwise, it fills the screen with error messages, and then stops, and shows the message --More-- at the bottom of the terminal screen. At this point you can press:

- The Enter key, to advance by one line.

- The Space key, to advance by one screenful.

- The Q key (for "quit"), to abort printing error messages, and get back to the command prompt.

Comments

Write the following code

```
// This program
// prints a number.
print!("{}", 34); // thirty-four
/* print!("{}", 80);
*/
```

that will print 34.

The first two lines start with a pair of slashes "//". Such a pair of characters indicates the start of a "line comment," ending at the end of the line. To write a comment on several lines, the pair of slashes must be repeated at every line of the comment, as in the second line of the program above.

Rust programmers use to leave a blank just after the double slash, to improve readability.

As it appears in the third line, a line comment may start after a statement, usually separated by at least one blank.

There is another kind of comment, exemplified in the fourth and fifth lines. Such a comment starts with the character pair "/*" and ends with the pair "*/"; it may extend on several lines, and so it is named "multi-line comment."

Rust programmers usually avoid the multi-line comment in production code, using only single line comments, and use multi-line comments only to exclude temporarily some code from compilation.

Rust comments look identical to modern C language comments. In fact, there is an important difference between Rust comments and C comments: Rust comments may be nested, and they must be nested correctly.

```
/* This is /* a valid*/
comment, even /* if /* it contains
comments*/ inside */itself.   */
```

```
/* This /* instead is not allowed in Rust,
while in C is tolerated (but it may generate a warning).*/
```

CHAPTER 2

Doing Arithmetic

In this chapter, you will learn:

- How to compute an arithmetic operation between integer numbers or between floating-point numbers
- How to write a program containing several statements
- How to print strings in several lines

Adding Integer Numbers

Let's see how to compute the sum of two integer numbers; for example, 80 and 34.

Put the following line as the only contents of the braces of the main function:

```rust
print!("The sum is {}.", 80 + 34);
```

The execution will print: "The sum is 114.".

The second argument of the print macro is the expression 80 + 34.

The compiler surely does not store in the executable such numbers in decimal format. If compiling optimizations are off, the compiler just converts the two numbers in binary format and stores into the executable such binary numbers and the addition operation. But if compiling optimizations are on, the compiler, realizing that this expression contains only constant values, evaluates directly that expression, obtaining the integer number 114, and stores into the executable program such number in binary format. In both cases, at runtime, such a number is formatted as the three-character decimal string 114, and then the placeholder {} of the literal string is replaced by such string. Finally, of course, the resulting string is printed to the console.

Notice that the string "The sum is 114." has been generated by the program; it is not present in source code; so it is still a string, but not a literal string.

© Carlo Milanesi 2018
C. Milanesi, *Beginning Rust*, https://doi.org/10.1007/978-1-4842-3468-6_2

Similarly, the two-character sequence 80 represents an integer number directly in source code, and so it is called a "literal integer". The same holds for the two characters 34. Instead, the integer number 114, saved into the executable in binary format, and loaded into memory at runtime, is not a literal integer, as it does not appear in source code.

It is also allowed to write:

```
print!("{} + {} = {}", 34, 80, 80 + 34);
```

whose execution will print "34 + 80 = 114".

In such case, the second argument of the macro will be put where there is the first placeholder, the third argument where there is the second placeholder, and the fourth argument where there is the third placeholder.

You can specify hundreds of arguments for the "print" macro, as long as the arguments after the first one are as many as the placeholders "{}" inside the first argument.

Other Operations Between Integer Numbers

All the integer arithmetic operators of C language can be used. For example:

```
print!("{}", (23 - 6) % 5 + 20 * 30 / (3 + 4));
```

This will print 87.

Let's see why.

Such a formula is evaluated by the Rust compiler exactly as the C compiler would.

First, the operations in parentheses, 23 - 6 and 3 + 4, are evaluated, obtaining, respectively, 17 and 7.

At this point, our expression has become 17 % 5 + 20 * 30 / 7.

Then, the multiplication and division operations are evaluated, as they have precedence over addition and subtraction, and, for operations of the same precedence, they are evaluated in order from left to right.

17 % 5 is the "remainder of the integer division" operation, and it has 2 as a result, that is, the remainder of the operation 17 / 5. The expression 20 * 30 is evaluated before the following division, as it is at its left.

At this point, our expression has become 2 + 600 / 7.

Then, the integer division (with truncation) 600 / 7 is performed, and our expression has become 2 + 85.

Finally, the sum is evaluated, the result is formatted in decimal notation, the placeholder is replaced by the formatted number, and the resulting string is printed.

These arithmetic operations are performed always on integer binary numbers, obtaining integer binary numbers, and the results are converted to decimal format only when they are used to replace the placeholders.

Usually, compilers generate machine language instructions, which are afterwards executed when the program is running; though, the Rust compiler is highly optimizing, and so it tries to evaluate directly at compile time the expressions that it is possible to evaluate using the information available in source code. Our expression is made only of literal integers, and so the whole expression will be evaluated already at compile time, storing in the executable program only the result to print. Though, conceptually, we can think that the computations are performed at runtime.

Floating-Point Arithmetic

Let's see how to compute the sum between two numbers with fractional parts, for example, 80.3 and 34.9.

Replace the statement with:

```
print!("The sum is {}", 80.3 + 34.8);
```

The run will print The sum is 115.1.

Now replace in the second number only the character "8" with a "9", obtaining:

```
print!("The sum is {}", 80.3 + 34.9);
```

The run will print The sum is 115.19999999999999.

This will surprise those who would expect 115.2 as the result.

This phenomenon happens also in many other programming languages, and it is due to the fact that Rust, like almost every programming language, performs computations involving non-integer numbers using the "floating-point" format. But here we won't treat this format any more.

Also expressions containing floating-point numbers can be evaluated:

```
print!("{}", (23. - 6.) % 5. + 20. * 30. / (3. + 4.));
```

This will print `87.71428571428571`.

Let's see why.

By putting a dot after a literal number, it is transformed into a literal floating-point number, having the same value. The precedence rules are the same of integer arithmetic, although division has a different result.

Let's see how the evaluation of the expression is performed.

The evaluation of `23. - 6.` and of `3. + 4.` is similar to that of integer numbers.

By evaluating `17. % 5.`, `2.` is obtained, similarly to integer numbers. Such an operator does not exist in C language for floating-point numbers, and it corresponds to the expression `fmod(17., 5.)` of the C language.

By evaluating `"20. * 30."`, `600.` is obtained, similarly to integer numbers.

By evaluating `"600. / 7."`, a floating-point number is obtained, that cannot be exactly represented neither in binary notation nor in the decimal one. Internally, a binary-format approximate representation is generated; if you ask Rust to convert such number into a decimal-format approximate representation, you would get the string `85.71428571428571`.

Finally, the value `2.` is added to such binary number, obtaining another value that cannot be exactly represented, which is printed in the way shown above.

Notice that, differing from C language, in Rust you cannot simply mix integer numbers and floating-point numbers. The following statement generates a compilation error:

```
print!("{}", 2.7 + 1);
```

A way to make it valid is to add a dot:

```
print!("{}", 2.7 + 1.);
```

However, this one is a syntax-only limitation, not an operative one, as anyway machine code cannot sum an integer number and a floating-point number, without before converting one of the two operands to the type of the other operand. A C compiler, when it encounters the expression `2.7 + 1`, emits implicitly the machine language instruction to convert the integer number 1 to a floating-point number, or better, being 1 a constant, it is converted to a floating-point number at compile time. In Rust, such conversions must be explicit.

At last, a note about the "%" operator. This is often improperly named "modulo" (or "modulus") operator. Well, it should be better named "remainder" operator, because the mathematical modulo operator has a different behavior for negative numbers. The "%" operator behaves in Rust like in C language:

```
print!("{} {}", -12 % 10, -1.2 % 1.);
```

This will print "-2 -0.19999999999999996".

Sequences of Statements

As the body of the main function, write:

```
print!("{} + ", 80);
print!("{} =", 34);
print!(" {}", 80 + 34);
```

This will print 80 + 34 = 114.

The program now contains three statements, each of them terminated by the ";" character. Such statements are executed in order of appearance.

If the body of the main function would become

```
print!("{} + ",80);print!("{} = ",34);
        print ! ( "{}"  ,
    80     + 34 )  ;
```

its result wouldn't change. Actually, additional whitespaces (blanks, tabs, and line breaks) are ignored.

However, Rust programmers have the following habits that are recommended:

- to indent lines by four spaces inside functions;

- to avoid adding several consecutive spaces inside statements;

- to avoid exceeding 80 columns, possibly splitting long statements on several lines.

Breaking Literal Strings

As said before, to avoid code lines that are too long, you can break them in any point between syntax symbols, like in C language; though, the syntax to break a literal string is different. This code is illegal:

```
println!("{}", "This"
    "is not allowed");
```

Actually, in Rust you cannot simply juxtapose literal strings, like in C.

Though, you can start a literal string in one line, and end it a few lines below. For example, this is a valid program:

```
fn main() {
    println!("{}", "These
        are
        three lines");
}
```

And this is what is printed:

```
These
        are
        three lines
```

As you can see, the literal string contains all the characters that in the source file are between the start and the end of the string, including newline characters and line leading spaces.

Maybe this is what you want, but you can do something different:

```
fn main() {
    println!("{}", "This \
        is \
        just one line");
}
```

This will print:

```
This is just one line
```

By adding a backslash character ("\") inside a literal string, just before the end of a line, the resulting string will contain neither that end-of-line character nor the following spaces; therefore, the leading spaces of the next line are omitted. Given that we wanted at least one blank, we inserted such a blank just before the backslashes.

Finally, if we want a single literal string containing several resulting lines, with no leading whitespace, we can write this:

```
fn main() {
    println!("{}", "These
are
three lines");
}
```

or this:

```
fn main() {
println!("{}", "These\n\
    are\n\
    three lines");
}
```

Both will print:

```
These
are
three lines
```

The first solution has the drawback of being disrespectful of indentation conventions, and therefore usually the second solution is preferable. In such a solution, at the end of the lines there is the sequence "\n", which is codified as a newline sequence, and then another backslash to exclude from the string the source code newline and the following spaces.

CHAPTER 3

Naming Objects

In this chapter, you will learn:

- The concepts of "value", "object", and "variable"
- The concept of "mutability" of variables
- The difference between initialization and re-assignment
- How to avoid warnings for unused variables
- The concept of "Boolean expression"
- Which type checks are performed by the compiler for assignments
- How some operators can perform both an arithmetic operation and an assignment
- How to invoke functions defined in the Rust standard library

Associating Names to Values

So far, we have seen three kinds of values: strings, integer numbers, and floating-point numbers.

But values should not be confused with objects and variables. So, let's define what the words "value", "object", and "variable" actually mean.

The word "value" indicates an abstract, mathematical concept. For example, when you say "the value 12" you mean the mathematical concept of the number 12. In mathematics, there is just one number 12 in the world. Even true or "Hello" are values that conceptually exist in one single instance in the universe, because they are concepts.

But *values* may be stored in the memory of a computer. You can store the number 12 or the string "Hello" in several locations of the memory. So, you can have two distinct memory locations that both contain the 12 value.

17

© Carlo Milanesi 2018
C. Milanesi, *Beginning Rust*, https://doi.org/10.1007/978-1-4842-3468-6_3

The portion of memory that contains a value is named "object". Two distinct objects, located in different positions of memory, are said to be "equal" if they contain the same value. Instead, two values are said to be "equal" if and only if they are not distinct, that is, they are actually the same value.

When Rust source code is compiled, the resulting executable program contains only objects that have a memory location and a value. Such objects do not have names. But in source code, you may want to associate names to objects, to reference them later. For example, you can write, as the body of the main function:

```
let number = 12;
let other_number = 53;
print!("{}", number + other_number);
```

This will print 65.

The word "let", as the already seen word "fn", is a keyword reserved by the language, that is, a word that cannot be used for other purposes.

The first statement introduces in the program an object containing the value 12 and associates the name number to such object. The second statement introduces another object and associates it to another name. The third statement accesses these two objects by using the names previously defined.

The first statement has the following effects:

- it reserves an object (i.e., an area of memory) large enough to contain an integer number;

- it stores the value 12 in such object, in binary format;

- it associates the name number to such object, so that such name can be used in later points of the source code to indicate such object.

Therefore, such a statement is not a simple "alias" declaration. It doesn't mean "From now on, every time we use the word number, we will mean the value 12"; rather, it means "A memory space shall be reserved to contain initially the value 12, and from now on, every time we use the word number, we will mean such memory space". So, such statement declares both an object and a name of that object. A synonym of "name of object" is "identifier".

Identifier-object pairs are called "variables". So, that statement is a declaration of a variable.

But it is more than a declaration. A simple declaration of a variable just reserves space for an object, and associates an identifier to such object. The value of the object remains undefined. Instead, this statement also assigns the initial value of such object. Assigning the initial value of an object is called "initializing" that object. So, we say that this statement *declares and initializes a variable*.

The operation of reserving a memory area for an object is named "allocation" of that object. Conversely, the removal of an object, causing its memory area to become available for allocating other objects, is named "deallocation" of that object. So we say that this statement allocates an object, assigns it to an identifier, and initializes that object (or the variable composed by the pair identifier-object).

These concepts are the same as those of C language.

The second statement is similar to the first one.

After having declared and initialized a variable, you can use the name of such variable inside expressions, and the evaluation of such variable gives the value stored in its object. Actually, the third statement above appears to add the names of the two variables, with the effect of adding their current values.

If any of the first two statements were omitted, the third statement would generate a compilation error, as it would use an undeclared variable; and this is forbidden.

In the second statement of the following code

```
let number = 12;
print!("{} {}", number, 47);
```

two numbers are printed, 12 and 47, but 12 is printed as it is the value of a *variable*, while 47 is a *literal*.

Mutable Variables

After having appropriately declared a variable, you can modify its value in another kind of statement, named "assignment":

```
let mut number = 12;
print!("{}", number);
number = 53;
print!(" {}", number);
```

This will print 12 53.

The first statement declares the variable number and initializes it to the value 12. The second statement prints the value of such variable. The third statement assigns the value 53 to the same variable. The fourth statement prints the new value of the variable.

The assignment does not allocate objects. It just modifies the value of an already allocated object.

You probably noticed that the first statement contains the word "mut"; it is a keyword of Rust, and it is an abbreviation of "mutable". In fact, the conventional name "variable" is somewhat improper, as it applies also to objects that actually cannot be mutated, and therefore are *constant*, and are not *variable*; someone tried to use the alternative name "binding", but the name "variable" is so entrenched in so many languages, that its meaning is almost universal. So, in this text, we'll always use the word "variable".

Given that the word "variable" is used both to associate a name to an object that may be changed, and to associate a name to an object that cannot be changed, the variables of the first kind are named "mutable variables", while the second ones are named "immutable variables".

The simple keyword "let" declares an immutable variable, whereas the sequence "let mut" is required to be able to declare a mutable variable.

In the previous section, we declared two immutable variables, and actually the values of those variables were never modified after their initialization.

Instead, in the last program shown above, given that we wanted to modify the value of the variable, we declared it as *mutable*. Otherwise, in the third statement, we would have gotten a compilation error with this message: re-assignment of immutable variable `number`.

The C language version equivalent to the first Rust program in the previous section is:

```
#include <stdio.h>
int main() {
    int const number = 12;
    int const other_number = 53;
    printf("%d", number + other_number);
    return 0;
}
```

while the version equivalent to the Rust program in this section is:

```c
#include <stdio.h>
int main() {
    int number = 12;
    printf("%d", number);
    number = 53;
    printf(" %d", number);
    return 0;
}
```

Notice that when a Rust declaration *does not contain* the "mut" keyword, the corresponding C declaration *contains* the "const" keyword, and conversely, when a Rust declaration *contains* the "mut" keyword, the corresponding C declaration *does not contain* the "const" keyword.

In other words, in the C language, the simplest declaration form defines a mutable variable, and you must add a keyword to obtain immutability, while in Rust the simplest declaration form defines an immutable variable, and you must add a keyword to obtain mutability.

Not Mutated Mutable Variables

As we said before, if, after initialization, you try to assign a new value to an immutable variable, you get a compilation error. On the other side, it is not an error to declare a variable as mutable, and then never assign new values to it. However, the compiler notices the inadequacy of such situation, and it reports it as a warning. The code

```rust
let mut number = 12;
println!("{}", number);
```

could generate the following compilation message (that could change according the version of the compiler and the compilation options):

```
warning: variable does not need to be mutable
 --> main.rs:2:9
  |
2 |     let mut number = 12;
  |         ---^^^^^^
```

```
|            |
|            help: remove this `mut`
|
= note: #[warn(unused_mut)] on by default
```

The second line of the warning message indicates the portion of source code that caused the warning. It is the file main.rs, starting from column 9 of row 2. The next six lines of the message show such a line of code, underlying the relevant portion of code, and suggesting a correction.

The last line indicates that there is a compilation directive that can be set to enable or to disable this specific kind of warning reports. As the warning indicates, the compiler's default behavior is to print warnings when some mutable variables are never changed.

Uninitialized Variables

So far, each time we declared a variable, we also initialized it in the same statement. Conversely, we are also allowed to declare a variable without initializing it in the same statement, like in the following program:

```
let number;
number = 12;
print!("{}", number);
```

It will print 12.

Then what does the following code do?

```
let number;
print!("{}", number);
```

It generates a compilation error. The compiler notices that in the second line the variable number is evaluated without being assigned any value, and so the second statement would have undefined behavior.

Instead, the following code is valid.

```
let number1;
let number2 = 22;
number1 = number2;
print!("{}", number1);
```

This program will print 22. Such a value first is used to initialize the variable `number2` in the second statement, and then to initialize the variable `number1` in the third statement.

Instead, the following code will generate another compilation error:

```
let number1;
print!("{}", number1);
number1 = 12;
```

Actually, in this case the variable `number1` is initialized in the third statement, but it is evaluated already in the second statement, when its value has not been defined yet.

But also the following statement, standing alone, is illegal:

```
let number;
```

The first assignment of a value to a variable is named "initialization" of such variable, both if it happens in the declaration statement itself, or in a following statement. Instead, further assignments are named "reassignments".

Therefore, the rule is that every variable, mutable or immutable, must have one initialization, and such initialization must happen before encountering statements that try to evaluate such variable. Immutable variables cannot have reassignments. If a mutable variable has no reassignments, the compiler can emit a warning.

The Leading Underscore

Sometimes though, it happens to declare a variable, assign a value to it, and never use such a variable again. Of course, all this has a well-defined behavior; but what use is it to initialize a variable, yet never use its value? The compiler rightly suspects it is a programming error, and reports it as a warning. If you compile this code:

```
let number = 12;
```

you get the following warning:

```
warning: unused variable: `number`
 --> main.rs:2:9
  |
2 |     let number = 12;
  |         ^^^^^^
  |
```

```
= note: #[warn(unused_variables)] on by default
= note: to avoid this warning, consider using `_number` instead
```

If such warning is annoying, a way to silence it is by using the directive indicated by the warning; but there is a simpler way, suggested by the last line of the warning:

```
let _number = 12;
```

This code generates no warnings. The underscore character ("_") is allowed in any part of an identifier, but if it is the first character, it has the effect of silencing this kind of warning. Therefore, by convention, you put a leading underscore to an identifier whenever you are going to not evaluate such variable after it has gotten an initial value.

Also the following statement generates no errors nor warnings:

```
let _ = 12;
```

This statement, though, has another meaning. It does not declare a variable. A single underscore character is not a valid identifier, but it is a placeholder that indicates that you don't want to specify any name. It is a "don't-care" symbol.

The difference appears when you try to evaluate that symbol. The following program is valid:

```
let _number = 12;
print!("{}", _number);
```

but the following one is not:

```
let _ = 12;
print!("{}", _);
```

It generates a compilation error containing the message "expected expression, found `_`".

Therefore, an isolated underscore is not a valid expression; instead, it is a placeholder of some syntax symbol that you don't want to specify. Of course, it is not allowed in any point of the code. We already saw that it is allowed not to specify the name of the variable that you are declaring, but it is not allowed in an expression to evaluate, because such symbol has no value.

Boolean Values

To represent truth values, the keywords true and false are used. Such keywords are expressions having a non-numeric type, named "Boolean."

Write the code

```
let truth = true;
let falsity = false;
print!("{} {}", truth, falsity);
```

This will print true false.

Boolean values, in addition to being generated by evaluating the keywords true and false, are generated by relational expressions. For example:

```
let truth = 5 > 2;
let falsity = -12.3 >= 10.;
print!("{} {} {}", truth, falsity, -50 < 6);
```

This will print true false true.

In the code above, the expression 5 > 2, which should be read "five is greater than two", is arithmetically true, and so it initializes the truth variable with the true Boolean value.

A similar operation is performed in the second line, where two floating-point numbers are compared with the greater-or-equal operator.

Finally, in the third line the "less-than" operator is used directly in the expression that is the fourth argument of the invocation of the print macro.

The relational operators are the following ones:

- ==: is equal to

- !=: is different from

- <: is less than

- <=: is less than or equal to

- >: is greater than

- >=: is greater than or equal to

As you can see, Rust relational operators are the same ones used in the C language.

Each of them is applicable to two integer numbers, or to two floating-point numbers, or even to values of other types, like strings. For example:

```
print!("{} {} {}", "abc" < "abcd", "ab" < "ac", "A" < "a");
```

This will print `true true true`.

However, the two values to be compared must be of the same type. For example, the expression `3.14 > 3` is invalid.

When comparing strings, the `"<"` operator, instead of being thought of as "is less than", should be thought of as "precedes", and the `">"` operator should be thought of as "follows". The sort criterion is that of language dictionaries, also known as "lexicographical".

Such a criterion is the following one. You start by comparing the first characters of the two strings and then proceed to compare characters in the same positions of the two strings, until one of the following situations happens:

- If both strings have no more characters, they are equal.

- If one string has no more characters, while the other has other characters, the shorter string precedes the longer one.

- If both strings have more characters, and the next corresponding characters are different, the string having the character preceding the other character in the alphabet precedes the other string.

In the first comparison in the example, after having processed the first three characters of both strings, the first string ends, while the second one proceeds, and so the first string precedes the second string in the order.

In the second comparison, the second character is different, and the "b" letter precedes the "c" letter, and so the whole string "ab" precedes the string "ac".

In the third comparison, an uppercase "A" is compared with a lowercase "a". Uppercase letters are defined to precede lowercase letters, and so also in this case the first string precedes the second one.

Boolean Expressions

Boolean values can be combined with the so-called *logical connectives*:

```
let truth = true;
let falsity = false;
println!("{} {}", ! truth, ! falsity);
println!("{} {} {} {}", falsity && falsity, falsity && truth,
    truth && falsity, truth && truth);
println!("{} {} {} {}", falsity || falsity, falsity || truth,
    truth || falsity, truth || truth);
```

This will print:

```
false true
false false false true
false true true true
```

Those who know C language will found nothing new.

The operator "!", read "not", produces a true value for a false argument, and a false value for a true argument.

The operator "&&", read "logical-and", produces a true value if both its arguments are true, and a false value in the other cases.

The operator "||", read "logical-or", produces a false value if both its arguments are false, and a true value in the other cases.

Logical connectives do not have the same precedence:

```
print!("{} {}", true || true && ! true,
    (true || true) && ! true);
```

This will print: "true false".

The operator "!" has top precedence, and it transforms the first expression into true || true && false; then the "&&" operator has a higher precedence than the "||" operator, and so it is evaluated next, and it transforms that expression into true || false; and finally the "||" operator is evaluated, and it transforms that expression into true.

If you'd like a different evaluation order, you can use parentheses, which actually change the value of the second expression, first into true && false, and then into false.

27

Type Consistency in Assignments

The program

```
let mut n = 1;
print!("{}", n);
n = 2;
print!(" {}", n);
n = 3;
print!(" {}", n);
```

will print 1 2 3.

But if we change the fifth line to

```
n = 3.14;
```

the compiler will report that the value 3.14 is of a wrong type. Actually, the first line creates a variable that, being initialized using an integer number, is of type "integer number"; the third line assigns to such variable a value that is still of type "integer number"; but the fifth line would assign to such variable a floating-point number value. This is not allowed, as to a variable of type "integer number" only values of type "integer number" can be assigned.

In general, in Rust every variable is of a type defined at compile time, and also every expression has a value defined at compile time.

For example, all the following expressions are of type "integer number": 12, 12 - 3, 12 - (7 % 5). The following expressions are of type "floating-point number": 12., 12. - 3., 12. - (7. % 5.). The expression "hello" is of "string" type, and the expressions false and 4 > 3 are of "Boolean" type.

The type of a variable can be deduced, or, as it is commonly said, *inferred*, from the type of the expression used to initialize such variable. A program containing only the line

```
let number;
```

is illegal, as we said before; but the reason is made clear by the compilation error message, which contains the text type annotations needed, and then the text cannot infer type.

Once the compiler understands which is the type of a variable, all the assignments to such variable must have at the right of the "=" sign an expression of such type.

In addition, notice this:

```
let number1 = 12;
let _number2 = number1;
```

Here, the literal integer number 12 is of type "integer number", and so the number1 variable is also of type "integer number", and so the initialization expression appearing in the second line at the right of the = sign is of that type, and so the variable _number2 is of the same type, as it is initialized by such expression.

Going back to the previous example, where we attempted to use the number 3.14, there are several ways to solve the problem of type mismatch. One is to write:

```
let mut n = 1.;
print!("{}", n);
n = 2.;
print!(" {}", n);
n = 3.14;
print!(" {}", n);
```

In this code, there are only floating-point numbers, and therefore there is no type error.

Change of Type and of Mutability

Another possibility is to write:

```
let mut n = 1;
print!("{}", n);
n = 2;
print!(" {}", n);
let n = 3.14;
print!(" {}", n);
```

In this case, the first statement declares the variable "n" of type "mutable integer number", and initializes it; the third statement changes the value of such variable; and the fifth statement re-declares the variable "n", and initializes it using an expression of type "floating-point number", and therefore the variable itself must be of that type.

In some programming languages, this is not allowed. Instead, Rust allows it, because re-declarations do not overwrite existing variables, but they create always new variables.

Of course, after such a declaration, the first variable is no more accessible, but it hasn't been destroyed. We say that the old variable has been "shadowed" by the new variable.

Notice that this last declaration creates a variable of another type and also of different mutability, that is, while the variable declared in the first statement was mutable, the one declared in the fifth statement is not. Therefore, for example, the following code generates a compilation error at the last statement:

```
let mut _n = 1;
_n = 2;
let _n = 3.14;
_n = 5.9;
```

As a re-declaration introduces a new variable that shadows the first one, such variable can be of any type:

```
let x = 120; print!("{} ", x);
let x = "abcd"; print!("{} ", x);
let mut x = true; print!("{} ", x);
x = false; print!("{}", x);
```

This will print 120 abcd true false.

Assignment Arithmetic Operators

In Rust, often the need to write code like this happens:

```
let mut a = 12;
a = a + 1;
a = a - 4;
a = a * 7;
a = a / 6;
print!("{}", a);
```

This will print 10. Similarly to C language, such expressions may be abbreviated in this way:

```
let mut a = 12;
a += 1;
a -= 4;
a *= 7;
a /= 6;
print!("{}", a);
```

Actually, those aren't only abbreviations, they are different operators, which however behave like arithmetic operators followed by an assignment; that is, for example, the operator += is equivalent to perform first an addition and then assign the resulting sum.

Using the Functions of the Standard Library

As any programming language, even Rust can do little using only the built-in features of the language, and most of its features are delegated to external libraries.

In addition to using downloadable libraries, every Rust installation provides an official library, the so-called "standard library". Differing from C language, which requires using the #include directive to include in the source code the needed file of the standard library, Rust, by default, includes its whole standard library, and the application code can immediately use the features of the standard library, with no need to include external modules:

```
print!("{} {}", str::len("abcde"), "abcde".len());
```

This will print 5 5.

Here a function, or routine, is invoked, or called. Its name is len, abbreviation of "length", and it is part of the standard library.

In Rust, to invoke many functions, including the len function, there are two possible syntax forms, and the example above shows both of them.

The len function returns the number of bytes contained in the string passed as an argument.

The first syntax form has a procedural style, while the second one has an object-oriented style.

In the first form, first the name of the module containing the function is specified, and in this case it is `str`, in which string manipulation functions are defined; then, the name of the function is specified, separated by a couple of colon characters (`::`); then, possible arguments are specified, enclosed in parentheses.

In the second form, first, the first argument is specified; then, the name of the function, separated by a dot; and finally, the possible other arguments, enclosed in parentheses.

The parentheses are required even if there are no arguments, like in C language.

CHAPTER 4

Controlling Execution Flow

In this chapter, you will learn:

- How to use if statements to execute different statements based on a Boolean condition

- How to use if expressions to generate different values based on a Boolean condition

- How to use while statements to repeat some statements as long as a Boolean condition holds

- How to use for statements to repeat some statements for a definite number of times

- What is the scope of validity of variables

Conditional Statements (if)

The main usage of Boolean values is in making decisions about how to let the execution of the program proceed. Suppose you want to print a word, but only if a given number is positive:

```rust
let n = 4;
if n > 0 { print!("positive"); }
```

This will print positive.

© Carlo Milanesi 2018
C. Milanesi, *Beginning Rust*, https://doi.org/10.1007/978-1-4842-3468-6_4

The second line contains an `if` statement, similar to that of many other languages. In such a statement, the Boolean expression following the `if` keyword is evaluated. Such an expression is referred to as the "condition". Only when the outcome of evaluating the condition is `true`, the statements enclosed in the following braces will be executed.

The braces can enclose zero or more statements. Therefore, they resemble the body of the "main" function. In general, a sequence of statements enclosed in braces is named "block".

This syntax differs from that of other languages, like C, for the following reasons:

- The condition must be of Boolean type. Therefore, the following syntax is not allowed: `if 4 { print!("four"); }`.

- It is not required to enclose the condition between parentheses, and usually it is not done. In fact, the compiler reports a warning if you do so.

- After the condition, a block (of statements) is required. Therefore, the following syntax is not allowed: `if 4 > 0 print!("four");` and neither the following one: `if (4 > 0) print!("four");`.

If you want to do something even in case the condition is evaluated to `false`, you can introduce the alternative case, preceded by the `else` keyword:

```
let n = 0;
if n > 0 {
    print!("number is");
    print!(" positive");
}
else {
    print!("non positive");
}
```

This will print `non positive`.

As you can see, as the whole `"if"` statement is very long, it has been split in seven lines, and the statements enclosed in blocks have been indented by four columns, to make evident the block.

If there are more than two cases, of course, you can insert `if` statements inside blocks, in this way:

```
let n = 4;
if n > 1000 {
    print!("big");
}
else {
    if n > 0 {
        print!("small");
    }
    else {
        if n < 0 {
            print!("negative");
        }
        else {
            print!("neither positive nor negative");
        }
    }
}
```

However, the following equivalent syntax is allowed to make it more readable.

```
let n = 4;
if n > 1000 {
    print!("big");
}
else if n > 0 {
    print!("small");
}
else if n < 0 {
    print!("negative");
}
else {
    print!("neither positive nor negative");
}
```

Notice that after an `else` keyword, you must put a block or another `if` statement.

Conditional Expressions

Instead of writing the previous code, you could write the equivalent code:

```
let n = 4;
print!("{}",
    if n > 1000 {
        "big"
    }
    else if n > 0 {
        "small"
    }
    else if n < 0 {
        "negative"
    }
    else {
        "neither positive nor negative"
    }
);
```

Here, a "conditional expression" is used, similar to the C-language ternary operator
"?:". The corresponding code in C language is:

```
#include <stdio.h>
int main(int argc, char **argv) {
    int n = 4;
    printf("%s",
        n > 1000 ?
            "big" :
        n > 0 ?
            "small" :
        n < 0 ?
            "negative" :
            "neither positive nor negative");
}
```

The last Rust program, instead of containing four invocations of the "print" macro, contains just one invocation, having two arguments. The first argument says simply to print the second argument, and the second argument is an expression extending over twelve lines. Such expression uses, like in the previous example, the "if" and "else" keywords, but, instead of containing statements in the blocks, it contains simple literal strings.

The evaluation of such a composite expression proceeds in a way that is similar to that of the if-else statement in the previous example, but, after it has been determined which block should be executed, while in the previous example the statements enclosed in the block were *executed*, in this example the expression enclosed in the block is *evaluated*, and the value obtained from such evaluation is considered as the value of the whole "if-else" expression. Afterwards, such value will be used by the macro to be printed.

The main difference with respect to the "?:" operator of C language is the fact that, in Rust, conditional expressions have the same syntax of conditional statements. What characterizes them as conditional expressions is the fact that all its blocks end without a semicolon. In such a case, the expressions contained in the blocks give the value of the composite if expression.

In order to have a unique type for the composite expression, it is required that such expression have at least one else branch, and that all its blocks end with expressions of the same type. For example, it is not allowed to write

```
let a = if true { "abc" };
```

as the value of a in the else case wouldn't be defined; and also it is not allowed to write

```
let a = if true { "abc" } else { 12 };
```

as the first block has a string as its value, while the second block has an integer number, and so the compiler wouldn't be able to determine a type for the a variable. Instead, it is allowed to write the statements

```
let _a = if true { "abc" } else { "xy" };
let _b = if true { 3456 } else { 12 };
let _c = if true { 56.9 } else { 12. };
```

as, in the first statement we have only strings, in the second only integer numbers, and in the third only floating-point numbers; and so _a is a string, _b is an integer number, and _c is a floating-point number.

Conditioned Loops (`while`)

Let's suppose you want to print the integer numbers from 1 to 10, including 1 and 10, squared. You can do that with the statements

```
let mut i = 1;
while i <= 10 {
    print!("{} ", i * i);
    i += 1;
}
```

that will print `1  4  9  16  25  36  49  64  81  100`.

Here, the "`while`" keyword is used, similarly to C language. The Boolean condition following it is evaluated, and if its value is `true`, the following block is executed. The `while` statement differs from the "`if`" statement because, after having executed the block, it repeats the evaluation of the condition and possibly re-executes the block, until the condition is evaluated to false, or until the block is exited for some other reason.

This syntax differs from other languages, like C, for the same aspects already seen about the syntax of "`if`" statements.

In our example, the mutable variable "`i`" is declared, as an integer number, and it is initialized to 1. Such value represents the number of which you want to print the square.

The "`while`" statement checks if such value is less or equal to the 10 value, and, as it is so, the block is executed, and then the Boolean condition is evaluated again. Inside the block the value of "`i`" is incremented, and so after ten iterations, the value of "`i`" is 11; at this point the condition of the loop is no more satisfied, and so the execution of the "`while`" statement ends.

While in C language there is also the `do ... while` statement, there is no such statement in Rust. Instead the same `break` and `continue` statements of C language exist also in Rust. Their purpose is respectively to exit prematurely from the whole loop, and to exit prematurely from the sole current iteration of the loop.

For example, if, for each integer number from 1 to 50, that wouldn't be divisible by 3, we would like to print its square, as long as such square is not larger than 400, we could write:

```
let mut i = 0;
while i < 50 {
    i += 1;
```

```rust
if i % 3 != 0 {
    if i * i <= 400 {
        print!("{} ", i * i);
    }
}
}
```

or, using `continue` and `break`, we can write the equivalent code:

```rust
let mut i = 0;
while i < 50 {
    i += 1;
    if i % 3 == 0 { continue; }
    if i * i > 400 { break; }
    print!("{} ", i * i);
}
```

These two versions have the same first three lines.

In the first version, if the remainder of i divided by three is different from zero, that is, the number *is not* divisible by three, the iteration goes on, while in the second version of the program, if the number *is* divisible by three, the `continue` statement is executed, and so the current iteration is immediately ended, and the next iteration is reached.

Notice that, to let the next iteration process the next number, it is needed to increment however such number. Therefore such increment is put at the beginning of the iteration.

The usage of the `continue` keyword allows us to improve readability, because it reduces by one the nesting level of blocks.

In addition, in the first version of the program, it is checked if the square is larger than 400, and the value is printed only if the limit is not exceeded. In the second version, it is taken into account the fact that, given that the number is steadily incremented, once its square exceeds 400, it will exceed it in every following iteration; therefore, as soon as the square exceeds 400, the `break` statement is executed, with the effect of immediately getting out of the whole loop.

The usage of the `break` keyword allows us to improve readability too, similarly to the `continue` keyword, but it allows us also to improve speed, as it avoids several useless iterations.

Infinite Loops (loop)

It happens to execute so-called infinite loops, meaning the execution flow exits from such loops only when the program is forcefully terminated, or by executing statements that get out of the loop, like the break keyword. For example, to print all the squares less than 200, we can write

```
let mut i = 1;
while true {
    let ii = i * i;
    if ii >= 200 { break; }
    print!("{} ", ii);
    i += 1;
}
```

that will print 1 4 9 16 25 36 49 64 81 100 121 144 169 196.

Though, the compiler will suggest to denote infinite loops with `loop { ... }`. The compiler advises to replace the while true clause with the more expressive loop keyword, so obtaining the equivalent program:

```
let mut i = 1;
loop {
    let ii = i * i;
    if ii >= 200 { break; }
    print!("{} ", ii);
    i += 1;
}
```

Counting Loops (for)

And the famous for loop of the C language (and many others languages)?

Even in Rust there is the for keyword, and also in Rust it is used to iterate a definite number of times, but its use in Rust is very different from that in C language.

Here is a program that solves the problem of printing the integer numbers from 1 to 10, including 1 and 10, squared:

```
for i in 1..11 {
    print!("{} ", i * i);
}
```

After the open brace, the syntax of the `for` statement is the same as that of the `while` statement, meaning that the `break` and `continue` statements are allowed, but the first part of the statement is very different.

Just after the `for` keyword, there is the name of a variable that will be created in such way. In our example, it is `"i"`.

Then, there is the `in` keyword, followed by two integer numeric expressions, separated by the symbol `".."`.

Executing this loop means assigning to the `i` variable the first numeric value, then executing the block with such value of the `i` variable, then incrementing by one the value of `i`, executing another time the block with such value of `i`, and so on. When the value of `i` reaches the second numeric value, the block is *not* executed, and the `for` statement ends. Therefore, while the first limit is included in the sequence of used values, the second one is excluded.

As the second limit is excluded from the loop, to iterate from 1 to 10 you must write 1..11.

As we said, the loop variable is declared by the loop statement, and it is destroyed when the loop ends. If there were already a variable having the same name, such variable would be shadowed, that is ignored, for the whole loop, and it would become valid again after the loop, as shown by this code:

```
let index = 8;
for index in 0..4 { print!("{} ", index); }
print!(":{}", index);
```

This will print: `"0 1 2 3 :8"`.

Notice that the two limits may be even complex expressions, but anyway both such expressions are evaluated *before* the beginning of the loop. The program

```rust
let mut limit = 4;
for i in 1..limit {
    limit -= 1;
    print!("{} ", i);
}
print!(":{}", limit);
```

will print "1 2 3 :1". Let's see why.

First, the `limit` variable is created, and it is initialized to the 4 value.

Then, the extremes of the loop are evaluated. The first extreme, included, is 1, while the final extreme, excluded, is 4.

Therefore the block is executed three times; the first one with `i=1`, the second time with `i=2`, and the third time with `i=3`. Each time that the block is executed, the value of `limit` is decremented by one, therefore passing from 4 to 1. However, this does not affect the number of iterations that will be executed.

This is different from the following C language program:

```c
#include <stdio.h>
int main() {
    int limit = 4;
    for (int i = 1; i < limit; i++) {
        limit -= 1;
        printf("%d ", i);
    }
    printf(":%d ", limit);
    return 0;
}
```

This will print "1 2 :2", because, as `limit` is decremented, the loop condition is no more satisfied after the second iteration).

Variables Scopes

We have already seen many statements using blocks: the "main" function, the "if" statement/expression, the "while" statement, the "loop" statement, and the "for" statement.

In such cases, using blocks is required, though you can use blocks everywhere you want to enclose some statements. For example:

```
print!("1");
{
    print!("2");
    print!("3");
    {
        print!("4");
        {
            print!("5");
            { { } }
            print!("6");
        }
    }
    print!("7");
}
```

This will print "1234567". Of course, braces must be correctly paired.

Indents and other spaces are optional, and they do not change the generated executable; their purpose is just to make the source code more readable.

But what's the purpose of all those braces? In the example above, they have no purpose, but if you compile the following code:

```
{ let i = 10; }
print!("{} ", i);
```

you get the error cannot find value `i` in this scope at the second line, as if the variable i hadn't ever been declared. It happens so, because each variable ceases to exist at the end of the block in which it has been declared.

The block where a variable has been declared is called the "scope" of the variable.

So, in our example, the scope of i lasts only for one line.

The scope of a variable also includes possible blocks nested in the block in which the variable has been declared. This code

```
{
    let i = 10;
    {
        let j = 4;
        {
            print!("{} ", i);
        }
        print!("{}", i + j);
    } // End of the scope of "j"
} // End of the scope of "i"
```

will print 10 14. In this case, the scope of i lasts for nine lines, while the scope of j lasts for six lines.

Now let's examine this code

```
{
    let i = 10;
    {
        let i = 4;
        print!("{} ", i);
    } // End of the scope of the second "i"
    print!("{} ", i);
} // End of the scope of the first "i"
```

that will print 4 10.

We already said that it is allowed to define a variable having the same name of a variable already existing, and that in such case this last variable is "shadowed" and not "overwritten" by the new declaration.

Here, first, a variable named i is declared, and it is initialized with the value 10. Then another variable with the same name is declared, and it is initialized with the value 4. Then, the value of a variable with such name is printed. As the second variable shadows the first one, the value of the second variable is used, and so 4 is printed. Then, the second variable gets out of its scope, and therefore it is destroyed, and so the first variable becomes visible again. So, the second print statement uses the value of the first variable, which hasn't been destroyed yet.

44

Therefore, we saw that pairs of braces may be inserted to purposely limit the scope of a variable.

But variable visibility rules hold also for the blocks of "if", "while", and "for" statements. Therefore the following code

```
let mut _i = 1;
if true { let _i = 2; }
print!("{} ", _i);

while _i > 0 { _i -= 1; let _i = 5; }
print!("{} ", _i);
```

will print 1 0.

Actually, it is true that in the second line the statement let _i = 2; is executed, but the effect of such statement is to create a new variable, and destroy it in the same line, and so in the third line the value of the first _i-named variable is printed.

In the last-but-one line, as _i was initially greater than zero, the body of the while statement is executed the first time. Inside such body, the value of _i is decremented to zero, and then another variable having the same name _i is created and immediately destroyed. Given than now the original _i is zero, the while statement ends, and finally the value of the first (and only remaining) variable is printed.

You should think that any variable declaration *creates* an object, and that such object is *destroyed* when the scope where such variable has been declared ends.

And each time you use a variable name, except for declaring it, the variable actually referred is the latest declared variable having such name, and not yet destroyed.

Using a metaphorical language, the creation of an object can be considered its birth, and the destruction of an object can be considered its death. So, we can say that each use of a variable name refers to the *youngest live variable* having such name.

CHAPTER 5

Using Data Sequences

In this chapter, you will learn:

- How to define sequences of objects of the same type, having fixed-length (arrays) or variable-length (vectors)

- How to specify the initial contents of arrays or vectors, by listing the items, or by specifying one item and its repeat count

- How to read or write the value of single items of arrays or vectors

- How to add items to a vector or to remove items from a vector

- How to create arrays with several dimensions

- How to create empty arrays or vectors

- How to print or copy whole arrays or vectors

Arrays

So far, we have seen how to store in a variable a string, a number, or a Boolean. If you want to store several strings in a single variable, you can write

```
let x = ["English", "This", "sentence", "a", "in", "is"];
print!("{} {} {} {} {} {}",
    x[1], x[5], x[3], x[2], x[4], x[0]);
```

that will print: `"This is a sentence in English."`

The first statement declares the x variable as an immutable object made of an array of six objects, all of string type, specified in the statement itself. Such a kind of objects is indeed named "array".

47

© Carlo Milanesi 2018
C. Milanesi, *Beginning Rust*, https://doi.org/10.1007/978-1-4842-3468-6_5

The second statement contains six expressions, each of them making a read access to a different element of x. Such accesses specify the item to access by means of a positional index, or subscript, put between brackets. Notice that indexes start always from zero, and so, as the array has six elements, the index of the last item is 5. This behavior is similar to that of C language arrays.

To determine how many elements are there in an array, you can do this:

```
let a = [true, false];
let b = [1, 2, 3, 4, 5];
print!("{}, {}.", a.len(), b.len());
```

It will print "2, 5."

The a variable is an array of two Booleans, while the b variable is an array of five integer numbers.

The third statement invokes on the objects a and b the len function of the standard library, to get the number of the objects contained in the array. Both the syntax and semantics of these invocations are similar to those of the expression "abc".len(), used to get the length in bytes of a string.

Notice that in the examples, every array contains elements of the same type; only strings, only Booleans, or only integer numbers.

If you try to write

```
let x = ["This", 4];
```

or

```
let x = [4, 5.];
```

you get a compilation error, indicating the array cannot contain objects of different types.

It is possible to create arrays of many types of items, as long as in every array all the items are of the same type.

It is so, because there is not a single type "array". The concept of "array" is that of a *generic* type, which is parameterized by its items type, and also by the number of its items. So, in the first example of the chapter, the variable x is of type "array of 5 strings"; while in the second example, a is of type "array of 2 Booleans"; and b is of type "array of 5 integer numbers".

In the following program, every line but the first one will generate a compilation error:

```rust
let mut x = ["a"]; // array of strings
x[0] = 3;
x[-1] = "b";
x[0.] = "b";
x[false] = "b";
x["0"] = "b";
```

The second statement is wrong because it tries to assign an integer number to an item of an array of strings. The following statements are wrong because the index is not a non-negative integer number, and array indexes must be integer numbers greater or equal to zero.

The following one is a different case:

```rust
let x = ["a"]; // array of strings
let _y = x[1];
```

This statement is allowed by the compiler, even if we know that it is senseless to read the index 1 item, which is the second item, in an array that has only one item.

However, when the program is running, its machine code, before accessing that array item, checks if such index is valid, and if, as in this case, the index is not valid, it terminates the execution of the program, emitting a runtime error message.

Notice that such abnormal termination is not caused by the operating system, but by instructions inserted by the Rust compiler into the executable program (in other words, it is not a "segmentation violation trap", but it is an "abortion"). In this way, the program, at every access to an array, checks if the index used for such access is valid, and terminates voluntarily the execution if it realizes that the index exceeds the array bounds.

Such premature termination of the execution of the program, in Rust jargon, is named "panic", and the action of terminating the program is named "panicking". In this way, every array access has well-defined behavior, while notoriously in C language out-of-bound array accesses have undefined behavior.

However, the compiler cannot always check such an index, and therefore it generates an executable program. Actually, in this case, as the index is a constant value, and array sizes are always constant, the compiler can check that this index is not valid, and so it emits the warning: `this expression will panic at runtime` and then `index out of bounds: the len is 1 but the index is 1`.

Mutable Arrays

The modification of the items of an array is possible only on mutable arrays:

```
let mut x = ["This", "is", "a", "sentence"];
x[2] = "a nice";
print!("{} {} {} {}.", x[0], x[1], x[2], x[3]);
```

This will print "This is a nice sentence."

The first sentence contains the "mut" keyword, and the second statement assigns the new string to the third item of the array. This operation is allowed by the compiler, because the following three conditions hold:

- The x variable is mutable.

- The type of the new value assigned is the same of the other items of x. Actually, they are all strings.

- The index is a non-negative integer number.

In addition, at runtime, the operation is performed without panicking, because the index is between the array bounds, that is, the conditions "0 <= 2" and "2 < 4" hold.

Instead, it is not allowed to add items to an array nor to remove items from an array. Therefore its length is a compile-time-defined constant.

A mutable variable of an array type, as any mutable variable, can be the target of an assignment from another array:

```
let mut x = ["a", "b", "c"];
print!("{}{}{}. ", x[0], x[1], x[2]);
x = ["X", "Y", "Z"];
print!("{}{}{}. ", x[0], x[1], x[2]);
let y = ["1", "2", "3"];
x = y;
print!("{}{}{}.", x[0], x[1], x[2]);
```

This will print "abc. XYZ. 123.".

In the first line, an array is created and assigned to the x variable. In the third line, another array is created and assigned to the same x variable, therefore replacing all the three existing strings. In the fifth line, another array is created and assigned to the y variable. In the sixth line, such array is assigned to the x variable, therefore replacing the three existing values.

If x weren't mutable, two compilation errors would be generated: one at the third line and one at the sixth.

The following code generates compilation errors both at the second and third lines:

```
let mut x = ["a", "b", "c"];
x = ["X", "Y"];
x = [15, 16, 17];
```

Actually, because of the first line, x is of type "array of three elements of type string". The statement in the second line tries to assign to x a value of type "array of two elements of type string"; while the statement in the third line tries to assign to x a value of type "array of three elements of type integer number". In the first case, the number of elements is wrong, even if the type of each element is correct; conversely, in the second case the number of the elements is correct, but the type of each element is wrong. In both cases, the type of the whole value that is being assigned is different from the type of the target variable.

Arrays of Specified Size

We already saw how to create an array by listing the items initially contained.

If you want to handle many items, instead of writing many expressions, you can write

```
let mut x = [4.; 5000];
x[2000] = 3.14;
print!("{}, {}", x[1000], x[2000]);
```

that will print. "4, 3.14".

The first statement declares the x variable as a mutable array of 5000 floating-point numbers, all initially equal to 4. Notice the usage of a semicolon between the square brackets, instead of a comma.

The second statement assigns the value 3.14 to the item at position 2000 of such array.

Finally the value, which *never changed*, at position 1000, and the value, which just *changed*, at position 2000 are printed. Notice that the valid indexes for this array go from 0 to 4999.

To scan the items of an array, the "for" statement is very useful:

```
let mut fib = [1; 15];
for i in 2..fib.len() {
    fib[i] = fib[i - 2] + fib[i - 1];
}
for i in 0..fib.len() {
    print!("{}, ", fib[i]);
}
```

This will print: "1, 1, 2, 3, 5, 8, 13, 21, 34, 55, 89, 144, 233, 377, 610,".

This program computes the first 15 numbers of the famous Fibonacci sequence, and then prints them. Such sequence is defined in this way: the first two numbers are both 1, and every other number is the sum of the two preceding numbers.

Examine the program.

The first statement creates a variable named fib and initializes it using an array of 15 numbers 1.

The statement in the following three lines is a for loop, in which the i variable is initialized to 2 and it is incremented up to 14. The body of such loop assigns to each item of the array, starting from the third one, the sum of the two preceding items. Given that, when each item is written, the preceding items have already received their correct value, such assignment uses always correct values.

Finally there is another "for" loop, but this time its index starts from 0.

Multidimensional Arrays

You can easily write arrays having several dimensions:

```
let mut x = [[[[23; 4]; 6]; 8]; 15];
x[14][7][5][3] = 56;
print!("{}, {}", x[0][0][0][0], x[14][7][5][3]);
```

This will print: "23, 56."

The first statement declares an array of 15 items, each of them being an array of 8 items, each of them being an array of 6 items, each of them being an array of 4 items, each of them initialized with the integer number 23.

The second statement accesses the 15th and last item of such array, so getting an array; then it accesses the 8th and last item of such array, so getting an array; then accesses the 6th and last item of such array, so getting an array; then accesses the 4th and last item of such array, so getting an item of type integer number; finally, it assigns the integer number 56 to such item.

The third statement prints the content of the very first item and the content of the very last item of the array.

Because multidimensional arrays are no more than arrays of arrays, it comes out easy to get the sizes of a given array:

```
let x = [[[[0; 4]; 6]; 8]; 15];
print!("{}, {}, {}, {}.",
    x.len(), x[0].len(), x[0][0].len(), x[0][0][0].len());
```

This will print: "15, 8, 6, 4."

A big limitation of arrays is the fact that their size must be defined at compilation time.

```
let length = 6;
let arr = [0; length];
```

The compilation of this code generates the error `attempt to use a non-constant value in a constant`. Actually the expression `length` is a variable, and therefore conceptually it is not a compile-time constant, even if it is immutable, and even if it has just been initialized by a constant. The size of an array cannot be an expression containing variables.

Vectors

To create sequences of objects whose size is defined at runtime, the Rust standard library provides the Vec type, shorthand for `vector`.

```
let x = vec!["This", "is"];
print!("{} {}. Length: {}.", x[0], x[1], x.len());
```

53

This will print: "`This is. Length: 2.`"

The first statement looks like the creation of an immutable array, with the only difference of the appearance of the `vec!` clause.

Such a clause is an invocation of the `"vec"` macro of the standard library. Also `"vec"` is an abbreviation of "vector."

The effect of such a macro is indeed to create a vector, initially containing the two strings specified between square brackets. Actually, when `len()` is invoked on such an object, 2 is returned.

Vectors allow us to do everything that is allowed for arrays, but they allow also us to change their size after having been initialized:

```
let mut x = vec!["This", "is"]; print!("{}", x.len());
x.push("a"); print!(" {}", x.len());
x.push("sentence"); print!(" {}", x.len());
x[0] = "That";
for i in 0..x.len() { print!(" {}", x[i]); }
```

This will print: "`2 3 4 That is a sentence.`"

The first line creates a mutable vector, initially containing two strings, and prints its length.

The second line invokes the *push* function on the just created vector, and prints its new length. Such a function adds its argument at the bottom of the vector. To be legal, it must have exactly *one* argument, and such argument must be of the same type of the items of the vector. The word "push" is the word commonly used for the operation of adding an item to a "stack" data structure.

The third line adds another string at the end of the vector, so making the vector to contain four items, and it prints the new length of the vector.

The fourth line replaces the value of the first item of the vector. This operation and the two preceding ones are allowed only because the x variable is mutable.

The fifth line scans the four items of the vector and prints them all on the terminal.

Let's see another example:

```
let length = 5000;
let mut y = vec![4.; length];
y[6] = 3.14;
y.push(4.89);
print!("{}, {}, {}", y[6], y[4999], y[5000]);
```

This will print: "`3.14, 4, 4.89`".

The second line declares a variable having as value a vector containing a sequence of values `4`. The length of such sequence is specified by the variable `length`. This wouldn't be allowed with an array.

The third line changes the value of the seventh item of the vector.

The fourth line adds a new item at the end of the vector. Because the vector had 5000 items, the new item will get position 5000, that is, the last position of any vector having 5001 items.

Finally, three items are printed: the changed item, the item that was the last before the addition, and the just added item.

So we saw that, differing from arrays, you can create vectors with a length defined at runtime, and you can change their length during execution. Also vectors, like arrays, are generic types, but while the type of every array is defined by two parameters, a type and a length, the type of every vector is defined by a single parameter, the type of its elements. The length of every vector is variable at runtime, and so it does not belong to the type, as in Rust all types are defined only at compile time.

Therefore, this is a valid program:

```
let mut _x = vec!["a", "b", "c"];
_x = vec!["X", "Y"];
```

as a vector of strings is assigned to a vector of strings, although they have different lengths. Instead, this is illegal:

```
let mut _x = vec!["a", "b", "c"];
_x = vec![15, 16, 17];
```

as a vector of numbers is assigned to a vector of strings.

As vectors can do all that arrays can do, what's the need to use arrays? The answer is that arrays are more efficient, and so, if at compile time you know how many items to put in your collection, you get a faster program by using an array instead of a vector.

Those who know the C++ language should have imagined that Rust arrays are equivalent to C++ `std::array` objects, while Rust vectors are equivalent to C++ `std::vector` objects.

Other Operations on Vectors

The standard library provides many operations regarding vectors. Here are some of them:

```
let mut x = vec!["This", "is", "a", "sentence"];
x.insert(1, "line");
x.insert(2, "contains");
x.remove(3);
x.push("about Rust");
x.pop();
for i in 0..x.len() { print!("{} ", x[i]); }
```

This program will print: "`This line contains a sentence.`"

Let's analyze it. The second line inserts the string "line" at position 1, that is, as the second place, just after the string `This`.

The third line inserts the string "contains" in the next position.

The fourth line removes the item that, after the last two insertions, is in position 3, that is, the string `is`, which initially was in position 1.

At this point, we have already the vector we need, but, just to show some other features of vectors, we add a string at the end, and next we remove it.

As it is shown, the `vector.push(item);` statement is equivalent to `vector.insert(vector.len(), item);`, while the statement `vector.pop()` is equivalent to `vector.remove(vector.len() - 1)`.

Given that `"push"` and `"pop"` operate only at the last position, while `"insert"` and `"remove"` can operate at any position, someone could think that the former two statements are much less used than the latter ones, or even almost useless. Well, he who thinks so would be wrong, because, using vectors, adding or removing items at the last position is quite typical; it is at least as common as adding or removing items at other positions.

Notice that the `insert` library function operates on three arguments: one is the vector in which the item is to be inserted, and it is written before the name of the function; another one is the position inside the vector, where the item is to be inserted, and it is passed as the first argument in the parentheses; and the third one is the value to insert, passed as the second argument in the parentheses.

If it were written, wrongly

```rust
let mut _x = vec!["This", "is", "a", "sentence"];
_x.insert("line", 1);
```

that would mean "insert into the vector _x the number 1 at position "line"". This kind of logic error is reported by the compiler because the insert function, like any Rust function, requires that its argument list has exactly the types defined by the function itself. The insert function applied to a vector of strings requires two arguments: the first one must be an integer number, and the second argument must be a string. Passing some more arguments, or some less arguments, or some arguments of different types causes compilation errors.

Ambiguity is possible only with a vector of integer numbers:

```rust
let mut _x = vec![12, 13, 14, 15];
_x.insert(3, 1);
```

This code is valid, but at a glance it is not obvious if it is inserting the number 1 in position 3 (and it is indeed so), or if it is inserting the number 3 in position 1 (and it is not so). Therefore, only with vectors of integer numbers the logic error of exchanging the two arguments wouldn't be detected by the compiler. In any other case, the compiler helps to avoid this kind of error.

Empty Arrays and Vectors

We saw that arrays and vectors are generic types, parameterized by the type of their items, and that such type is inferred by the type of the expressions used to initialize such arrays or vectors.

Now, let's assume we want to invoke a function f, which accepts two arguments: an array of options, where each option is a string; and a vector of options, where each option is an integer number. We could invoke it using this valid statement:

```rust
f(["help", "debug"], vec![0, 4, 15]);
```

However, if we want to tell such function that we don't want to pass any option, we could try to write:

```rust
f([], vec![]);
```

This is not allowed, though, because of there not being any item whose type is used to infer the type of the arguments, the compiler is not able to determine the type of the array nor the type of the vector.

Then, how can we declare an empty array or an empty vector?

If we compile

```
let _a = [];
```

we get a compilation error with the message "type annotations needed" and then "cannot infer type."

Instead, if we write

```
let _a = [""; 0];
```

the compilation is successful, and creates an empty array, whose type is that of an array of strings. The empty string specified is never used at runtime; it is used only by the compiler to understand that the expression is an array of strings.

Similarly, the code

```
let _a = vec![true; 0];
let _b = vec![false; 0];
```

declares two variables having the same type, and initially also the same value, as the "true" and "false" expressions are used only to specify the type as Boolean.

Therefore, our function above can be invoked in this way:

```
f([""; 0], vec![0; 0]);
```

Debug Print

As we saw, the "print" and "println" macros accept only a string as their first argument, but the possible further arguments can be of various types, including integer numbers, floating-point numbers, and Boolean values. However, if you want to print the contents of an array or of a vector, the following code is not allowed:

```
print!("{} {}", [1, 2, 3], vec![4, 5]);
```

because both the array passed as second argument, and the vector passed as third argument have no standard display format, and so two error messages are emitted.

Though, when debugging a program, it is useful to display the contents of such structures, without having to resort to "for" loops. For this purpose, you can write

```
print!("{:?} {:?}", [1, 2, 3], vec![4, 5]);
```

that will print "[1, 2, 3] [4, 5]".

By inserting the characters :? enclosed in the braces of a placeholder, you are telling the print macro (and the println macro) to generate a debug format for the corresponding data. So, whenever you want to print the contents of any variable, even if "{}" does not work, you may hope that "{:?}" works.

Copying Arrays and Vectors

If you want to copy an entire array or an entire vector, you are not required to write the code that scans its items:

```
let mut a1 = [4, 56, -2];
let a2 = [7, 81, 12500];
print!("{:?} ", a1);
a1 = a2;
print!("{:?}", a1);
```

This will print: "[4, 56, -2] [7, 81, 12500]". Indeed, the a1 array is exactly overwritten by the contents of the a2 array.

Using vectors, in this case, the behavior is the same:

```
let mut a1 = vec![4, 56, -2];
let a2 = vec![7, 81, 12500];
print!("{:?} ", a1);
a1 = a2;
print!("{:?}", a1);
```

However, the following code, using arrays

```
let mut a1 = [4, 56, -2];
let a2 = [7, 81];
print!("{:?} ", a1);
a1 = a2;
print!("{:?}", a1);
```

generates the compilation error mismatched types; while the following one, that instead uses vectors

```
let mut a1 = vec![4, 56, -2];
let a2 = vec![7, 81];
print!("{:?} ", a1);
a1 = a2;
print!("{:?}", a1);
```

is valid, and will print: "[4, 56, -2] [7, 81]".

All this happens because, as we saw before, the type of every array is characterized also by its size, while the type of each vector does not. And, in general, in Rust you can never copy an expression of one type onto a variable of another type.

CHAPTER 6

Using Primitive Types

In this chapter, you will learn:

- How to write numeric literals in hexadecimal, octal, or binary notation

- How to use the underscore character to make numeric literals easier to read

- How to use the exponential notation to write huge or tiny numbers in a compact form

- Which are the ten primitive integer numeric types, and the two primitive floating-point numeric types; which are their ranges; and when it is better to use each of them

- How to specify numeric literals of concrete types or of unconstrained types

- How to convert a numeric value to another numeric type

- The other primitive types: Booleans, characters, and empty tuples

- How type inference works

- How to express the types of arrays and vectors

- How to assign a name to a compile-time constant

- How to use the compiler to discover the type of an expression

© Carlo Milanesi 2018
C. Milanesi, *Beginning Rust*, https://doi.org/10.1007/978-1-4842-3468-6_6

Non-Decimal Numeric Bases

The way we write numbers every day uses the so-called "decimal notation" or "base-ten notation", but sometimes it is handy to write numbers in a base different from ten:

```
let hexadecimal = 0x10;
let decimal = 10;
let octal = 0o10;
let binary = 0b10;
print!("{} {} {} {}",
    hexadecimal, decimal, octal, binary);
```

This will print: "16 10 8 2". It is so because, if a literal integer number starts with a zero digit followed by an "x" (that is the third letter of "hexadecimal"), that number is expressed in hexadecimal notation; instead, if it starts with a zero followed by an "o" (that is the initial of "octal"), it is a number expressed in octal notation; and instead, if it starts with a zero followed by a "b" (that is the initial of "binary"), it is a number expressed in binary notation. In every other case, the number is expressed in decimal notation.

The numbers of this example are expressed in different notations, but they are all of the same type: integer numbers. Actually you can write:

```
let hexadecimal = 0x10;
let octal = 0o10;
let binary = 0b10;
let mut n = 10;
print!("{} ", n);
n = hexadecimal;
print!("{} ", n);
n = octal;
print!("{} ", n);
n = binary;
print!("{} ", n);
```

This will print: "10 16 8 2".

The n variable could receive the assignments from the other variables as they are all of the same type.

CHAPTER 6   USING PRIMITIVE TYPES

Instead, floating-point numbers can be expressed only in decimal notation.

Notice that such representations exist only in source code, as the machine code generated by the Rust compiler uses always a binary notation, both for integer numbers and for floating-point numbers.

For example, the program:

```
print!("{} {}", 0xA, 0b100000000);
```

and the program

```
print!("{} {}", 10, 256);
```

generate exactly the same executable program.

A last point: the letters used as hexadecimal digits may be indifferently uppercase or lowercase. For example, the number 0xAEf5b is equal to the number 0xaeF5B.

Instead, the letters used to indicate the numeric base must be lowercase. Therefore, the expressions 0X4, 0O4 e 0B4 are illegal.

Underscore in Numeric Literals

We saw that we can write the integer number "one billion", as 1000000000. But are you sure that it contains exactly nine zeros?

The integer number "one billion" comes out to be more readable if you write it as 1_000_000_000. The underscore characters ("_") can be inserted in any literal number, even floating point, and they are ignored by the compiler.

Even the number 3___4_.56_ is a valid number, and it is equal to 34.56. Though usually the underscore characters are used only to group decimal digits or octal digits by three, or hexadecimal or binary digits by four, as in:

```
let hexadecimal = 0x_00FF_F7A3;
let decimal = 1_234_567;
let octal = 0o_777_205_162;
let binary = 0b_0110_1001_1111_0001;
print!("{} {} {} {}",
    hexadecimal, decimal, octal, binary);
```

This will print "16775075 1234567 134023794 27121".

The Exponential Notation

Floating-point numbers can reach huge values, both positive and negative, like one billion of billions of billions of billions, and also hugely small values, which is very near to zero, like one billionth of billionth of billionth of billionth. If we wrote the literals of such hugely large or small numbers using the notation used so far, we typically should write many zeros, and the resulting numbers would be hard to read, even using underscores.

But you can write floating-point literal numbers also in another way:

```
let one_thousand = 1e3;
let one_million = 1e6;
let thirteen_billions_and_half = 13.5e9;
let twelve_millionths = 12e-6;
```

The first line uses a literal meaning "one times ten raised to the third power". In decimal notation, it is equivalent to write the number before the "e" and then shifting the decimal point *to the right* by as many places as are indicated after the "e", adding zeros, if there are not enough digits. In our case, we write "1", and then we shift the point by three places, adding as much zeros, and so we get the number "1000".

The number before the "e" is named "mantissa", while the number following it is named "exponent". They are both signed decimal numbers. The mantissa may have also a decimal point, and it may be followed by a fractional part.

This notation is named "exponential". The literals written in exponential notation are still floating-point numbers, even if they are written with no decimal point.

The second literal in the example means "one times ten raised to the sixth power", that is, the number "1000000".

The third literal means "thirteen point five times ten raised to the ninth power". There is already one decimal digit beyond which we have to shift the period, and after it we must add eight zeros, to get the value "13500000000". This number could be written also as 1.35e10, that means "one point thirty-five times ten raised to the tenth power", or as 135e8, or also as 13500e6, and in other ways, all generating the same machine code.

Finally, the fourth literal means "twelve times ten raised to the sixth negative power", or, equivalently, "twelve divided by ten raised to the sixth power". Using a negative exponent of ten is equivalent to writing the mantissa and then shifting the point *to the left* by as many digits as are indicated after the minus sign of the exponent, adding the needed zeros. So, the number 12e-6 is equal to the number 0.000012.

The Various Kinds of Signed Integer Numbers

So far, we said that there are two types of numbers: integer numbers and floating-point numbers.

There are programming languages having only floating-point numbers, without having a specific type for integer numbers; with respect to such languages, having two distinct numeric types is more complicated. But in Rust there are actually ten different integer numeric types, and two floating-point numeric types, so it is comparatively very complicated. Having further numeric types can have advantages, so that many programming languages have several numeric types.

So far we used integer numbers and floating-numbers, without further specifications, but it is possible to be more precise when defining the internal format of such numbers.

Here an important aspect of Rust appears: efficiency. Actually Rust has been designed to be extremely efficient.

A simple language could use only 32-bit integer numbers. But if we want to store a long sequence of small numbers, say between 0 and 200, and if every value were stored in a 32-bit object, some memory would be wasted, because it is possible to represent any number between 0 and 200 using only 8 bits, which is a quarter of 32 bits.

And this is not only for saving RAM space or storage space, but also to optimize speed; as the larger our objects are, the more cache space they use; and cache space is strictly limited. If an object cannot be contained in cache, its access will slow down the program. To have a fast program, you should keep in cache as many processed data as possible. To this purpose, objects should be as small as possible. In our example, we shouldn't use more than 8 bits to store our numbers.

On the other side, 32-bit numbers could be not large enough to represent all the values required by the application. For example, a program could need to store with accuracy a number larger than ten billions. In such case, a type having more than 32 bits is needed.

Therefore, Rust provides the opportunity to use 8-bit integer numbers, 16-bit integer numbers, 32-bit integer numbers, and also 64-bit integer numbers. And in case many of them are needed, like in an array or in a vector, it is advisable to use the smallest data type able to represent all the values required by application logic.

Let's see how we can use these numbers:

```rust
let a: i8 = 5;
let b: i16 = 5;
let c: i32 = 5;
let d: i64 = 5;
print!("{} {} {} {}", a, b, c, d);
```

The ": i8" clause, inserted in the first statement, and the similar ones in the three following statements, define the *type* of the variable that is being declared, and also of the object represented by such variable.

The words i8, i16, i32, and i64 are Rust keywords that identify, respectively, the type "8-bit signed integer number", the type "16-bit signed integer number", the type "32-bit signed integer number", and the type "64-bit signed integer number" The i letter is the initial of "integer".

Such types identify with precision how many bits will be used by the object. For example, the "a" variable will use eight bits, that will be able to represent 256 distinct values, and being a signed number, such an object will be able to contain values between -128 and +127, extremes included.

The variables "a", "b", "c", and "d" are of four different types, and so if we append an assignment statement from one of these variables to another, like b = d;, we will get a compilation error.

We already saw that it is not possible to compute an addition between an integer number and a floating-point number, as they have different types. Similarly, it is not possible to sum two integer numbers having a different number of bits:

```rust
let a: i8 = 5;
let b: i16 = 5;
print!("{}", a + b);
```

This statement generates a compilation error with the message "mismatched types".
Instead, the following code is valid and will print "23 23 23":

```rust
let a: i16 = 5;
let b: i16 = 18;
let c: i64 = 5;
let d: i64 = 18;
let e: i32 = 5;
```

```
let f: i32 = 18;
print!("{}", a + b);
print!("{}", c + d);
print!("{}", e + f);
```

Maybe someone will wonder why the number of bits of an integer number must be exactly 8, 16, 32, or 64, and not, for example, 19.

This is due to three reasons, all regarding efficiency:

- Every modern processor has instructions for arithmetic and data transfer that apply efficiently only to numbers having 8, 16, 32, and 64 bits. A 19-bit number would be handled anyway by the same machine language instructions that handle 32-bit numbers, and therefore there is no advantage in distinguishing a 19-bit type from 32-bit type.

- Memory management is more efficient when manipulating objects having as size a power of two. Therefore, having objects of different sizes causes less efficient code or the need to allocate additional space to reach a power of two (this operation is named "padding").

- If the same conceptual operation is executed on objects of the different sizes, the compiler must generate different machine language instructions. If there are many different types, there must be a lot of machine code, even if the source code is the same for all those types. Such phenomenon is known as "code bloat". It uses badly the instruction cache, and so causes the program to be slow. Instead, if a program contains only few types, the compiler can generate more compact code, which fits better in the CPU cache.

The third reason could suggest to not always use the smallest possible type, but to use just one type, which could be a large type. Actually, the rule of using the smallest possible type holds only for rather large collections of data, while for individual objects (also known as "scalars") or very small collections it is more efficient to use as few data types as possible. The general rule to maximize cache efficiency is therefore "minimize the memory used by machine code plus data".

Unsigned Integer Number Types

If we had to define an object containing an integer number that can have values between 0 and 200, which type is best to use? According to the last section, it may be better to use the smallest type among those that can represent all such values. The i8 type is the smallest, but it can represent only values between -128 and +127, and therefore it's no good. So, with the type encountered so far, we must use i16.

This is not optimal, as all the values between 0 and 255, including extremes, could be represented using only eight bits, if we reinterpret them. And such reinterpretation is already included in the machine language of all modern processors, and so it would be a pity (read "inefficient") to not use it.

Therefore, Rust allows to use four other numeric types:

```
let a: u8 = 5;
let b: u16 = 5;
let c: u32 = 5;
let d: u64 = 5;
print!("{} {} {} {}", a, b, c, d);
```

Here we introduced other four types of integer numbers. The "u" letter, shorthand for "unsigned", indicates it is an unsigned integer number. The number after the "u" letter indicates how many bits are used by such object; for example, the "a" variable uses eight bits, using which it can represent 256 distinct values, and therefore, being it an unsigned number, such values will be the integer numbers from 0 to 255, extremes included.

But there is at least another reason to prefer unsigned numbers to signed numbers. If we want to check if a *signed* integer number x is between zero included and a positive value n excluded, we should write the Boolean expression 0 <= x && x < n. But if x is an *unsigned* number, such a check can be done simply using the expression x < n.

Notice that the variables "a" "b", "c", and "d" have four different types, which are distinct among them, and also from the corresponding signed types.

Target-Dependent Integer-Number Types

So far we have seen eight different types to represent integer numbers, but Rust still has other integer numeric types.

When you access an item in an array or in a vector, which type should have the index?

You could think that, if you have a small array, you could use an i8 value or a u8 value, while if you have a somewhat larger array it would be required to use instead an i16 value or a u16 value.

It isn't so. It comes out that the most efficient type to use as index of an array or of a vector:

- on 16-bit computers, it is an unsigned 16-bit integer;

- on 32-bit computers, it is an unsigned 32-bit integer;

- on 64-bit computers, it is an unsigned 64-bit integer.

In other words, the index of an array or vector should be unsigned, and it should have the same size of a memory address.

At present, Rust is not supported for 16-bit systems, but it is both for 32-bit systems and for 64-bit systems. And so, which type should we use, to write some source code that should be optimal both on 32-bit computers and on 64-bit computers?

Notice that it is not relevant on which system the compiler runs, but on which system the program generated by the compiler will run. Actually, by a so-called "cross-compilation", a compiler can generate machine code for a system having a different architecture from the one where the compiler is run. The system for which machine code is generated is named "target." So there is a need to specify an integer numeric type having a size dependent on the target, which is a 32-bit integer if the target is a 32-bit system, and a 64-bit integer if the target is a 64-bit system.

To such purpose, Rust contains the isize type and the usize type:

```
let arr = [11, 22, 33];
let i: usize = 2;
print!("{}", arr[i]);
```

This will print "33".

In the word usize, the "u" letter indicates it is an unsigned integer, and the "size" word indicates it is a type thought to measure the length of some (possibly very large) object.

The compiler implements the usize type as the u32 type, if it is generating machine code for a 32-bit system, while implements it as the u64 type, if it is generating machine code for a 64-bit system. If 16-bit systems were supported, when generating code for such systems, probably it would implement the usize type as the u16 type.

In general, the `usize` type is useful every time there is a need for an unsigned integer, having the same size of a memory address (aka pointer).

In particular, if you have to index an array:

```
let arr = [11, 22, 33];
let i: usize = 2;
print!("{}", arr[i]);
let i: isize = 2;
print!("{}", arr[i]);
let i: u32 = 2;
print!("{}", arr[i]);
let i: u64 = 2;
print!("{}", arr[i]);
```

This code will generate three compilation errors, one for each call to `print`, except the first one. Actually, only the `usize` type is allowed as an index of an array.

Similar error messages are printed if you use a vector instead of an array.

In such a way, Rust allows us to access arrays and vectors only in the most efficient way.

Notice that it is not allowed even to use an index of u32 type on a 32-bit system, nor to use an index of u64 type on a 64-bit system. This guarantees source code portability.

For symmetry, there is also the `isize` type, which is a *signed* integer, having the same size of a memory address in the target system.

Type Inference

In the previous chapters, we were declaring variables without specifying their type, and we were talking about the types "integer number", "floating-point number", and so on.

In this chapter we started to add to the variable declarations the data type annotations.

But if no type is specified, do variables still have a specific type, or are they of a generic type?

```
let a = [0];
let i = 0;
print!("{}", a[i]);
```

This program is valid. How come? Didn't we say that to index an array, only `usize` expressions are valid?

In fact, each variable and each expression has always a well-defined type, but it is not always required to specify explicitly such a type. In many cases, the compiler is able to deduce it, or, as it is usually said, *infer* it, from the way in which the variable or expression in question is used.

For instance, in the preceding example, after having assigned to "i" the integer value 0, the compiler infers that the type of "i" must be that of an integer number, but it has not yet determined exactly which one, among the ten integer types available in Rust. We say that the type of such variable is that of a *generic*, or better, *unconstrained*, integer number.

However, when the compiler realizes that such variable is used to index an array, an operation allowed only to the `usize` type, the compiler assigns the `usize` type to the "i" variable, as it is the only allowed type.

In this program,

```
let i = 0;
let _j: u16 = i;
```

the compiler first determines that "i" is of type "unconstrained integer number", then it determines that "_j" is of type u16 as such type is explicitly annotated, and then, as "i" is used to initialize "_j", operation allowed only to expressions of type u16, it determines that "i" is of such type.

Instead, the compilation of this program

```
let i = 0;
let _j: u16 = i;
let _k: i16 = i;
```

generates an error at the third line, with the message `expected i16, found u16`.

Indeed, the compiler, following the above reasoning, at the second line has determined that "i" must be of type u16, but at the third line "i" is used to initialize a variable of type i16.

Conversely, this program is valid:

```
let i = 0;
let _j: u16 = i;
let _k = i;
```

71

In this case, it is the variable "_k" to come out to be of type u16.

Notice that such reasoning is performed always at compile time. In the final stage of every successful compilation, every variable has one concrete, constrained type.

If the compiler cannot infer the type of a variable, it generates a compilation error.

Instead, if the compiler succeeds to infer only that the type in an integer one, but it cannot constrain it to a specific integer type, then, as "default" integer type, it takes the type i32.

For example:

```
let i = 8;
let j = 8_000_000_000;
print!("{} {}", i, j);
```

This program will print: "8 -589934592".

Here both variables are of type i32. Too bad that the second one is initialized with a number that is too large to be contained in an i32 object.

The compiler realizes that, and so it emits the warning literal out of range for i32. In Rust, for efficiency reasons, similarly to C language, integer numeric overflow does not generate errors either at compile time or at runtime. Yet, the effect is that the number is stored in a truncated binary format that leaves only the least significant 32 bits, and then such bits are interpreted by the print macro as they were a signed integer number.

The Type Inference Algorithm

We saw that the compiler always tries to determine a concrete type for each variable and for each expression. For what we saw so far, the used algorithm is the following one.

If a type is explicitly specified, of course, the type must be the specified one.

If the type of a variable or of an expression hasn't yet been determined at all, and such variable or expression is used in an expression or in a declaration that can be valid only with a specific type, then such type is determined in this way for such variable or expression. Such determination may be of a constrained kind, or it may be of an unconstrained kind. A constrained type is a specific type, like i8 or u64, while an unconstrained type is a category of types, like {integer}.

If, at the end of the parsing, the compiler has determined only that a variable is of an unconstrained integer numeric type, such type is defined to be i32. Instead, if the type is completely undetermined, a compilation error is generated.

Floating-Point Numeric Types

Regarding the floating-point numeric types, the situation is similar to that of integer numbers but much simpler: at present in Rust there are only two floating-point types.

```
let a: f64 = 4.6;
let b: f32 = 3.91;
print!("{} {}", a, b);
```

This program will print: "4.6 3.91".

The "f64" type is that of 64-bit floating-point numbers, while the "f32" type is that of 32-bit floating-point numbers. The "f" letter is shorthand for "floating-point". Such types correspond exactly and respectively to the "double" and "float" types of the C language.

So far, Rust has no other numeric types, but if a 128-bit floating-point type were added, probably its name would be "f128".

What we said about integer types holds also for these types. For example:

```
let a = 4.6;
let mut _b: f32 = 3.91e5;
_b = a;
```

This program is valid. The compiler, parsing the first line, determines that the variable "a" has an *unconstrained* floating-point numeric type. Then, parsing the third line, it determines that the variable "a" is of type f32, as this is the only type allowed to assign a value to a variable of f32 type.

The "default" floating-point type is the 64-bit one. Therefore, if there wasn't the last line in this program, the "a" variable would be of f64 type.

For floating-point numbers, the criteria to choose between 32-bit and 64-bit numbers are similar to those for integer numbers, but somewhat fuzzier. It is still true that 32-bit numbers occupy exactly half as much memory and cache as 64-bit numbers. And it is still true that the maximum value that can be represented by a 64-bit number is larger than the maximum value that can be represented by a 32-bit number. However, the latter is so large that is rarely exceeded.

Instead, a more important fact if that 64-bit numbers have much more digits in mantissa, and that makes such numbers much more precise. Indeed, 32-bit numbers have a 24-bit mantissa, while 64-bit numbers have a 53-bit mantissa.

To give you an idea, 32-bit numbers can represent exactly all the integer numbers only up to around 16 million, while 64-bit numbers can represent exactly all the integer numbers up to around 9 million of billions. Put in other words, each value of f32 type, expressed in decimal notation, has almost 7 significant digits, while every f64 has almost 16 significant digits.

Explicit Conversions

We have said several times that Rust performs a strict type of checking: every time that the compiler expects an expression of a certain type, it generates an error if it finds an expression of another type, even if similar; and in every arithmetic expression, the compiler expects that its operands are of the same type.

These rules would seem likely to forbid any calculation involving objects of different types, but it isn't so:

```
let a: i16 = 12;
let b: u32 = 4;
let c: f32 = 3.7;
print!("{}", a as i8 + b as i8 + c as i8);
```

This will print: "19".

The variables "a", "b", and "c" are of three different types. The last one is not even an integer number. However, by using the "as" operator, followed by the name of a type, you can do many conversions, including the three shown above.

All of the three objects of the example are converted into objects of type i8, and so such resulting objects can be summed up.

Notice that if the destination type is less *expressive* than the original type, you may lose information. For example, when you convert the fractional value 3.7 into the integer type i8, the fractional part is discarded, and 3 is obtained.

This code has a behavior somewhat difficult to predict:

```
let a = 500 as i8;
let b = 100_000 as u16;
let c = 10_000_000_000 as u32;
print!("{} {} {}", a, b, c);
```

Perhaps surprisingly, it will print: "-12 34464 1410065408".

Such behavior is easily understandable only when thinking about the binary code that is used to represent the integer numbers.

The value 500 cannot be expressed using only 8 bits, but at least 9 bits are required. If we take its binary representation, we extract its least significant 8 bits, and then we interpret such 8-bit sequence as an "i8" object, when we print in decimal notation such object, we get -12.

Similarly, the least significant 16 bits of the binary representation of one hundred thousand, interpreted as an unsigned integer, are printed in decimal notation as 34464; and the least significant 32 bits of the binary representation of ten billions, interpreted as an unsigned number, are printed in decimal notation as 1410065408.

Therefore the as operator, if applied to an integer number object, extract from such object enough least significant bits to represent the specified type, and it generates such value as the result of the expression.

Type Suffixes of Numeric Literals

So far, we used two kinds of numeric literals: the integer ones, like -150; and the floating-point ones, like 6.022e23. The former is of type "unconstrained integer number", and the latter of type "unconstrained floating-point number".

If you want to constrain a number, there are several ways:

```
let _a: i16 = -150;
let _b = -150 as i16;
let _c = -150 + _b - _b;
let _d = -150i16;
```

All these four variables are of type i16, and they have the same value.

The first one has been declared explicitly to be of such type. In the second line, the unconstrained integer numeric expression has been converted into a specific type. In the third line, the expression contains the subexpressions "_b" of a specific type, and so the whole expression gets such type. At last, in the fourth line a new notation is used.

If, after an integer numeric literal, a type is specified, the literal gets such type, as if an "as" keyword were interposed. Notice that between the literal and the type, no blank is allowed. If you like, you can add some underscores, like in -150_i16 or 5__u32.

Similarly, you can decorate floating-point numeric literals: 6.022e23f64 is a 64-bit floating-point number, while -4f32 and 0_f32 are 32-bit floating-point numbers. Notice that the decimal point is not needed, if there is no fractional digit.

All the Numeric Types

In summary, here is an example that uses all the Rust numeric types:

```
let _: i8 = 127;
let _: i16 = 32_767;
let _: i32 = 2_147_483_647;
let _: i64 = 9_223_372_036_854_775_807;
let _: isize = 100; // The maximum value depends on the target architecture
let _: u8 = 255;
let _: u16 = 65_535;
let _: u32 = 4_294_967_295;
let _: u64 = 18_446_744_073_709_551_615;
let _: usize = 100; // The maximum value depends on the target architecture
let _: f32 = 1e38;
let _: f64 = 1e308;
```

And here is the list of all Rust built-in integer numeric types:

Type	Occupied bytes	Minimum value	Maximum value
i8	1	-128	+127
i16	2	-32,768	+32,767
i32	4	-2,147,483,648	+2,147,483,647
i64	8	-2^{63}	$+2^{63} - 1$
isize	4 or 8	on a 32-bit target: -2,147,483,648; on a 64-bit target: -2^{63}	on a 32-bit target: +2,147,483,647; on a 64-bit target: $+2^{63} - 1$
u8	1	0	+255
u16	2	0	+65,535
u32	4	0	+4,294,967,295
u64	8	0	$+2^{64} - 1$
usize	4 or 8	0	on a 32-bit target: +4,294,967,295; on a 64-bit target: $+2^{64} - 1$

Instead, there are just two floating-point numeric types:

- **f32**, having 32 bits, is equivalent to the float type of the C language.

- **f64**, having 64 bits, is equivalent to the double type of the C language.

Booleans and Characters

In addition to numeric types, Rust defines some other primitive built-in types:

```
let a: bool = true; print!("[{}]", a);
let b: char = 'a'; print!("[{}]", b);
```

This will print: "[true][a]".

The bool type, that we saw already, is equivalent to the type of C++ language having the same name. It admits only the two values: false and true. It is used mainly for the condition in the if and while statements.

The char type, which actually we haven't seen yet, looks like the type of C language having the same name, but in fact it differs a lot from it. To start with, a C language char typically occupies only one byte, while an isolated Rust char occupies four bytes. This is due to the fact that Rust chars are Unicode characters, and the Unicode standard defines more than one million of possible values.

Literal characters are enclosed in single quotes, and they can be also non-ASCII characters. For example, this code

```
let e_grave = 'è';
let japanese_character = 'さ';
println!("{} {}", e_grave, japanese_character);
```

will print "è さ".

Notice that, differing from C language, neither bool nor char are in any way considered numbers, and so both the following statements are illegal:

```
let _a = 'a' + 'b';
let _b = false + true;
```

However, both types may be converted to numbers:

```
print!("{} {} {} {} {}", true as u8, false as u8,
    'A' as u32, 'à' as u32, '€' as u32);
```

This will print: "1 0 65 224 8364".

In this way we just discovered that true is represented by the number 1, false by the number 0, the "A" character by the number 65, the grave "a" by the number 224, and the euro symbol by the number 8364.

Instead, if you want to convert numbers into Booleans or into characters, you can use these features:

```
let truthy = 1;
let falsy = 0;
print!("{} {} {} {}", truthy != 0, falsy != 0,
    65 as char, 224 as char);
```

This will print: "true false A à".

Instead, you cannot use the as bool clause with a number, because not every numeric value corresponds to a Boolean; in fact only zero and one have this property, and so in general such conversion would not be well defined.

So, if for a number the zero value is meant to represent falsity, to convert such number into a Boolean, which is to see if it corresponds to truth, it is enough to check if it is different from zero.

The situation of characters is similar. Each character is represented by a 32-bit number, and so it may be converted to it, but not every 32-bit number represents a character, and so some (actually, most) 32-bit numbers wouldn't be convertible into characters. Therefore, the expression 8364 as char is illegal.

To convert any number into a character, you need to use a library function, not described here.

Though, for each number between 0 and 255 there is a Unicode character corresponding to it, and so it is allowed to convert into a character any number of u8 type. Actually, that has been done, in the example above, for the numbers 65 and 224.

It may be interesting, for those who don't know yet Unicode, to see all the characters corresponding to the first 256 numbers:

```
for i in 0..256 {
    println!("{}: [{}]", i, i as u8 as char);
}
```

This will print 256 lines, each one containing a number and its corresponding character. Some of those characters are terminal control codes, like "line-feed" and "carriage-return," and others are non-printable.

Notice that i must be converted to u8 type, before being able to convert it into a char.

The Empty Tuple

There is another primitive, weird type, whose name in Rust is "()", which is a pair of parentheses. Such type has only one value, which is written in the same way as its type, which is "()". This type somewhat corresponds to the "void" type of the C language, or to the "undefined" type of JavaScript, as it represents the absence of type information. To be able to pronounce its name, it is named "empty tuple".

This type appears in several cases, like the following ones:

```
let a: () = ();
let b = { 12; 87; 283 };
let c = { 12; 87; 283; };
let d = {};
let e = if false { };
let f = while false { };
print!("{:?} {:?} {:?} {:?} {:?} {:?}",
    a, b, c, d, e, f);
```

This code will print: "() 283 () () () ()".

The first line declares a variable of type "()", and initializes it using the only possible value. In the last line, the "print" macro cannot match such type with the placeholder "{}", and so the debug placeholder "{:?}" must be used.

The second line declares a variable and initializes it with the value of a block. From here, some new concepts appear.

The first concept is that a simple number like "12" or "87" can be used in place of any statement, because any expression can be used in place of a statement. Of course, such a statement does nothing, and so it will generate no machine code.

The second concept is that the value of a block is defined to be the value of its last expression, if there is such an expression; so, in the case of the second line, the value of the block is the integer number "283", and such value is used to initialize the "b" variable, which therefore will be of i32 type.

79

The third line shows the case where the contents of a block end with the statement terminator, the semicolon character. In such case, the value of the block is "()", and such value is used to initialize the "c" variable, which therefore will be of "()" type.

The fourth line declares the "d" variable, and it initializes it with the value of an empty block. Also empty blocks have empty tuples as their values.

In the fifth line there is a conditional expression without the "else" branch. When the "else" branch is missing, the "else { }" clause is implied. Therefore, such statement is meant to be "let e = if false { } else { }". Such a conditional expression is valid, as both branches have the same type.

The sixth line shows that also the "while" statement has the value of an empty tuple. Actually both the "while" statement block and the "while" statement itself must always have as value an empty tuple, and therefore it has little sense to use the "while" construct as an expression. This holds also for "loop" and "for" loops.

Array and Vector Types

When presenting arrays and vectors, we said that if we change the type of the contained items, we implicitly change also the type of both arrays and vectors; and if we change the number of the contained items, we implicitly change also the type of arrays, but not the type of vectors.

If you want to make explicit the type of arrays or vectors, you should write:

```
let _array1: [char; 3] = ['x', 'y', 'z'];
let _array2: [f32; 200] = [0f32; 200];
let _vector1: Vec<char> = vec!['x', 'y', 'z'];
let _vector2: Vec<i32> = vec![0; 5000];
```

As it is shown, the expression that represents the type of an array contains both the type of the items, and their number, separated by a semicolon and enclosed in square brackets.

Instead, the type of a vector is written as the word Vec (with an uppercase initial), followed by the type of the contained items, enclosed in angular brackets.

Constants

The following program is illegal:

```
let n = 20;
let _ = [0; n];
```

It is so because arrays must be of a length known at compile time, and even if "n" is immutable, and so, in a sense, constant, its initial value could be determined at runtime, and so it is not allowed to specify the size of an array.

But the following program is valid:

```
const N: usize = 20;
let _ = [0; N];
```

The "const" keyword allows us to declare an identifier having a value defined at compile time, and of course no more changeable at runtime. In its declaration, it is required to specify its type.

Rust constants correspond to C++ language const items.

A Rust constant can be considered a name that at compile time is associated to a value, not to an object. The compiler replaces such value in every place in the program where the constant's name is used.

Discovering the Type of an Expression

You will often come across an expression, wondering what the type of such expression is.

This could be answered by an interpreter, an integrated development environment, or the written documentation, but there is a trick to answer such kind of questions using only the compiler.

Say we want to know the type of the expression 4u32 / 3u32, that in some languages is a floating-point number.

We just add a statement that tries to use that expression to initialize a bool variable. If the program compiles with no errors, that means that our expression is of bool type. But in our case we have:

```
let _: bool = 4u32 / 3u32;
```

The compilation of this program generates the error `mismatched types`, and the detail of the error message explains `expected bool, found u32`. From such explanation, we learn that our expression is of `u32` type.

Sometimes, the error message is more vague.

```
let _: bool = 4 / 3;
```

For this program the error explanation is `"expected bool, found integral variable"`, and then `"expected type 'bool' found type '{integer}'"`. That expression "integral type", and the equivalent "{integer}", does not indicate a concrete type; it indicates a still unconstrained type, which the compiler has determined to be an integral type, but not yet which of the several existing integral types.

CHAPTER 7

Enumerating Cases

In this chapter, you will learn:

- How enums help in defining variables that can take on values only from a finite set of cases

- How enums can be used to implement discriminated union types

- How to use the match pattern-matching construct to handle enums

- How to use the match construct to handle other data types, like integer numbers, strings, and single characters

- How to use Boolean guards to generalize the pattern-matching of the match construct

Enumerations

Instead of writing the following code:

```
const EUROPE: u8 = 0;
const ASIA: u8 = 1;
const AFRICA: u8 = 2;
const AMERICA: u8 = 3;
const OCEANIA: u8 = 4;

let continent = ASIA;

if continent == EUROPE { print!("E"); }
else if continent == ASIA { print!("As"); }
else if continent == AFRICA { print!("Af"); }
else if continent == AMERICA { print!("Am"); }
else if continent == OCEANIA { print!("O"); }
```

© Carlo Milanesi 2018
C. Milanesi, *Beginning Rust*, https://doi.org/10.1007/978-1-4842-3468-6_7

CHAPTER 7   ENUMERATING CASES

It is better to write the following equivalent code:

```
enum Continent {
    Europe,
    Asia,
    Africa,
    America,
    Oceania,
}

let contin = Continent::Asia;

match contin {
    Continent::Europe => print!("E"),
    Continent::Asia => print!("As"),
    Continent::Africa => print!("Af"),
    Continent::America => print!("Am"),
    Continent::Oceania => print!("O"),
}
```

The "enum" keyword introduces the new Continent type, specified just after it. Such a type is called "enumerative", because it lists a set of items, associating internally a unique number to each item. In the example, the allowed values for the type Continent are Europe, Asia, Africa, America, and Oceania, which respectively are represented internally by the values 0u8, 1u8, 2u8, 3u8, and 4u8.

In the simplest cases, like the one shown above, such type is similar to the homonymous construct of the C language.

After having defined an enumerative type, it is possible to create objects of such type, named "enumerations", or "enum" for shorthand. In the example, the contin enum variable, of Continent type, has been defined.

The enums can have as value only one of the items listed in the definition of their type. Such items are named "variants."

Notice that the use of a variant must be qualified by the name of its type, like in Continent::Asia.

The following code

```
enum T {A, B, C, D};
let n: i32 = T::D;
let e: T = 1;
```

generates a compilation error at the second line, and another one at the third line, both of the kind `mismatched types`. The first error is described as `expected i32, found enum 'main::T'`; instead, the second error is described as `expected enum 'main::T', found integral variable`. Therefore, enums cannot implicitly be converted to numbers, and numbers cannot implicitly be converted to enums.

The match Construct

In the last part of the first example, the just-created enum is used by a new kind of construct, beginning with the `"match"` keyword.

The `match` statement is the basic Rust tool to use enumerations, similarly to the `switch` statement in the C language, even if they differ about many aspects.

In the first place, notice that the expression following the `match` keyword doesn't have to be enclosed in parentheses.

Then, the various cases, also called "arms", are made of a pattern, followed by the symbol `"=>"`, followed by an expression. Such arms are separated by commas.

Both in the declaration of the enumerative type, and in the `"match"` statement, after the last item, it is optional to put another comma. Usually, if you put each item in a different line, such comma is written, so that every line containing items ends with a comma; instead, the comma is omitted just before a closed brace, like in:

```
enum CardinalPoint { North, South, West, East };
```

The behavior of our `match` statement is the following one.

First, the statement following `match` is evaluated, so obtaining a value, in our case `Continent::Asia`. Then, such value is compared with each one of the (five) patterns, in the order that they appear written, and as soon as a pattern matches, the right side of its arm is evaluated, and the statement is ended.

Notice that the right side of every arm must be a single expression. So far, we always used `print!` as if it were a statement, but actually it is an expression.

In fact, any expression becomes a valid statement, if you add a semicolon character after it:

```
let a = 7.2;
12;
true;
4 > 7;
5.7 +  5. * a;
```

This code is valid, although, of course, it does nothing.

Given that an invocation of the print! macro is a valid expression, when we added the ";" character we could use it as a statement.

However, notice that there are statements that aren't valid expressions. For example, "let a = 3;" and "fn empty() {}" are statements that aren't valid expressions even without the semicolon character. If we wrote:

```
match contin {
    Continent::Europe => let a = 7;,
    Continent::Asia => let a = 7,
    Continent::Africa => fn aaa() {},
    Continent::America => print!("Am"),
    Continent::Oceania => print!("O"),
}
```

We would have gotten an error for each of the first three cases, as at the right of the "=>" symbol, there aren't valid expressions.

And what if you wish to evaluate several expressions in the right side of an arm? Or a statement that isn't also an expression? In such cases you can use a block:

```
enum Continent {
    Europe,
    Asia,
    Africa,
    America,
    Oceania,
}

let mut contin = Continent::Asia;
```

```
match contin {
    Continent::Europe => {
        contin = Continent::Asia;
        print!("E");
    },
    Continent::Asia => { let a = 7; },
    Continent::Africa => print!("Af"),
    Continent::America => print!("Am"),
    Continent::Oceania => print!("O"),
}
```

Here contin has been declared as mutable, and then, in case its value was Europe, it would be changed to Asia, and the letter E would be printed. Instead, in case its value was Asia, another variable would be declared, initialized, and immediately destroyed.

Such two arms have a block as their right side, and, because any block is an expression, this syntax is valid.

Relational Operators and Enums

Enums are not comparable using the "==" operator. Actually, the following program is illegal:

```
enum CardinalPoint { North, South, West, East };
let direction = CardinalPoint::South;
if direction == CardinalPoint::North { }
```

The compiler generates for the last statement the message "binary operation `==` cannot be applied to type `main::CardinalPoint`". Consequently, to check the value of an enum, you are required to use a match statement.

Enums are important as they are used in many places of the standard library, and also in other Rust libraries. And the match construct is important as it is required to use enums, even if often it is encapsulated in other constructs.

With enums, not only the "==" operator is forbidden, but also the other relational operators. Therefore, the following code will also generate a compilation error:

```
enum CardinalPoint { North, South, West, East };
if CardinalPoint::South < CardinalPoint::North { }
```

Handling All the Cases

If you try to compile the following program

```rust
enum CardinalPoint { North, South, West, East };
let direction = CardinalPoint::South;
match direction {
    CardinalPoint::North => print!("NORTH"),
    CardinalPoint::South => print!("SOUTH"),
}
```

you get the error "non-exhaustive patterns: `West` and `East` not covered". The compiler complains that among the allowed values for the expression direction, only two of them were considered, and the cases in which the expression's value would be West or East weren't considered. This happens as Rust requires that the match statement handles explicitly every possible case.

Instead, the following program is valid, as it considers all the possible values of the argument of match:

```rust
enum CardinalPoint { North, South, West, East };
let direction = CardinalPoint::South;
match direction {
    CardinalPoint::North => print!("NORTH"),
    CardinalPoint::South => print!("SOUTH"),
    CardinalPoint::East => {},
    CardinalPoint::West => {},
}
```

However, here the last two variants (East and West) do nothing, and it is annoying to list them anyway. To avoid having to list all the variants that do nothing, it is possible to use an underscore sign, in the following way:

```rust
enum CardinalPoint { North, South, West, East };
let direction = CardinalPoint::South;
match direction {
    CardinalPoint::North => print!("NORTH"),
    CardinalPoint::South => print!("SOUTH"),
    _ => {},
}
```

The underscore sign always matches with any value, and so it avoids the compilation error, given that in this way all cases have been handled. Of course, such a "catch-all" case must be the last one, to avoid catching even cases that should be handled differently:

```
enum CardinalPoint { North, South, West, East };
let direction = CardinalPoint::South;
match direction {
    CardinalPoint::North => print!("NORTH"),
    _ => {},
    CardinalPoint::South => print!("SOUTH"),
}
```

This program does not print anything, because the matching `CardinalPoint::South` case is never reached.

The "`_`" pattern corresponds to the "`default`" case of the C language.

Using `match` with Numbers

The `match` construct, in addition to be needed with enums, is also usable and useful with other data types:

```
match "value" {
    "val" => print!("value "),
    _ => print!("other "),
}
match 3 {
    3 => print!("three "),
    4 => print!("four "),
    5 => print!("five "),
    _ => print!("other "),
}
match '.' {
    ':' => print!("colon "),
    '.' => print!("point "),
    _ => print!("other "),
}
```

This will print: "other three point".

The first match statement has a string as its argument, and so it expects strings as left sides of its arms. In particular, no arm matches exactly, and so the default case is taken.

The second match statement has an integer number as its argument, and so it expects integer numbers as left sides of its arms. In particular, the pattern of the first arm matches, and so it is taken.

The third match statement has a character as its argument, and so it expects single characters as left sides of its arms. In particular, the pattern of the second arm matches, and so it is taken.

Also for the match statements with arguments that aren't enums, it is required that all possible cases are handled. However, except for enums and for Booleans, it is not feasible to specify all single cases; and so, it is required to use the underscore "catch-all" case.

Enumerations with Data

Rust enumerations aren't always as simple as the one seen above:

```
enum Result {
    Success(f64),
    Failure(u16, char),
    Uncertainty,
}

// let outcome = Result::Success(23.67);
let outcome = Result::Failure(1200, 'X');

match outcome {
    Result::Success(value) =>
        print!("Result: {}", value),
    Result::Failure(error_code, module) =>
        print!("Error n. {} in module {}",
            error_code, module),
    Result::Uncertainty => {},
}
```

This will print: "Error n. 1200 in module X".

Instead, if the comment is changed so to reactivate the commented-out line and to comment-out the next line, the program will print: "Result: 23.67".

In this code, the definition of the Result enumerative type has the first variant with a data type enclosed in parentheses (f64), the second variant with two types (u16 and char), and the third variant with no type (and no parentheses).

The effect of such a declaration is that every object having such a Result type, like the variable outcome in the example, can have the following values: its value may be Result::Success, and in addition it contains also an object of type f64; or its value is Result::Failure, and in addition it contains also an object of type u16 and an object of type char; or its value is Result::Uncertainty, and it contains no further data. No other possibility.

Therefore, with respect to the C language, Rust enumerative types combine the enum feature with the union feature.

The C language program corresponding to this example is:

```
#include <stdio.h>
int main() {
    enum eResult {
        Success,
        Failure,
        Uncertainty
    };

    struct sResult {
        enum eResult r;
        union {
            double value;
            struct {
                unsigned short error_code;
                char module;
            } s;
        } u;
    } outcome;
```

```
    /*
    outcome.r = Success;
    outcome.u.value = 23.67;
    */
    outcome.r = Failure;
    outcome.u.s.error_code = 1200;
    outcome.u.s.module = 'X';

    switch (outcome.r) {
        case Success:
            printf("Result: %g", outcome.u.value);
            break;
        case Failure:
            printf("Error n. %d in module %c",
                outcome.u.s.error_code,
                outcome.u.s.module);
            break;
        case Uncertainty:
            break;
    }
    return 0;
}
```

Going back to the above Rust code, you can see that to assign a value to the outcome variable, the name of the variant (Result::Success or Result::Failure) is specified, and it is followed by some comma-separated values, enclosed in parentheses, like in a function call ((23.67) in the first case, and (1200, 'X') in the second case).

When you assign a value to an enumeration of such a type, you must specify in parentheses the arguments having the types requested by the enumerative type. In the example, in the Success case, a floating-point number is passed; in the Failure case, an integer number and a character are passed; and in the Uncertainty case, no parameter is passed. If you pass arguments of other types or in different numbers, you'll get a compilation error.

In the "match" statement, the pattern of the first arm is Result::Success(value); and the pattern of the second arm is Result::Failure(error_code, module). So, in every pattern there are as many arguments as defined in their respective declaration. Here too, doing differently causes errors.

In such patterns, in place of the type present in the declaration, a name is placed, not necessarily declared before. For example, in place of f64, a value has been placed. Such names are in fact declarations of variables, and the scope of such variables is restricted to the arm where they are declared.

When a specific arm is taken, for example, the Success arm, the variables in parentheses in such arm, if present, are initialized using the value contained in the variant. In the example, the value variable is initialized using the value 23.67. When such a variable will be used in the right side of the arm, it will have the value by which it has been initialized.

If you don't need to use the value of a variable in a pattern of a "match" statement, to avoid a compiler warning, you can do it this way:

```
enum Result {
    Success(f64),
    Failure(u16, char),
    Uncertainty,
}

let outcome = Result::Success(23.67);

match outcome {
    Result::Success(_) => print!("OK"),
    Result::Failure(error_code, module) =>
        print!("Error n. {} in module {}",
            error_code, module),
    Result::Uncertainty => {},
}
```

This will print: "OK". The arm "Result::Success" would need an argument, and not putting it is illegal, but we don't need the value of such argument, and we don't want to forge a variable name for something that we don't need. In such case, the underscore sign tells the compiler: "I know that here you would like to pass me an argument, but I don't have any use for it, so throw it away".

"match" Expressions

Similarly to the "if" expressions, there are also "match" expressions:

```
enum CardinalPoint { North, South, West, East };
let direction = CardinalPoint::South;
print!("{}", match direction {
    CardinalPoint::North => 'N',
    CardinalPoint::South => 'S',
    _ => '*',
});
```

This will print: "S."

We already saw that if the "if" keyword is used to create an if expression, it must have also an else block, and its returned type must be the same of the block before the else keyword.

The same applies for match expressions: all the arms of match expressions must have the right sides of the same type. In the example, the three arms have the values 'N', 'S', and '*', and so they are all of char type.

If the third arm were replaced by "_ => {},", you would get the compilation error "match arms have incompatible types". Indeed, as two arms are of char type, and one of () type, it is impossible to determine the type of the whole match expression.

Use of Guards in match Constructs

Let's assume we want to classify the integer numbers in the following categories: all the negative numbers, the zero number, the one number, and all the other positive numbers:

```
for n in -2..5 {
    println!("{} is {}.", n, match n {
        0 => "zero",
        1 => "one",
        _ if n < 0 => "negative",
        _ => "plural",
    });
}
```

This program will print:

```
-2 is negative.
-1 is negative.
0 is zero.
1 is one.
2 is plural.
3 is plural.
4 is plural.
```

The "for" statement iterates the integer numbers from "-2" included to "5" excluded.

For each processed number, that number, followed by its classification, is printed. Such classification is performed by the "match" construct, which here is used as an expression having a string as its value. Indeed, each of its arms has a literal string as its value.

The third arm differs from the others. Its pattern is an underscore, and so such an arm should match always, but such a pattern is followed by a clause made by the "if" keyword and a Boolean condition. Such a clause causes this pattern to match only if such Boolean condition is true.

CHAPTER 8

Using Heterogeneous Data Structures

In this chapter you will learn how to define and use other composite types:

- Tuples
- Structs
- Tuple-Structs

They are useful to group objects of different types.

At the end of the chapter, you'll see some code style conventions.

The Tuples

Arrays and vectors can contain several items, yet such items must all be of the same type. If you wish to store in a single object several sub-objects of different types, you can do in this way:

```
let data = (10000000, 183.19, 'Q');
let copy_of_data = data;
print!("{}, {}, {}",
    data.0, copy_of_data.1, data.2);
```

This will print: "10000000, 183.19, Q".

The "data" variable is a composite object, as it is composed of three objects. Even arrays are composite objects, but they are constrained to be composed of objects of the same type, while the "data" variable is composed of objects of different types: an integer number, a floating-point number, and a character.

© Carlo Milanesi 2018
C. Milanesi, *Beginning Rust*, https://doi.org/10.1007/978-1-4842-3468-6_8

Therefore, our object is not an array, but a "tuple."

The declaration of tuples looks like that of arrays. The only difference is that round parentheses are used instead of square brackets.

Each item of a tuple is named "field."

Also the type of tuples can be made explicit:

```
let data: (i32, f64, char) = (10000000, 183.19, 'Q');
```

The type has the same format as the value, where the value of each field is replaced by its type.

As it is shown in the second statement, an entire tuple may be used to initialize another tuple of the same type.

You can access the fields of a tuple by their position, using the dot-notation. When accessing the seventh item of the "arr" array, you must write "arr[6]"; to access the seventh field of the "data" tuple, you must write "data.6".

Also tuples can be mutable:

```
let mut data = (10000000, 183.19, 'Q');
data.0 = -5;
data.2 = 'x';
print!("{}, {}, {}", data.0, data.1, data.2);
```

This will print: "-5, 183.19, x".

Similarly to arrays, tuples can also have any number of fields, including zero. Given that the type of a tuple is defined by the sequence of the types of its fields, enclosed in parentheses, if there are no fields only the parentheses remain, and so its type is "()". And given that the value of a tuple is expressed by the sequence of the values of its fields, enclosed in parentheses, if there are no fields, only the parentheses remain, and so its value is "()".

But we already saw this type and this value. So now it is explained why they are named "empty tuples".

A difference between tuples and arrays is that tuples cannot be accessed by a variable index:

```
let array = [12, 13, 14];
let tuple = (12, 13, 14);
let i = 0;
print!("{}", array[i]);
print!("{}", tuple.i);
```

In this program the last line is illegal, and there is no way to get the value of a field of a tuple using an index determined at runtime.

The Structs

Tuples are useful as long as they contain no more than a handful of items, but when they have many fields, it is too easy to mistake them, and the code that uses them comes out to be poorly understood:

```
let data = (10, 'x', 12, 183.19, 'Q', false, -9);
print!("{}", data.2 + data.6);
```

Is it clear that this code will print 3?

In addition, the type of any tuple is defined only by the sequence of the types of its fields, and if there are many fields, such a type is too long to specify, and poorly understood:

```
let data1 = (10, 'x', 12, 183.19, 'Q', false, -9);
let mut data2: (u16, char, i16, f64, bool, char, i16);
data2 = data1;
```

This code is illegal. Can you spot the error?

In addition, if a field is added at the beginning of a tuple, all the indexes to objects of such a type must be incremented in source code. For example, "data.2" must become "data.3".

Therefore, it comes out very useful to have a specific statement to declare the type of a structure, giving it a name, and labeling all the fields of that structure:

```
struct SomeData {
    integer: i32,
    fractional: f32,
    character: char,
    five_bytes: [u8; 5],
}
let data = SomeData {
    integer: 10_000_000,
    fractional: 183.19,
```

```
    character: 'Q',
    five_bytes: [9, 0, 250, 60, 200],
};
print!("{}, {}, {}, {}",
    data.five_bytes[3], data.integer,
    data.fractional, data.character);
```

This will print 60, 10000000, 183.19, Q.

The first statement occupies six lines: it starts with the "struct" keyword and proceeds with a block. Its effect is to declare the "SomeData" type. Any object of such a type is a sequence of four fields. For each field, its name and its type are declared, separated by a colon. The list of field declarations is comma-separated, with an optional ending comma. Let's name "struct" such a kind of data type.

Also the second statement occupies six lines. It declares the variable "data", and initializes it with an object of the type just declared. Notice that the initialization syntax looks like the type declaration syntax, where the "struct" keyword is removed, and each field type is replaced by the value to assign to such a field. Let's name "struct-object" such kind of an object, which is any object whose type is a struct.

The third statement accesses the fields of the just-defined struct-object, using the so-called dot-notation. This notation consists of an expression representing the struct-object, followed by a dot, followed by the name of the field to access.

This code is similar to the following C language program:

```
#include <stdio.h>
int main() {
    struct SomeData {
        int integer;
        float fractional;
        char character;
        unsigned char five_bytes[5];
    };
    struct SomeData data = {
        10000000,
        183.19,
        'Q',
        {9, 0, 250, 60, 200},
    };
```

```
    printf("%d, %d, %g, %c",
        data.five_bytes[3], data.integer,
        data.fractional, data.character);
    return 0;
}
```

Let's see where this C code differs from the above Rust code.

While in C the fields are separated by semicolons, in Rust they are separated by commas.

In Rust, the type is written after the name of the field, like in the Pascal language.

In C, you can declare several fields of the same type, by specifying the type just once, that is, in this way: "int a, b;". In Rust, instead, you must specify the type once for every field, in this way: "a: i32, b: i32,".

In C, the initialization of "data" is done simply by listing the values, similarly to Rust tuples. In Rust, instead, for each field you must specify also the name of the field.

Both in C and in Rust, the dot-notation is used.

If you declare a variable as mutable, you can also change the values of its fields, using the same dot-notation:

```
struct SomeData {
    integer: i32,
    fractional: f32,
}
let mut data = SomeData {
    integer: 10,
    fractional: 183.19,
};
data.fractional = 8.2;
print!("{}, {}", data.fractional, data.integer);
```

This will print: "8.2, 10".

Like tuples, structs may be empty also, so you can declare a tuple containing no fields.

The Tuple-Structs

We already saw that there are two kinds of structures containing objects of different types:

- tuples, whose types have no name and are not to be previously declared, and whose fields have no name;

- structs, whose types have a name, and must be previously declared, and whose fields have a name.

So, there are several differences between these two kinds of structures. Yet sometimes something halfway is needed: a kind of structure whose types have names and must be previously declared, like structs, but whose fields have no name, like tuples. Because they are a hybrid between tuples and structs, they are named "tuple-structs":

```
struct SomeData (
    i32,
    f32,
    char,
    [u8; 5],
);
let data = SomeData (
    10_000_000,
    183.19,
    'Q',
    [9, 0, 250, 60, 200],
);
print!("{}, {}, {}, {}",
    data.2, data.0, data.1, data.3[2]);
```

This will print: "Q, 10000000, 183.19, 250".

As it is shown in the example, the tuple-struct is defined before instantiating it, by using the keyword `"struct"` like a struct, but enclosing its fields in parentheses, and without specifying the names of the fields, like a tuple. The initialization starts with the name of the type, like a struct, but goes on like a tuple.

Its fields are accessed, by necessity, like a tuple, as they have no name.
Differing from both tuples and structs, empty tuple-structs are not allowed.
Tuple-structs are not actually used often.

Lexical Conventions

Now that we have seen a good deal of different Rust constructs (but not yet all of them!),
it is a good time to think about some lexical conventions adopted by almost every Rust
programmer, so that they are strongly recommended to everyone. Such conventions are
so entrenched, that even the compiler emits a warning if they are violated.

Here is a program showing them:

```rust
const MAXIMUM_POWER: u16 = 600;
enum VehicleKind {
    Motorcycle,
    Car,

    Truck,
}
struct VehicleData {
    kind: VehicleKind,
    registration_year: u16,
    registration_month: u8,
    power: u16,
}
let vehicle = VehicleData {
    kind: VehicleKind::Car,
    registration_year: 2003,
    registration_month: 11,
    power: 120,
};
if vehicle.power > MAXIMUM_POWER {
    println!("Too powerful");
}
```

The conventions shown in this example are:

- Names of constants (for example: MAXIMUM_POWER) contain only uppercase characters, with words separated by underscore.

- Type names defined by application code or by the standard library (for example: VehicleKind and VehicleData) and enum variant names (for example: Car) are comprised of words stuck together, where every word has an uppercase initial letter, followed by lowercase letters.

- Any other name (for example, keywords like let, primitive types like u8, and field identifiers like registration_year) use only lowercase letters, with words separated by underscores.

Defining Functions

In this chapter you will learn:

- How to define your own procedures (better known as "functions") and how to invoke them
- When and how you can have several functions with the same name
- How to pass arguments to a function, by-value or by-reference
- How to return simple and composite values from a function
- How to exit prematurely from a function
- How references to objects can be manipulated

Defining and Invoking a Function

If it happens that you write the same code several times, you can encapsulate that code in a block, and then give that block a name. In this way you define a "function". Then you can execute that code by invoking that function by name:

```
fn line() {
    println!("----------");
}
line();
line();
line();
```

This will print:

```
----------
----------
----------
```

© Carlo Milanesi 2018
C. Milanesi, *Beginning Rust*, https://doi.org/10.1007/978-1-4842-3468-6_9

To define a function you write the "fn" keyword, followed by the name you want to associate to that function, followed by a pair of parentheses, followed by a block.

That block is named the "body" of the function, and all that precedes the body is named the "signature" of the function.

This syntax should look quite familiar, as all the programs we have written so far are nothing but definitions of a function named "main".

Although the "main" function is a special function, as it is invoked by the program startup machine code, our "line" function above is executed only when our code invokes it.

Indeed, the second part of our small program invokes the line function three times. To invoke (or "call") it, it is enough to write its name, followed by a pair of parentheses.

Notice that we defined the line function inside the main function. Actually, differing from C language, in Rust you can define functions inside the body of other functions. And you can also invoke functions defined externally of the main function. Here is a complete Rust program (not to be inserted in a main function):

```rust
fn f1() { print!("1"); }
fn main() {
    f1();
    fn f2() { print!("2"); }
    f2(); f1(); f2();
}
```

This will print: "1212".

Functions Defined After Their Use

This code is illegal:

```rust
a;
let a = 3;
```

as it uses the a variable before having defined it.

The following one is valid instead:

```rust
f();
fn f() {}
```

as you may invoke a function even before defining it, as long as it is defined in the current scope or in an enclosing scope.

Functions Shadowing Other Functions

We already saw that after having defined a variable, you can define another variable having the same name, and that second variable will shadow the first one. With functions you cannot do that, inside the same scope:

```
fn f() {}
fn f() {}
```

This will generate the compilation error that the name `f` is defined multiple times.

However, you can define several functions with the same name, as long as they are in different parallel blocks:

```
{
    fn f() { print!("a"); }
    f(); f();
}
{
    fn f() { print!("b"); }
    f();
}
```

This will print: "aab".

Every function is valid only in the block where it is defined, so you cannot invoke it from the outside of that block:

```
{
    fn f() { }
}
f();
```

This will generate, on the last line, the compilation error: "cannot find function `f` in this scope".

Finally, a function can shadow another function defined in an outer block. Here is a complete program:

```
fn f() { print!("1"); }
fn main() {
    f(); // Prints 2
    {
        f(); // Prints 3
        fn f() { print!("3"); }
    }
    f(); // Prints 2
    fn f() { print!("2"); }
}
```

This will print 232.

Indeed, externally to the main function, a function that prints 1 is defined, but inside the main function another function is defined, having the same name, and printing 2, and so the first statement in the main function invokes the function declared inside the main one, even if it is defined six lines below. In the nested block, still another function with the same name is defined and invoked, and it prints 3. Then that block ends, and so the function printing 2 gets back to be the active one. The external function, which would print 1, is never invoked, and so the compiler reports that in a warning.

Passing Arguments to a Function

A function that prints always the same text every time it is invoked is not very useful. A function that prints the sum of any two numeric values that are passed to it is more interesting:

```
fn print_sum(addend1: f64, addend2: f64) {
    println!("{} + {} = {}", addend1, addend2,
        addend1 + addend2);
}
print_sum(3., 5.);
print_sum(3.2, 5.1);
```

This will print:

```
3 + 5 = 8
3.2 + 5.1 = 8.3
```

Now you can understand the use of parentheses! In a function definition, they enclose the list of argument definitions; and in function invocations, they enclose the expressions whose values are passed as arguments.

The definitions of the arguments of a function behave much like definitions of variables.

So, the program above is to be interpreted as if it were the following one:

```
{
    let addend1: f64 = 3.; let addend2: f64 = 5.;
    println!("{} + {} = {}", addend1, addend2,
        addend1 + addend2);
}
{
    let addend1: f64 = 3.2; let addend2: f64 = 5.1;
    println!("{} + {} = {}", addend1, addend2,
        addend1 + addend2);
}
```

The main difference between the definition of a variable and the definition of an argument of a function is that, in function argument definitions, the type specification is required, that is, you cannot rely only on type inference.

Type inference is used anyway by the compiler to check that the value received as the argument is actually of the type declared for that argument. Indeed, this code

```
fn f(a: i16) {}
f(3.);
f(3u16);
f(3i16);
f(3);
```

generates an error at the first invocation of f, as a floating-point number is passed to an integer argument; and it generates an error also at the second invocation, as a value of u16 type is passed to an argument of i16 type.

The last two invocations, instead, are allowed. Actually, the third invocation passes a value that has exactly the type expected by the function; while the fourth invocation passes an argument of unconstrained integer type, which is constrained to the "i16" type by the invocation itself.

Passing Arguments by Value

Notice also that arguments are not simply new names for the passed objects, that is, they are not aliases; instead they are *copies* of such objects. Such copies are created when the function is invoked, and they are destroyed when the function ends and the control returns to the caller code. This example clarifies this concept:

```
fn print_double(mut x: f64) {
    x *= 2.;
    print!("{}", x);
}
let x = 4.;
print_double(x);
print!(" {}", x);
```

This will print: "8 4".

Here, apparently, a variable named "x" is declared and initialized, and it is passed to the function "print_double", where it keeps its name "x"; the value of such variable is changed, its new value is correctly printed, the functions ends, returning to the caller, and the value of our variable is printed ... as it were before the function invocation!

Actually, it is not *the variable* that is passed to the function, but *the value* of the variable. It is a so-called *pass-by-value* passing mechanism, like in C language. The value of the "x" variable is used to initialize a new variable, which accidentally here is also named "x", which is the argument of the function. The new variable is then changed and printed inside the function body, and it is destroyed by the function ending. In the caller function, our variable has never changed its value.

Notice that in the signature of "print_double", before the argument "x", there is the "mut" keyword. This is required to allow the first statement inside the function body; yet, as said before, such a statement changes only the value of the argument of the function, not the variable defined externally to the function, which actually has no need of the mut specification.

Returning a Value from a Function

Functions, in addition to being able to receive values to process, can send back to the caller a result of the computation:

```
fn double(x: f64) -> f64 { x * 2. }
print!("{}", double(17.3));
```

This will print "34.6".

The value returned by a function is normally the value of its body.

We already saw that the body of any function is a block, and that the value of any block is the value of its last expression, if there is a last expression, or otherwise an empty tuple.

The content of the body of the double function above is x * 2.. The value of such expression is the value returned by the function.

The type of the value returned by functions, while in C language is written before the name of the function, in Rust is written afterwards, separated by an arrow symbol "->". The double function above, according to its signature, returns an f64 value.

If no return value type is specified, it is implied to be the empty tuple type, that is "()":

```
fn f1(x: i32) {}
fn f2(x: i32) -> () {}
```

These functions "f1" and "f2" are equal, as they both return an empty tuple.

The value returned by any function must be of the same type specified by the function signature as the return value type, or an unconstrained type that may be constrained to that type.

So, this code is valid:

```
fn f1() -> i32 { 4.5; "abc"; 73i32 }
fn f2() -> i32 { 4.5; "abc"; 73 }
fn f3() -> i32 { 4.5; "abc"; 73 + 100 }
```

While this code is not:

```
fn f1() -> i32 { 4.5; "abc"; false }
fn f2() -> i32 { 4.5; "abc"; () }
fn f3() -> i32 { 4.5; "abc"; {} }
fn f4() -> i32 { 4.5; "abc"; }
```

111

It generates four mismatched type errors: for the f1 function, the error expected i32, found bool; for the f2, f3, and f4 functions, the error expected i32, found ().

Early Exit

So far, to exit from a function, we had to get to the end of its body. However, if you write a function containing many statements, it happens often to realize in the middle of the function that you have no more computations to do, and so you want to get out quickly from the function.

A possibility is to break out from a loop, another one if to create a large "if" statement enclosing the rest of the statements of the function; a third possibility is to set a Boolean variable indicating that no more processing is necessary, and checking the value of such variable using if statements every time you must do something.

Typically, though, the most convenient way is to ask the compiler to get out immediately from the function, returning a value of the type required by the function signature:

```
fn f(x: f64) -> f64 {
    if x <= 0. { return 0.; }
    x + 3.
}
print!("{} {}", f(1.), f(-1.));
```

It will print: "4 0".

The "return" statement evaluates the expression that follows it, and the resulting value is immediately returned to the caller.

The return keyword is the same of the C language, with the difference that in Rust it is not normally used as a last statement, but only for early exits. Yet, you can write:

```
fn f(x: f64) -> f64 {
    if x <= 0. { return 0.; }
    return x + 3.;
}
print!("{} {}", f(1.), f(-1.));
```

This program is equivalent to the preceding one, but it is considered bad style. Also this program is equivalent, and it is usually considered better:

```
fn f(x: f64) -> f64 {
    if x <= 0. { 0. }
    else { x + 3. }
}
print!("{} {}", f(1.), f(-1.));
```

The return statement is considered convenient only when it allows you to decrease the number of lines of code or the indentation level.

Also for the "return" statement, the return value type must be equal to the one declared in the function signature.

If the function signature specifies the empty tuple as a return value type, such value may be omitted in the "return" statement. Therefore, this is a valid program:

```
fn f(x: i32) {
    if x <= 0 { return; }
    if x == 4 { return (); }
    if x == 7 { return {}; }
    print!("{}", x);
}
f(5);
```

Any function invocation may be considered a valid statement:

```
fn f() -> i32 { 3 }
f();
```

In such a case, the returned value is ignored and immediately destroyed.

Instead, if the returned value is used, like in this valid code,

```
fn f() -> i32 { 3 }
let _a: i32 = f();
```

then it must be of the proper type. As a counterexample, the following program is illegal:

```
fn f() -> i32 { 3 }
let _a: u32 = f();
```

Returning Several Values

If you want to return several values from a function, you can use a tuple:

```
fn divide(dividend: i32, divisor: i32) -> (i32, i32) {
    (dividend / divisor, dividend % divisor)
}
print!("{:?}", divide(50, 11));
```

This will print "(4, 6)"

Or you can return an enum, a struct, a tuple struct, an array, or a vector:

```
enum E { E1, E2 }
struct S { a: i32, b: bool }
struct TS (f64, char);
fn f1() -> E { E::E2 }
fn f2() -> S { S { a: 49, b: true } }
fn f3() -> TS { TS (4.7, 'w') }
fn f4() -> [i16; 4] { [7, -2, 0, 19] }
fn f5() -> Vec<i64> { vec![12000] }
print!("{} ", match f1() { E::E1 => 1, _ => -1 });
print!("{} ", f2().a);
print!("{} ", f3().0);
print!("{} ", f4()[0]);
print!("{} ", f5()[0]);
```

This will print: "-1 49 4.7 7 12000".

Let's explain these five numbers.

The invocation of f1 in the first print! invocation returns the enumeration E2, which is tried to match with E1, and, as it doesn't match, the catch-all case is taken, and so -1 is printed.

The invocation of f2 returns a struct object containing the fields a and b, and from it the a field is extracted.

The invocation of f3 returns a tuple-struct containing two fields, and from it the first field is extracted.

The invocation of f4 returns an array containing four items, and from it the first item is extracted.

The invocation of f5 returns a vector containing just one item, and from it the first and only item is extracted.

How to Change a Variable of the Caller

Let's assume we have an array containing 10 numbers, some of them being negative, and we want to double the value of the negative numbers only.

We can do that in this way:

```
let mut arr = [5, -4, 9, 0, -7, -1, 3, 5, 3, 1];
for i in 0..10 {
    if arr[i] < 0 { arr[i] *= 2; }
}
print!("{:?}", arr);
```

This will print: "[5, -8, 9, 0, -14, -2, 3, 5, 3, 1]".

Now let's assume we want to encapsulate such an operation into a function. We could incorrectly write:

```
fn double_negatives(mut a: [i32; 10]) {
    for i in 0..10 {
        if a[i] < 0 { a[i] *= 2; }
    }
}
let mut arr = [5, -4, 9, 0, -7, -1, 3, 5, 3, 1];
double_negatives(arr);
print!("{:?}", arr);
```

This will print: [5, -4, 9, 0, -7, -1, 3, 5, 3, 1]. Our array hasn't changed at all.

Indeed, when passing this array by value, the entire array has been copied into another array, created by the function invocation. This last array has been changed inside the function, and then it has been destroyed when the function ended.

The original array was never changed, and the compiler is aware of that, as it reports the warning variable does not need to be mutable. That is, given that arr is never changed, you may also remove the mut clause from its declaration.

To obtain that our array is changed, you can make the function return the changed array:

```
fn double_negatives(mut a: [i32; 10]) -> [i32; 10] {
    for i in 0..10 {
        if a[i] < 0 { a[i] *= 2; }
    }
    a
}
let mut arr = [5, -4, 9, 0, -7, -1, 3, 5, 3, 1];
arr = double_negatives(arr);
print!("{:?}", arr);
```

This will print the expected result. However, this solution has one drawback: all the data is copied twice. First, at function invocation, all of the array is copied into the function, then the function works on such local copy of the data, and at last all the local data is copied back in place of the original data. These copies have a computational cost, which can be avoided.

Passing Arguments by Reference

To optimize the passing of a (long) array to a function, you can pass to that function only the address of the array, letting the function work directly on the original array:

```
fn double_negatives(a: &mut [i32; 10]) {
    for i in 0..10 {
        if (*a)[i] < 0 { (*a)[i] *= 2; }
    }
}
let mut arr = [5, -4, 9, 0, -7, -1, 3, 5, 3, 1];
double_negatives(&mut arr);
print!("{:?}", arr);
```

Even this program prints the expected result, but without copying arrays.

You obtain this result through the so-called *by reference* argument pass. The syntax is quite similar to the pass by pointer technique of C language.

CHAPTER 9 DEFINING FUNCTIONS

Let's see it in detail.

The new symbols "&" and "*" have appeared. They have the same meaning in Rust than in C language. The "&" symbol means "the (memory) address of the object ...", and the "*" symbol means "the object that is present at the (memory) address ...".

The a argument of the `double_negatives` function now is of type `&mut [i32; 10]`. By putting an & symbol before the type specification, it is specified that it is an *address* (also known as *pointer*, or *reference*) of an object of the type specified just afterwards. Therefore, in this case, a is of type "address of a mutable array of ten 32-bit signed integer numbers."

In the function body, we are not interested in handling the address itself, but the object referred to by such address, and so we use the * symbol to access such object. In general, given a reference a, the *a expression indicates the object referred to by such reference.

In the second line of the function, the object positioned at the address received as argument is accessed twice, by using the *a expression. Such an object is an array, and so you can access its i index item.

The parentheses around the *a expression are required, as square brackets have precedence over the star operator, and so the *a[i] expression would be taken as *(a[i]), which means "take the i-th item of the object a, and then, considering such item as an address, take the object having such address". This is not what we want to do, and however it would generate the compilation error `type `i32` cannot be dereferenced`, that is, "you cannot get the object whose memory address is contained in a value of type i32".

Using this kind of argument passing, the `double_negatives` function receives only the address of an array, by which it can read and write the items of such array.

After having declared this function, we can use it. The array must be declared and initialized as mutable, as its contents will have to be changed. Then the function is invoked without expecting a returned value, but passing as argument the address of the array. Notice that it is required to repeat the mut keyword also where the argument is passed, to make explicit that the referred object is expected to be changed by the function.

In fact this function may be simplified as the following equivalent version:

```
fn double_negatives(a: &mut [i32; 10]) {
    for i in 0..10 {
        if a[i] < 0 { a[i] *= 2; }
    }
}
```

We removed two asterisks, and so their parentheses, which have become useless.

We said that here a is not an array, but the address of an array, and so the a[i] expression should be illegal. Yet Rust makes the following simplification regarding such addresses: every time a reference is used improperly, that is, as if it were a non-reference value, Rust tries to pretend it is preceded by an asterisk, that is, it tries to dereference it, and so it considers the referenced object in place of the reference itself.

The resulting syntax is that of C++ references, with the difference that in Rust it is allowed also to apply an explicit dereference, that is, before a reference, you are allowed to write or to omit the asterisk, while in C++ you must put it before a pointer and must not put it before a reference.

Using References

References are used mainly as function arguments, but you may use them elsewhere too:

```
let a = 15;
let ref_a = &a;
print!("{} {} {}", a, *ref_a, ref_a);
```

This will print: "15 15 15".

Actually, the same object is printed three times.

The a variable contains simply a 32-bit object whose value is the number 15.

The ref_a variable contains the memory address of such object, that is of the a variable. Therefore, it is a reference to a number.

In the last statement, first the value of a is printed; then, the object referred by ref_a is taken and printed; finally, the compiler attempts to print directly the ref_a variable, but as it is not allowed to print directly a reference in this way, the referred object is taken and printed.

Using references, you can do some virtuosity:

```
let a = &&&7;
print!("{} {} {} {}", ***a, **a, *a, a);
```

This will print: "7 7 7 7".

In the first statement, the 7 value is taken, and it is put in memory in a nameless object. Then, the address of such object is taken, and such address is put in memory in a second nameless object. Then, the address of such object is taken, and it is put in memory in a third nameless object. Then, the address of such object is taken, and it is put in memory in a fourth object, and the name a is associated to such object. This fourth object is the a variable, which therefore is a reference to a reference to a reference to a number.

In the second statement, first the ***a expression is printed. Here, considering that a is a reference, the object referenced by a is taken, by using the rightmost asterisk of the three; then, considering that also this object is a reference, the object referenced by it is taken, by using the middle asterisk; then, considering that also this object is a reference, the object referenced by it is taken, by using the leftmost asterisk; finally, considering that this object is a number, it is printed as a number.

If you add one or more additional asterisks, a compilation error would result, because it is not allowed to dereference an object that is a number and not a reference.

After having printed the first 7 using a completely explicit syntax, the same object is printed three other times, using expressions that imply, respectively, one, two, or three asterisks.

Mutability of References

Let's see how to use the mut keyword with references:

```
let mut a: i32 = 10;
let mut b: i32 = 20;
let mut p: &mut i32 = &mut a; // line 3
print!("{} ", *p);
*p += 1; // line 5
print!("{} ", *p);
p = &mut b; // line 7
print!("{} ", *p);
*p += 1; // line 9
print!("{} ", *p);
```

This will print: "10 11 20 21".

Here, we have the two numeric variables a and b, and the reference p, initially referring to a.

For a moment ignore all those mut words.

Initially, the value of a is 10, p refers to a, and so, by printing *p, 10 is printed.

Then, at line 5, the object referred to by p is incremented, becoming 11, and so, by printing *p, 11 is printed.

Then, at line 7, p is made to refer to b, whose value is 20, and indeed, by printing *p, 20 is printed.

Then, at line 9, also the object now referred to by p is incremented, becoming 21, and so, by printing *p, 21 is printed.

Notice that, at line 5, p indirectly increments the a variable, and so a must be mutable; at line 9, p indirectly increments the b variable, and so b must be mutable; and at line 7, p itself is changed, and so also p must be mutable. But the reasoning of the compiler is different.

The actual reasoning is the following.

At line 5 and at line 9, the objects referred to by p are incremented, that is, they are read and written, and this is allowed only if *p is mutable. So p cannot be of type &i32; it must be of type &mut i32, which is "reference to a mutable i32".

The expression &a is of type &i32, and so it cannot be assigned to p, that is, of type &mut i32. Instead the expression &mut a has the correct type, as it has the same mutability of p. So, the initialization in line 3 is correct.

But the expression &mut a, which can be read "reference to a mutable a", allows us to change a, and Rust allows this only if a is mutable. Therefore, the initialization at line 3 is allowed only if the a variable is declared as mutable. Similarly, the initialization at line 7 is allowed only if the b variable is mutable.

Then, notice that at line 7 p itself is changed, that is, it is made to refer to some other object. This is allowed only if the p variable is mutable.

And with this, any use of mut in this program has been explained.

However, it is better to insist that at line 3, the first mut word has a different meaning that the two others.

The first mut word means that the p variable can be changed, meaning it can be re-assigned, making it to refer to another object, like it has been done at line 7. Without such mut word, p would refer always to the same object.

The second and third mut words mean that the type of p allows it to change the value of the referred object. Without such mut words, p wouldn't be able to change the value of its referred object.

CHAPTER 10

Defining Generic Functions and Structs

In this chapter, you will learn:

- How to write a single function definition, whose invocations can efficiently handle different data types

- How to use type inference to avoid the need to specify the types used by generic functions

- How to write a single struct, tuple-struct, or enum type, whose instances can contain efficiently different data types

- How to use two important standard generic enums, Option and Result, to represent optional data or fallible functions results

- How some standard functions ease the handling of Option and Result

Need of Generic Functions

Rust performs a strict data type check, so when you define a function that uses an argument of a certain type, say fn square_root(x: f32) -> f32, the code that invokes such a function must pass to it an expression of exactly that type, like in square_root(45.2f32), or it must perform explicit conversions every time that function is used, like in square_root(45.2f64 as f32). You cannot pass a different type, like in square_root(45.2f64).

This is inconvenient for those who write the code that invokes the function, but also for who writes the function itself. As Rust has many different numeric types, when you write a function, you must cope with the problem of which type to choose. For example,

© Carlo Milanesi 2018
C. Milanesi, *Beginning Rust*, https://doi.org/10.1007/978-1-4842-3468-6_10

if you decide to specify that an argument of your function must be of i16 type, but then for every invocation an i32 type is preferred, it would be preferable to change that function definition.

And if your function is going to be used by several modules or even by several applications, as far as we have seen, there is no way to satisfy every user of your function.

For example:

```rust
// Library code
fn f(ch: char, num1: i16, num2: i16) -> i16 {
    if ch == 'a' { num1 }
    else { num2 }
}

// Application code
print!("{}", f('a', 37, 41));
```

This will print: "37".

In application code, if you replace 37 with 37.2, and 41 with 41., you would get a compilation error; and moreover, if you add as i16 after each number, obtaining the statement print!("{}", f('a', 37.2 as i16, 41. as i16)); the program would still print 37, instead of the desired 37.2.

In you decide to change library code, replacing i16 with f32 or with f64, the program will work correctly in all the above cases, but will force all the callers to use floating-point numbers.

Defining and Using Generic Functions

The idiomatic way to solve this problem in Rust is to write the following code:

```rust
// Library code
fn f<T>(ch: char, num1: T, num2: T) -> T {
    if ch == 'a' { num1 }
    else { num2 }
}

// Application code
let a: i16 = f::<i16>('a', 37, 41);
let b: f64 = f::<f64>('b', 37.2, 41.1);
print!("{} {}", a, b);
```

This will print 37 41.1.

In the function definition, just after the name of the function, there is the T word enclosed in angular brackets. This symbol is a type parameter of the function declaration.

It means that what is being declared is not a concrete function, but a generic function, which is parameterized by the T type parameter. Such function will become a concrete function only when, still at compile time, a concrete type will be specified for such T parameter.

Such T parameter is defined only in the scope of the function definition. Indeed it is used, three times, only in the signature of the function, and it could have been used also in the body of the function, but not elsewhere.

While the ch argument is of char type, the num1 and num2 arguments, as well as the function returned value are of the T generic type. When such a function will be used, it will be required to replace such T parameter with a concrete type, so obtaining a concrete function.

The first line of the application code, instead of using the f generic function, uses the f::<i16> function, that is, the concrete function obtained by replacing the T parameter with the i16 type. Similarly, the second line of the application code invokes the f::<f64> function, that is, the concrete function obtained by replacing the T parameter with the f64 type.

Notice that where the i16 type has been used, two integer values that may be constrained to the i16 type are passed as second and third arguments of the f generic function, and the value returned by the function is assigned to a variable having type i16.

Instead, where the f64 type has been used, two floating-point values, which may be constrained to the f64 type, are passed as second and third arguments of the f generic function, and the value returned by the function is assigned to a variable having type f64.

If the types of the function arguments or the types of the variables that receive the returned value or both had been swapped, some mismatched types compilation errors would have been obtained.

In such a way, by writing library code without useless repetitions, it has been possible to write application code that uses two distinct types, and other types could easily be added, without having to change the existing library code.

C language does not allow generic functions, but C++ language allows them: they are the function templates.

Inferring the Parametric Types

The above application code may be further simplified, though:

```
// Library code
fn f<T>(ch: char, num1: T, num2: T) -> T {
    if ch == 'a' { num1 }
    else { num2 }
}
```

```
// Application code
let a: i16 = f('a', 37, 41);
let b: f64 = f('b', 37.2, 41.1);
print!("{} {}", a, b);
```

As it appears, the `::<i16>` and `::<f64>` clauses have been removed, obtaining anyway an equivalent program. Indeed, the compiler, when parsing an invocation of a generic function, uses the types of the values passed as arguments to determine the type parameter.

It is said that the parametric type is *inferred* from the type of the values used in the expression containing the invocation of the generic function.

Of course, the various types used must be consistent:

```
fn f<T>(a: T, _b: T) -> T { a }
let _a = f(12u8, 13u8);
let _b = f(12i64, 13i64);
let _c = f(12i16, 13u16);
let _d: i32 = f(12i16, 13i16);
```

This generates a compilation error at the last-but-one statement, and two other errors at the last one. Indeed, the first and the second invocations pass two numbers of the same type, while the third invocation passes two values of different types, even if they must be of the same type, represented by the T generic type.

In the last statement, the two arguments have the same type, but the returned value is assigned to a variable of a different type.

If you need to parameterize a function with several values of different types, you can do that by specifying several type parameters:

```
fn f<Param1, Param2>(_a: Param1, _b: Param2) {}
f('a', true);
f(12.56, "Hello");
f((3, 'a'), [5, 6, 7]);
```

This program is valid, even if it does nothing.

Defining and Using Generic Structs

Parametric types are useful also for declaring generic structs and generic tuple-structs:

```
struct S<T1, T2> {
    c: char,
    n1: T1,
    n2: T1,
    n3: T2,
}
let _s = S { c: 'a', n1: 34, n2: 782, n3: 0.02 };

struct SE<T1, T2> (char, T1, T1, T2);
let _se = SE ('a', 34, 782, 0.02);
```

The first statement declares the generic struct S, parameterized by the two types T1 and T2. The first one of such generic types is used by two fields, while the second one is used by only one field.

The second statement creates an object having a concrete version of such generic type. The parameter T1 is implicitly replaced by i32, as the two unconstrained integers 32 and 782 are used to initialize the two fields n1 and n2, and the parameter T2 is implicitly replaced by f64, as an unconstrained floating-point number 0.02 is used to initialize the field n3.

The third and fourth statements are similar, but they use a tuple-struct instead of a struct.

Also for structs the type parameter concretizations can be made explicit:

```
struct S<T1, T2> {
    c: char,
    n1: T1,
    n2: T1,
    n3: T2,
}
let _s = S::<u16, f32> { c: 'a', n1: 34, n2: 782, n3: 0.02 };

struct SE<T1, T2> (char, T1, T1, T2);
let _se = SE::<u16, f32> ('a', 34, 782, 0.02);
```

C language does not allow generic struct, but C++ language allows them: they are the class templates and the struct templates.

Genericity Mechanics

To understand better how genericity works, you should take the role of the compiler to follow the process of compilation. Indeed, conceptually, generic code compilation happens in several stages.

Let's follow the conceptual mechanics of compilation, applied to the following code:

```
fn swap<T1, T2>(a: T1, b: T2) -> (T2, T1) { (b, a) }
let x = swap(3i16, 4u16);
let y = swap(5f32, true);
print!("{:?} {:?}", x, y);
```

In the first stage, the source code is scanned, and every time the compiler finds a generic function declaration (in the example, the declaration of the swap function), it loads in its data structures an internal representation of such function, in all its genericity, checking only that there is no syntax error in the generic code.

In the second stage, the source code is scanned again, and every time the compiler encounters an invocation of a generic function, it loads in its data structures an association between such usage and the corresponding internal representation of the generic declaration, of course after having checked that such correspondence is valid.

Therefore, after the first two stages in our example, the compiler has a generic `swap` function, and a concrete `main` function, and this last function contains two references to the generic `swap` function.

In the third stage, all the invocations of generic functions are scanned (in the example, the two invocations of `swap`). For each of such usages, and for each generic parameter of the corresponding definition, a concrete type is determined. Such a concrete type may be explicit in the usage, or (like in the example) it may be inferred from the type of the expression used as the argument of the function. In the example, for the first invocation of `swap`, the parameter T1 is associated to the `i16` type, and the parameter T2 is associated to the `u16` type; instead, in the second invocation of `swap`, the parameter T1 is associated to the `f32` type, and the parameter T2 is associated to the `bool` type.

After having determined the concrete type by which the generic parameters are to be replaced, a concrete version of the generic function is generated. In such a concrete version, every generic parameter is replaced by the concrete type determined for the specific function invocation. And the invocation of the generic function is replaced by an invocation of the just generated concrete function.

For the example, the generated internal representation corresponds to the following Rust code:

```rust
fn swap_i16_u16(a: i16, b: u16) -> (u16, i16) { (b, a) }
fn swap_f32_bool(a: f32, b: bool) -> (bool, f32) { (b, a) }
let x = swap_i16_u16(3i16, 4u16);
let y = swap_f32_bool(5f32, true);
print!("{:?} {:?}", x, y);
```

As you can see, there are no more generic definitions or generic function invocations. The generic function definition has been transformed into two concrete function definitions, and the two function invocations now invoke each one a different concrete function.

The fourth stage consists in compiling this code.

Notice that it was needed to generate two different concrete functions, as the two invocations of the generic `swap` function specified different types.

But this code

```
fn swap<T1, T2>(a: T1, b: T2) -> (T2, T1) { (b, a) }
let x = swap('A', 4.5);
let y = swap('g', -6.);
print!("{:?} {:?}", x, y);
```

is internally translated to this code:

```
fn swap_char_f64(a: char, b: f64) -> (f64, char) { (b, a) }
let x = swap_char_f64('A', 4.5);
let y = swap_char_f64('g', -6.);
print!("{:?} {:?}", x, y);
```

Even if there are several invocations of the generic function swap, only one concrete version is generated, because all the invocations required the same types for the parameters.

In general, it is always applied the optimization of generating only one concrete version of a generic function declaration, when several invocations specify exactly the same type parameters.

The fact that the compiler can generate, in a single program, several concrete versions of machine code corresponding to a single function has consequences:

- This multi-stage compilation is somewhat slower, with respect to compiling non-generic code.

- The generated code is highly optimized for each specific invocation, as it uses exactly the types used by the caller, without needing conversions or decisions. Therefore the run-time performance of each invocation is optimized.

- If many invocations with different data types are performed for a generic function, a lot of machine code is generated. We already talked about this phenomenon, said "code bloat," regarding the fact that, to optimize performance, it is better to not use many different types in a single processing, as distinct code is used for distinct types, and this burdens the CPU caches.

All that was said in this section about generic functions holds also for generic structs and tuple-structs.

Generic Arrays and Vectors

Regarding arrays and vectors, there is no news. We saw them from the beginning as generic types.

Actually, while arrays are part of the Rust language, vectors are structs defined in the Rust standard library.

Generic Enums

In Rust, enums can also be generic.

```
enum Result1<SuccessCode, FailureCode> {
    Success(SuccessCode),
    Failure(FailureCode, char),
    Uncertainty,
}
let mut _res = Result1::Success::<u32,u16>(12u32);
_res = Result1::Uncertainty;
_res = Result1::Failure(0u16, 'd');
```

This program is valid. Instead, the following one causes a compilation at the last line, because the first argument of Failure is of type u32, while it should be of type u16, according the initialization of _res, two lines before.

```
enum Result1<SuccessCode, FailureCode> {
    Success(SuccessCode),
    Failure(FailureCode, char),
    Uncertainty,
}
let mut _res = Result1::Success::<u32,u16>(12u32);
_res = Result1::Uncertainty;
_res = Result1::Failure(0u32, 'd');
```

Generic enums are used a lot in the Rust standard library.

One of the most used enums defined in the Rust standard library solves the following common problem. If a function *can fail*, what should it do, when it fails?

For example, the function pop removes the last item from a vector, and returns the removed item, if that vector contains some items. But what should the expression vec![0; 0].pop() do? It is removing an item from an empty vector!

Some languages leave this behavior undefined, leading probably to a crash or to unpredictable results. Rust avoids as much as possible undefined behavior.

Some languages raise an exception, to be handled by an enclosing block or by the callers of the current function, or leading to a crash. Rust does not use the concept of *exception.*

Some languages return a specific *null* value. But a vector can contain almost any possible type, and many types have no null value.

Here is the Rust solution:

```
let mut v = vec![11, 22, 33];
for _ in 0..5 {
    let item: Option<i32> = v.pop();
    match item {
        Some(number) => print!("{}, ", number),
        None => print!("#, "),
    }
}
```

This will print: "33, 22, 11, #, #,".

The v variable is a vector initially containing three numbers.

The loop performs five iterations. Each of them tries to remove an item from v. If the removal is successful, the removed item is printed, otherwise the # character is printed.

The pop function applied to an object of Vec<T> type returns a value of Option<T> type.

Such generic type is defined by the Rust standard library as this:

```
enum Option<T> {
    Some(T),
    None,
}
```

This enum means: "This is an optional value of T type. It has the option of being a T and the option of being nothing. It can be something or nothing. If it is something, it is a T."

Probably such a definition would have been clearer if it had been:

```
enum Optional<T> {
    Something(T),
    Nothing,
}
```

It should be thought as such. However, Rust tries always to abbreviate names, and so the previous definition is the valid one.

Getting back to the example, at the first iteration of the loop, the value of the variable item is Some(33); at the second iteration it is Some(22); at the third iteration it is Some(11); and then the v vector has become empty, and so pop can only return None, which is assigned to item at the fourth and fifth iterations.

The match statement discriminates when Some number has been popped, and when there was None. In the former case, that number is printed, and in the latter case, just a # is printed.

Error Handling

The Rust standard library also defines a generic enum to handle the case in which a function cannot return a value of the expected type.

```
fn divide(numerator: f64, denominator: f64) -> Result<f64, String> {
    if denominator == 0. {
        Err(format!("Divide by zero"))
    } else {
        Ok(numerator / denominator)
    }
}
print!("{:?}, {:?}", divide(8., 2.), divide(8., 0.));
```

This will print Ok(4), Err("Divide by zero").

The divide function should return the result of the division of the first number by the second number, but only if the second number is not zero. In this latter case, it should return an error message.

The Result type is similar to the Option type, but while the Option type represents as None the case of a missing result, the Result type can add a value that describes such an anomalous condition.

The definition of this generic enum in the standard library is:

```
enum Result<T, E> {
    Ok(T),
    Err(E),
}
```

In our example, T was f64, because that is the type resulting from the division of two f64 numbers, and E was String, because we wanted to print a message.

We used the results of the invocations only to print them as debug information. In a production program, though, that is not acceptable. A more appropriate code would be the following one.

```
fn divide(numerator: f64, denominator: f64) -> Result<f64, String> {
    if denominator == 0. {
        Err(format!("Divide by zero"))
    } else {
        Ok(numerator / denominator)
    }
}
fn show_divide(num: f64, den: f64) {
    match divide(num, den) {
        Ok(val) => println!("{} / {} = {}", num, den, val),
        Err(msg) => println!("Cannot divide {} by {}: {}", num, den, msg),
    }
}
show_divide(8., 2.);
show_divide(8., 0.);
```

This will print:

```
8 / 2 = 4
Cannot divide 8 by 0: Divide by zero
```

Enum Standard Utility Functions

The Option and Result standard generic types allow us to capture in a flexible and efficient way all the cases that happen in real-world code; though, to use a match statement to get the result is quite inconvenient.

Therefore, the standard library contains some utility functions to ease the decoding of an Option or a Result value.

```
fn divide(numerator: f64, denominator: f64) -> Result<f64, String> {
    if denominator == 0. {
        Err(format!("Divide by zero"))
    } else {
        Ok(numerator / denominator)
    }
}
let r1 = divide(8., 2.);
let r2 = divide(8., 0.);
println!("{} {}", r1.is_ok(), r2.is_ok());
println!("{} {}", r1.is_err(), r2.is_err());
println!("{}", r1.unwrap());
println!("{}", r2.unwrap());
```

This program first prints:

```
true false
false true
4
```

and then panics with the message: thread 'main' panicked at 'called `Result::unwrap()` on an `Err` value: "Divide by zero"'.

The is_ok function returns true if it is applied to an Ok variant. The is_err function returns true if it is applied to an Err variant. As they are the only possible variants, is_err() is equivalent to ! is_ok().

The unwrap function return the value of the Ok variant, if it is applied to an Ok variant, and it panics otherwise. The meaning of this function is "I know that probably this value is a value wrapped in an Ok variant, and so I want just to get that contained value, getting rid of its wrapping; in the strange case it is not an Ok variant, an irrecoverable error has happened, and so I want to terminate immediately the program".

There is an unwrap function also for the Option enum. To print all the values in a Vec, you can write:

```
let mut v = vec![11, 22, 33];
for _ in 0..v.len() {
    print!("{}, ", v.pop().unwrap())
}
```

This will print: "33, 22, 11,". The invocation of unwrap gets the number inside the Ok enum returned by pop(). We avoided to call pop() on an empty vector; otherwise, pop() would have returned a None, and unwrap() would have panicked.

The unwrap function is much used in quick-and-dirty Rust programs, where possible errors are not required to be handled in a user-friendly way.

CHAPTER 11

Allocating Memory

In this chapter, you will learn:

- The various kinds of memory allocation, their performance characteristics, and their limitations

- How to specify in Rust which memory allocation to use for an object

- The difference between a reference and a Box

The Various Kinds of Allocation

To understand the Rust language, but also any other systems programming language, like the C language, it is important to understand well the various concepts of memory allocation, like static allocation, stack allocation, and heap allocation.

This chapter is entirely dedicated to such issues. In particular, we'll see the four kinds of memory allocation:

- In processor registers

- Static

- In the stack

- In the heap

In C and C++ language, static allocation is that of the global variables and of the variables declared using the `static` keyword; the stack allocation is the one used for all non-`static` local variables, and also for function arguments; while heap allocation is the one used by invoking the `malloc`function of the C language standard library, or the `new` operator of the C++ language.

© Carlo Milanesi 2018
C. Milanesi, *Beginning Rust*, https://doi.org/10.1007/978-1-4842-3468-6_11

Linear Addressing

In any computer hardware, there is one readable and writable memory, also known as RAM, which is comprised of a long sequence of bytes, accessible by their position. The first byte of the memory has position zero, while the last byte has a position equal to the size of installed memory minus one.

Simplifying, in our era there are two kinds of computers:

- Those where a single process at a time can run, and where such process uses directly the physical memory addresses. These are called "real-memory systems."

- Those with a multiprogramming operating system, which offers a virtual address space to each of the running processes. These are called "virtual-memory systems."

In the computers of the first kind, now used only as controllers, there could be no operating system (and so they are known also as "bare-metal systems"), or there could be an operating system residing in the first part of the memory. In this last case, the addresses greater than a certain value are available to the application program.

In the computers of the second kind, the capability to access any part of system memory is reserved to the operating system, which runs in a privileged mode (also known as "protected mode", or "kernel mode"), and such software assigns portions of memory to the various running processes.

Yet, in multiprogramming systems, the processes "see" their memory differently from how the operating system "sees" it. Consider this: a process asks the operating system the permission to use 200 more memory bytes, and the operating system satisfies such request by reserving for such process, say, the portion of memory from machine location 300 to machine location 499. Then, the operating system communicates the process of having allocated 200 bytes, but it does not communicate to it that the starting address of such portion of memory is 300. Indeed every process has a distinct address space, properly called "virtual", which the operating system maps to the physical memory, properly called "real".

Actually, when a process asks the operating system for some memory, the operating system just reserves a portion of the address space of the process, and no real memory is actually reserved for the process. As a result, such allocation is extremely fast even for very large memory portions.

As long as the process tries to access such memory, even if only to initialize it to zero, the operating system realizes that the process is accessing portions of virtual memory not yet mapped to real memory, and it performs immediately the mapping of the accessed virtual memory portion to a corresponding real memory portion.

Therefore, the processes do not operate directly on the real memory, but on the virtual memory that the operating system has made available to them, and has mapped to real memory.

In fact, often the virtual memory of a single process is even larger than the whole real memory of the computer. For example, you could have a computer with one gigabyte of physical (real) memory, and four processes running on such computer, with each process having a virtual memory space of three gigabytes. If all the virtual memory were mapped to the real memory, to handle such situation twelve gigabytes of memory would be required. Instead, most bytes of the virtual memory are not mapped to real memory; only the bytes actually used by the process are mapped to real memory. As long as the processes begin to use portions of their address space not yet mapped to real memory, the operating system maps such portions of virtual memory to corresponding portions of real memory.

Therefore, every time a process accesses, for reading or for writing, an address, if such address belongs to a virtual memory portion (called "page") reserved and mapped to a corresponding portion of real memory, the process accesses immediately such real memory; if, instead, the page is reserved but not presently mapped, the operating system, before allowing such access, kicks in, in a mechanism called "page fault", by which it allocates a real memory page and maps it to the virtual memory page containing the accessed address; if instead the accessed address does not belong to a page reserved by the operating system as part of the address space of the process, an addressing error happens (often called "segmentation fault"). Usually, addressing errors cause the immediate termination of the process.

Of course, if programs use memory too liberally, the operating system could take a lot of time to do such mappings, resulting in huge slowdowns of the processes, or even their termination for memory shortage.

Therefore, in modern computers, both single-programmed and multiprogrammed ones, every process "sees" its memory like an array of bytes. In one case it is real memory, and in the other case it is virtual memory, but anyway it is a contiguous address space, or, as it is usually said, "linear addressing" is used. This differs from old computer systems that used a "segmented" address space, more cumbersome to use by application programmers.

All this has been said to clarify that, in a virtual-memory system, the operating system manages a kind of memory allocation, which is the mapping from virtual memory to real memory. Though, from now on, we'll never talk anymore about such memory allocation, and we will define memory allocation as the operation of reserving a portion of the memory "seen" by the process, and associating such a memory portion to an object.

Static Allocation

There are various allocation policies, though.

The simplest allocation policy is the "static" allocation. According to such policy, the compiler determines how many bytes are needed by each object of the program, and takes from the address space the corresponding byte sequences, consecutively. Therefore, the address of each variable is determined at compile time. Here is an example in Rust:

```
static _A: u32 = 3;
static _B: i32 = -1_000_000;
static _C: f64 = 5.7e10;
static _D: u8 = 200;
```

The `static` keyword is similar to the `let` keyword. Both are used to declare a variable and optionally to initialize it.

The differences between `static` and `let` are:

- `static` uses the static allocation, while `let` uses stack allocation.

- `static` requires the explicit specification of the type of the variable, which is optional using `let`.

- Normal code cannot change the value of a static variable, even if it has the `mut` specification. Therefore, for safety reasons, in Rust static variables are normally immutable.

- The style guidelines require that the names of static variables contain only uppercase letters, with words separated by underscore. If such rule is violated, the compiler reports a warning.

Of these four aspects, here we'll see only the first one, regarding the allocation kind.

The _A and _B variables take up 4 bytes each, _C takes 8 bytes, while _D takes just 1 byte. If the address of the process would start at zero (that is usually false), the compiler would assign to _A the address 0, to _B the address 4, to _C the address 8, and to _D the address 16, for a total of 17 bytes allocated at compile time.

When the program is launched, the process asks the operating system to use 17 bytes of memory. Then, during execution, no further memory request is performed. When the process terminates, all the process memory is automatically released to the operating system.

A drawback of static allocation is the impossibility of creating recursive functions, which are functions that, directly or indirectly, invoke themselves. Indeed, if the arguments and local variables of a function are allocated statically, there is just one copy of them, and when the function invokes itself, it cannot have another copy of its arguments and local variables.

Another drawback of static allocation is that all the variables of all the subroutines are allocated at the start of the program, and if the program contains many variables, but each particular execution uses only a small fraction of them, many variables are allocated uselessly, making the program memory-hungry.

In addition, `static` variables are unsafe to modify.

Therefore, in Rust, they are not used a lot.

However, static allocations are used extensively for two other kinds of data: all the executable binary code (that actually is not really "data"), and all the strings literals.

Stack Allocation

Because of the shortcomings of static allocation, Rust allocates an object in the "stack", every time a variable is declared using the `let` keyword, and every time an argument is passed to a function invocation. The so-called "stack" is a portion of the address space of every process.

In fact, there is a stack for every thread, not only one for every process. If the operating system supports threads, then, every time a program is launched, that is every time a process is created, a thread is created and launched inside such process. Afterwards, inside the same process, other threads may be created and launched. Every time a thread is created, including the main thread of the process, the operating system is requested to allocate a portion of address space, which is the stack of that thread. In real-memory systems, only one stack is created at the beginning of the execution of the program.

Each thread keeps stored the addresses of the ends of its stack. Typically, the end having a higher value is considered the base of the stack, and the end having the lower value is considered the top of the stack.

Let's consider the following code, similar to the previous one, but using stack allocation instead of static allocation:

```
let _a: u32 = 3;
let _b: i32 = -1_000_000;
let _c: f64 = 5.7e10;
let _d: u8 = 200;
```

This program has only one thread. Now assume, quite unrealistically, that this thread has a stack of only 100 bytes, with addresses going from 500 included to 600 excluded. When this program is run, the four variables are allocated getting down from the base address, which is 600.

Therefore, as shown in Figure 11-1, the _a variable will occupy the 4 bytes having addresses from 596 to 599, the _b variable will occupy the 4 bytes having addresses from 592 to 595, the _c variable will occupy the 8 bytes having addresses from 584 to 591, and the _d variable will occupy just the byte having address 583.

Addresses	Memory
500	stack
501	
.	
.	
.	
583	d: u8
584	
585	
586	
587	_c: f64
588	
589	
590	
591	
592	
593	_b: i32
594	
595	
596	
597	_a: u32
598	
599	
600	

Figure 11-1.

However, when you need to indicate the address of an object, you must specify always the lower address. So, we say that _a is at the address 596, _b at the address 592, _c at the address 584, and _d at the address 583.

The word "stack" refers to the fact that if we got a stack of China dishes, we shouldn't insert a dish in the middle of the stack, nor remove a dish from the middle of the stack. We are allowed only to add a dish to the top of the stack, if it has not reached the ceiling yet, or remove a dish from the top of the stack, if the stack is not empty.

Similarly, the characteristic of stack allocation is that you can add an item only at the top of the stack, and you can remove only from the top of the stack.

Stack allocation and deallocation are very fast, because they consist, respectively, in decrementing or incrementing the address of the last item inserted and not yet removed, which is the address of the "top" of the stack. Such address is named "stack pointer", and it is kept constantly in a processor register, until there is a context switch, and control passes to another thread.

The stack limitation of acting only on the top applies only to allocations and deallocations, not to other kinds of access. Indeed, once an object is added to a stack, this object can be read and written even if other objects have been added, as long as such writing does not increase or decrease the size of that object.

When a function is invoked, enough stack space for all its arguments and for all its local variables is allocated. Such allocation is performed by decrementing the stack pointer by the sum of the sizes of all such objects. And when the execution of such function terminates, such stack space is deallocated, by incrementing the stack pointer by the same value. So, after a function returns, the stack pointer is restored to the value it had just before the function invocation.

However, a function may be invoked from several points in a program, and in such points the stack could have contents of different sizes. So, arguments and local variables of any function are allocated in different positions according to where such function is invoked. Here is an example:

```rust
fn f1(x1: i32) {
    let y1 = 2 + x1;
}
fn f2(x2: i32) {
    f1(x2 + 7);
}
let k = 20;
f1(k + 4);
f2(30);
```

Let's follow the execution of this program. This table shows, after each operation, the contents of the first four positions of the stack.

Operation	1	2	3	4	Description
k →	20				The invocation of main adds the value 20 of its local variable k to the stack
x1 →	20	24			The invocation of f1 adds the value 24 of its argument x1 to the stack
y1 →	20	24	26		The beginning of the execution of f1 adds the value 26 of its local variable y1 to the stack
← y1	20	24			The termination of f1 removes the value 26 of its local variable y1 from the stack
← x1	20				The termination of f1 removes the value 24 of its argument x1 from the stack
x2 →	20	30			The invocation of f2 adds the value 30 of its argument x2 to the stack
x1 →	20	30	37		The invocation of f1 adds the value 37 of its argument x1 to the stack
y1 →	20	30	37	39	The beginning of the execution of f1 adds the value 39 of the local variable y1 to the stack
← y1	20	30	37		The termination of f1 removes the value 39 of its local variable y1 from the stack
← x1	20	30			The termination of f1 removes the value 37 of its argument x1 from the stack
← x2	20				The termination of f2 removes the value 30 of its argument x2 from the stack
← k					The termination of main removes the value 20 of its local variable k from the stack

Actually, whenever a function is invoked, further data is added to the stack, and whenever that function terminates, such data is removed from the stack, but here we can ignore that additional data. As you can see in the table above, the f1 function is invoked twice. The first time, its argument x1 is represented by an object put at the second place of the stack with the value 24, and its local variable y1 is represented by an object put in the third place of the stack with the value 26. Instead, the second time f1 is invoked, its argument x1 is represented by an object put in the third place of the stack with the value 37, and its local variable y1 is represented by an object put at the fourth place of the stack with the value 39.

Therefore, the machine code generated for the function f1 cannot use absolute addresses to refer to its arguments and to its local variables. Instead, it uses addresses relative to the "stack pointer". Initially, the stack pointer contains the base address of the stack. In machine code, the addresses of the stack-allocated variables are all relative to the stack pointer. Let's see again the example above.

This table shows, after each operation, the contents of the first four positions of the stack, the value of the stack pointer, and the absolute addresses of the objects associated to the variables x1 and y1, where SP means "stack pointer".

Operation	1	2	3	4	Stack pointer	x1	y1
					base		
k →	20				base - 4		
x1 →	20	24			base - 12	SP + 4	SP
y1 →	20	24	26		base - 12	SP + 4	SP
← y1	20	24			base - 12		
← x1	20				base - 4		
x2 →	20	30			base - 8		
x1 →	20	30	37		base - 16	SP + 4	SP
y1 →	20	30	37	39	base - 16	SP + 4	SP
← y1	20	30	37		base - 16		
← x1	20	30			base - 8		
← x2	20				base - 4		
← k					base		

At the beginning of the program, the stack pointer value is the stack base address, the contents of the stack are undefined, and the variables x1 and y1 have not yet been defined.

When the main function is invoked by the system, the stack pointer becomes base - 4, as the main function has no arguments and has just one local variable, k, which occupies 4 bytes.

When the f1 function is invoked for the first time, the stack pointer becomes base - 12, as the f1 function has one argument, x1, and one local variable, y1, each one occupying 4 bytes.

The creation and destruction of y1 does not change the stack pointer, as its appropriate value has already been set at function invocation.

When the function f1 terminates, the stack pointer is restored at the value it had before the function invocation, which is base - 4.

When the function f2 is invoked, the stack pointer is incremented by the size of its argument x2, setting it to the value of base - 8.

When the f1 function is invoked for the second time, the stack pointer becomes base - 16, as it is decremented by the same amount as for the first invocation, which is 8 bytes.

As each of the f1, f2, and main function terminates, the stack pointer is incremented, first to base - 8, then to base - 4, and then to base.

As it is shown in the last two columns of the table, in the f1 function, the address of the argument x1 is always the value of the stack pointer minus 4; and the address of the local variable y1 is always the value of the stack pointer itself.

Limitations of Stack Allocation

The stack allocation is very convenient and efficient, but it has some limitations:

- The stack has usually a quite limited size. Such size depends on the operating system, and it can be further reduced for some applications, but, as order of magnitude, it is around a few megabytes.

- Rust allows us to allocate in the stack only objects whose size is known at compilation type, like primitive types and arrays, and does not allow us to allocate in the stack objects whose size is determined only at runtime, like vectors.

- It is not allowed to allocate explicitly objects in the stack or
to deallocate explicitly objects from the stack. Any variable is
automatically allocated when the function in which it is declared is
invoked, even if it is declared in an inner block inside that function,
and it is deallocated when the execution of that function terminates.
You cannot override such behavior.

Regarding the second limitation, we actually declared local variables of Vec<_> type, and so the corresponding object was allocated in the stack, but under the hood such objects allocate also some memory outside of the stack.

Regarding the first limitation, it is easy to build an example program that exceeds the stack capacity.

Caution   The following programs in this chapter surely crash the running program, but may also cause malfunction in the whole system. So, you'd better run them in a virtual machine, and save any pending changes before running such examples, because they may force you to reboot your system.

Here is an example of a program exceeding the stack capacity, causing the so-called "stack overflow":

```
const SIZE: usize = 100_000;
const N_ARRAY: usize = 1_000_000;
fn create_array() -> [u8; SIZE] { [0u8; SIZE] }
fn recursive_func(n: usize) {
    let a = create_array();
    println!("{} {}", N_ARRAY - n + 1, a[0]);
    if n > 1 { recursive_func(n - 1) }
}
recursive_func(N_ARRAY);
```

This program most probably crashes, typically emitting a message like "Segmentation fault", or something similar. Indeed, it tries to allocate on the stack more than 100 GB of data.

Assuming your target is not a micro-controller, its stack should be larger than 100 KB; therefore it can allocate at least one 100-KB-large array. However, it probably cannot allocate one million of such arrays.

Let examine this program.

After the declaration of the constants SIZE and N_ARRAY, and the declarations of the functions create_array and recursive_func, there is just one statement, which is an invocation of the recursive_func function, with N_ARRAY as the argument.

The recursive_func function first declares the a variable, and initializes it with the result of the invocation of the create_array function; then, it prints two numbers; then, if the argument n is greater than 1, it invokes itself, and so it is really a recursive function.

Notice that every recursive invocation passes an argument decremented by one, and so eventually the argument becomes no greater than one, and so the recursion eventually ends.

If N_ARRAY were 3, the argument n would be 3 for the first invocation, it would be 2 for the second invocation, it would be 1 for the third invocation, and then there would be no further invocations. Therefore, in this case, recursive_func would be invoked three times in all.

Indeed, the number of invocations is equal to the value of the argument of the original invocation, which is one million.

Now, look at the function create_array. It simply returns an array of 100,000 bytes. Such an array is then assigned to the variable a, which therefore is inferred to be of type [u8; 100000].

Remember that the variable a is allocated when the recursive_func function is invoked, and deallocated only when that function terminates. Therefore, at every recursive invocation, a new copy of a is allocated, without previously deallocating the existing copies. As a consequence, this program tries to allocate in the stack one million arrays of one hundred thousand bytes each. Of course, it cannot do that, and after having printed some lines, it terminates, usually showing an error message, like "Segmentation fault" or "Stack overflow".

The last line printed could be something like 83 0.

The first number indicates how many levels of recursion have been performed, and so, how many arrays have been allocated. If the number printed is 83, it means that more than 8.3 million bytes were successfully allocated in the stack before exceeding the available space.

The second number, which is the first item of the array, is there just to prevent a possible compiler optimization. Indeed, if the variable a were never read, the compiler, after emitting a warning, could remove it completely, as such removal would improve the performance of the program without changing its behavior (before crashing).

Heap Allocation

It's a pity to have a program that crashes for stack overflow, when there is so much more memory available. But heap allocation comes to the rescue:

```
const SIZE: usize = 100_000;
const N_ARRAY: usize = 1_000_000;
fn create_array() -> Box<[u8; SIZE]> { Box::new([0u8; SIZE]) }
fn recursive_func(n: usize) {
    let a = create_array();
    println!("{} {}", N_ARRAY - n + 1, a[0]);
    if n > 1 { recursive_func(n - 1) }
}
recursive_func(N_ARRAY);
```

Eventually, even this program crashes for stack overflow or for insufficient memory, but only after having printed many more lines than the previous program, and that means that it has successfully allocated much more memory.

In this program, with respect to the previous program, only the third line has changed.

Now, the `create_array` function, instead of returning an array, returns a value of type `Box<[u8; SIZE]>`.

That type is a "boxed" array of SIZE bytes.

In Rust, you can box most objects, not only arrays. The Rust standard library contains the generic struct type `Box<T>`. An object of type `Box<T>` is a reference to another object, which has type T, and that is placed in a part of memory, named "heap", different both from the static area and the stack.

The body of the `create_array` function is `Box::new([0u8; SIZE])`. This expression is an invocation of the `new` function declared in the `Box` scope. Such function receives as an argument an array of SIZE bytes, all of them equal to zero. The behavior and purpose of the `Box::new` function are to allocate an object in the heap that must be large enough to contain a copy of the received argument, copy the value of the received argument into such newly allocated object, and return the address of such object.

148

Therefore, the stack space occupied by the a variable is just that of one pointer. The actual array is allocated in the heap. Well, actually the Box::new function allocates that array temporarily in the stack, but it deallocates it as soon as it returns. So, it is enough that the stack can contain one instance of that array, which occupies one hundred thousand bytes.

Heap Management

Let's see how the heap memory is managed.

When a program starts, its heap is virtually empty (or very small).

At any time, each byte of the heap may be in two possible states: "reserved" (aka "used") or "free" (aka as "unused").

When the program needs to allocate an object in the heap, first it searches if the heap contains some sequence of free bytes that is at least as long as the size of the object to allocate. If there is such a sequence of bytes, the program reserves from it a subsequence as long as the object size. Instead, if the heap contains no long enough sequence, a request is made to the operating system to enlarge the size of the heap, so that the object can be allocated.

When an object allocated in the heap is not needed anymore, it can be explicitly deallocated, returning the memory space it used to the state of free.

Notice that usually the size of the heap of a process is never shrunk.

A serious problem of heap management is that it may become fragmented. If a million of f64 objects are allocated in a heap, that heap must become as large as at least 8 MB. If then every object of odd position is deallocated from that heap, after those deallocations the heap contains half a million of free spaces, for a total of 4 MB, interleaved with half a million of reserved spaces. There is a lot of free space, but if you need to allocate an object large 9 or more bytes, there is no large enough space for it, and you need to enlarge that heap.

In addition, a naive algorithm that searches a large-enough space in a heap can be very costly. There are smarter search algorithms that can improve the performance of heap allocation, but they cause the heap deallocation to become more costly.

Therefore, stack allocation is always more efficient than heap allocation, both in time and in space. Heap allocation is nearly as efficient as stack allocation only when it behaves like a stack, which is only when the last allocated object is deallocated. Of course, often the application requirements do not allow this allocation pattern.

The Behavior of Box

As we said, for any variable of type Box<T>, a pointer is allocated in the stack as soon as the function containing such variable is invoked. Instead, the heap allocation happens only when the function Box::new is invoked. So, the allocation of Box<T> happens in two steps: first the pointer, and then the referenced object.

Similarly, the deallocation also happens in two steps. The deallocation from the stack of the pointer happens only when the function containing the variable terminates, but the deallocation of the object from the heap happens before that, and possibly even much before.

```
fn f(p: &f64) {
    let a = Box::new(*p);
    {
        let b = Box::new([1, 2, 3]);
        print!("{} {:?}", *a, *b);
    }
    let c = Box::new(true);
    print!(" {} {}", a, c);
}
f(&3.4);
```

This will print: "3.4 [1, 2, 3] 3.4 true".

When the function main is invoked, the value 3.4, of type f64, is allocated on the stack, without being associated to any variable.

When the function f is invoked, four pointers are allocated in the stack, one for the argument p, and one for each of the three variables a, b, and c.

When the first statement of this function is executed, an f64 object is allocated in the heap, and it is initialized with the value of the expression *p, which is 3.4.

When the second statement of the function is executed, an array of three i32 values is allocated and initialized in the heap, and its address is used to initialize the b variable. The third statement prints the values referenced by a and b. The dereference operator is the same used for simple references. The c variable could not be printed here, because it is not yet visible. Immediately after this statement, the scope of b ends, and so the array referenced by b is deallocated from the heap, freeing the space it used, making it available for other allocations.

150

This last action is important. When b exits its scope, it becomes available no more; and automatically, the heap object referred to by it is deallocated.

When the fourth statement of the function is executed, a Boolean object is allocated and initialized in the heap, and its address is used to initialize the c variable. It may be that such Boolean object overlaps that of the previous array in the heap, as the space used by the array was freed. The fifth statement prints the values referenced by a and c. Also for boxes, like for simple references, the asterisks are optional and omitted. The b variable could not be printed here, because it is no more visible. Immediately after this statement, the scope of both a and c ends, and so the objects they are referencing are deallocated from the heap. This is also the end of the function execution, and so the four pointers are also deallocated from the stack.

Finally, the main function ends, and so the 3.4 unnamed object is deallocated from the stack.

Here it is rather pointless, but it is worth noting that if several variables are declared in the same scope, they exit their scope in reverse order of declaration. In our example, a has been declared before c, and so a exits its scope after c. This causes that the object referenced by a is deallocated from the heap after the object referenced by c. This is quite reasonable, considering that it is a stack, and so the top item is always the next to be removed.

Notice that here no deallocation function is invoked. Actually the Rust language and its standard library have no deallocation functions to call. This prevents forgetting to call them.

Similarity with C and C++

Even in C and in C++ you can use the heap. In the C language, you have the malloc, calloc, and realloc functions to allocate a buffer in the heap, and the free function to deallocate a previously allocated buffer. In addition, in the C++ language, you have the new and the new[] operators to allocate respectively an object or an array of objects in the heap, and the delete and delete[] operators to deallocate what has been allocated by, respectively, the new or the new[] operators.

Actually, the Rust Box<T> generic type is quite different from all the above kinds of heap allocation. But since 2011, in standard C++ there exists a type that is quite similar to Box<T>: it is the unique_ptr<T> class template. It is a so-called "smart pointer", which, like Box<T>, allocates an object in the heap and deallocates it when it exits from its scope.

Boxing and Unboxing

So, for a given T generic type, both Box<T> and &T are kinds of reference. Let's see how they can interact.

```
let a = 7;
let a_box: Box<i32>;
let mut a_ref: &i32 = &a;
print!("{} {};", a, *a_ref);
a_box = Box::new(a + 2);
a_ref = &*a_box;
print!(" {} {} {}", a, *a_ref, *a_box);
```

This will print: "7 7; 7 9 9". Let's examine it.

The stack will contain three objects: the number 7, represented by the a variable; and two pointers, represented by the a_box and a_ref variables. The pointer declared in the second line, a_box, is initialized only at the fifth line, while the other variables are initialized in the same statements in which they are declared.

Both pointer variables are type-annotated, but such annotations are optional and could be removed, because the type can be inferred from their usage. However, they show that a_box is a "smart" pointer, while a_ref is a "dumb" pointer, meaning that a_box takes care of allocating and deallocating its referred object, while a_ref does not take care of either allocation or deallocation of its referred object.

In the two print macro invocations, the three asterisks are optional and could be removed.

In the fifth and sixth lines, the two pointers are assigned a value. But for a_box, it's an initialization, and so the variable does not have to be mutable; instead, a_ref had been already initialized, and so, to be reassigned, it had to be declared with the mut clause.

The third line just set the a_ref variable value as the address of the a variable. Instead, the fifth line does something more complex. It allocates an i32 object in the heap, initializes such object using the value of the expression a + 2, which is the value 9, and then it sets the a_box variable value as the address of this object.

In the sixth line, the value of a_box (not the value referred to by a_box), which is a pointer, is copied to the variable a_ref; in other words, the dumb pointer is made to point to the same object pointed to by the smart pointer. This is confirmed by the last print statement. Though, this assignment cannot be simply a_ref = a_box;, because the two variables have different types, and also the statement a_ref = a_box as &i32;

would be illegal. Instead, the trick of dereferencing using *, and then referencing using &
allows to convert a Box into a reference, or better said, it allows us to take the address of
the object referenced to by the box.

Notice that the inverted operation would be illegal: a_box = &*a_ref;. Actually, the
expression &*a_ref is still of type &i32, and so it cannot be assigned to a variable of type
Box<i32>.

Finally, at the end of the program, first a_ref exits from its scope, doing nothing; then
a_box exists from its scope, deallocating its referenced object from the heap; then a exits
from its scope, doing nothing; and at last the three objects are deallocated from the stack.

This program is similar:

```
let a = 7;
let mut a_box: Box<i32>;
let a_ref: &i32 = &a;
print!("{} {};", a, a_ref);
a_box = Box::new(a + 2);
print!(" {} {} {};", a, a_ref, a_box);
a_box = Box::new(*a_ref);
print!(" {} {} {}", a, a_ref, a_box);
```

It will print 7 7; 7 7 9; 7 7 7.

Here it is a_box to be mutable, while a_ref is immutable.

The penultimate statement line reassigns the box. That, conceptually, causes a
heap deallocation followed by an allocation of a new object of the same type but a
different value.

Register Allocation

In Assembly language, and sometimes also in C language, the concept of "processor
register allocation" is used. In Rust language, this concept is absent, because it would
constrain the code to specific target hardware architectures. However, the code
optimizer can move the location of a stack-allocated object into a processor register, as
long as the resulting behavior of the program is equivalent. Therefore, what at source-
code level appears to be a stack-allocated object, at machine-code level may end up to
be a register-allocated object. This of course depends on the target architecture, because
the more registers the target processor has, the more variables can be register allocated.

This register allocation is usually irrelevant for the programmer. But if you use a source-level debugger to examine the contents of the memory of a highly optimized program, you will find that register-allocated variables have disappeared. So, when debugging, you should instruct your compiler to generate non-optimized executable code, unless you want to debug directly machine code.

CHAPTER 12

Data Implementation

In this chapter, you will learn:

- How to know how many bytes of stack are taken by objects of various types

- How to shorten the path to access functions declared in external modules

- How bits are stored in primitive type objects

- How to know where an object is stored in memory

- Why padding can increase the size taken by some objects

- How vectors are implemented

Discovering the Size of Objects

Given a source file, the Rust compiler is free to generate any machine code, as long as it behaves in the way specified by the language Rust for that source code.

Therefore, for example, given a variable, it is not defined how many memory bits it uses, and where it is located in memory. The compiler could even remove that variable from memory, because it is never used, or because it is kept in a processor register.

However, it is instructive to see a possible typical implementation of the arrangement of the data used by a Rust program.

For such a purpose, some Rust features are available:

```
print!("{} ", std::mem::size_of::<i32>());
print!("{} ", std::mem::size_of_val(&12));
```

This will print: "4 4".

© Carlo Milanesi 2018
C. Milanesi, *Beginning Rust*, https://doi.org/10.1007/978-1-4842-3468-6_12

In the first statement, the compiler enters the standard library module std (shorthand for "standard"), then it enters its submodule mem (shorthand for "memory"), and then it takes its generic function size_of.

The compiler concretizes such a generic function using the type i32, and then it generates the invocation of such resulting concrete function without passing any arguments. Such a function will return the number of bytes (or "octets of bits", to be precise) occupied by any object of the specified type. Typically, such function invocation will be inlined, and so the code generated is just a constant number. Actually, a 32-bit number comes out to occupy 4 bytes.

Notice that you may invoke this function even if in the program there is no object of the specified type.

In the second statement, the compiler enters in the same library module, but it accesses the generic function size_of_val (meaning "size of value"). In this case, the type of the parameter needed to concretize the generic function is inferred from the argument, and so it wasn't required to specify it explicitly. Instead, in the first statement there were no arguments, and so the type parameter was required.

When the concretized function size_of_val is invoked, an immutable reference to an object is passed to it. The function returns the size in bytes of such object.

The use Directive

If the path to reach a library function must be specified several times, it is convenient to "import" all or part of such path into the current scope, using the use directive.

The previous example can be rewritten in this way:

```
use std::mem;
print!("{} ", mem::size_of::<i32>());
print!("{} ", mem::size_of_val(&12));
```

or in this one:

```
use std::mem::size_of;
use std::mem::size_of_val;
print!("{} ", size_of::<i32>());
print!("{} ", size_of_val(&12));
```

The Rust use keyword is similar to the C++ using keyword.

There is an even more compact form of it:

```
use std::mem::*;
print!("{} ", size_of::<i32>());
print!("{} ", size_of_val(&12));
```

The asterisk is a wildcard that causes all the names at that level to be imported.

The Sizes of the Primitive Types

Now you should imagine the sizes of the objects having a primitive type:

```
use std::mem::*;
print!("{} {} {} {} {} {} {} {} {} {} {} {}",
    size_of::<i8>(),
    size_of::<u8>(),
    size_of::<i16>(),
    size_of::<u16>(),
    size_of::<i32>(),
    size_of::<u32>(),
    size_of::<i64>(),
    size_of::<u64>(),
    size_of::<f32>(),
    size_of::<f64>(),
    size_of::<bool>(),
    size_of::<char>());
```

In any computer, this will print 1 1 2 2 4 4 8 8 4 8 1 4.

Some other data types have sizes that depend on the target platform of the compiler:

```
use std::mem::*;
print!("{} {} {} {}",
    size_of::<isize>(),
    size_of::<usize>(),
    size_of::<&i8>(),
    size_of::<&u32>());
```

In a 64-bit system, this will print: 8 8 8 8, while in a 32-bit system, it will print: 4 4 4 4.

The last two printed values are references. Independently from the referenced object, a reference (aka a "pointer") has the size of a memory address.

The Representation of Primitive Types

Rust discourages accessing the internal representation of objects, and so it is not easy to do; but there is a trick to do that.

```rust
fn as_bytes<T>(o: &T) -> &[u8] {
    unsafe {
        std::slice::from_raw_parts(
            o as *const _ as *const u8,
            std::mem::size_of::<T>())
    }
}
println!("{:?}", as_bytes(&1i8));
println!("{:?}", as_bytes(&2i16));
println!("{:?}", as_bytes(&3i32));
println!("{:?}", as_bytes(&(4i64 + 5 * 256 + 6 * 256 * 256)));
println!("{:?}", as_bytes(&'A'));
println!("{:?}", as_bytes(&true));
println!("{:?}", as_bytes(&&1i8));
```

In an x86_64 system, this could print:

```
[1]
[2, 0]
[3, 0, 0, 0]
[4, 5, 6, 0, 0, 0, 0, 0]
[65, 0, 0, 0]
[1]
[129, 165, 54, 102, 23, 86, 0, 0]
```

The generic function as_bytes uses some Rust constructs we haven't seen yet, and that will not be explained here, because their knowledge is not required to understand what it does. It simply takes a reference to an argument of any type, and returns an object that represents the sequence of bytes contained in such an object. By printing such an object, you can see the representation of any object as the sequence of bytes it stores in memory.

First, an i8 having value 1 is stored in a single byte. And that is just the same in any supported hardware architecture.

Then, an i16 having value 2 is stored as a pair of bytes, of which the first one is 2 and the second one is 0. This happens both on 32-bit and 64-bit processors, but only in the so-called "little-endian" hardware architectures, which are those that store multi-byte numbers placing the least significant byte at the lowest address. Instead, a "big-endian" hardware architecture would have printed [0, 2].

Similar behavior appears in the following printed lines.

Notice that a char is stored as a 32-bit number containing the Unicode value of such character, and a bool is stored as a single byte, which is 1 for true and 0 for false.

Finally, the last statement prints the address of an i8 number. Such an address occupies eight bytes for a 64-bit processor, and differs from run to run.

Location of Bytes in Memory

You can also discover the (virtual) memory location of any object, which is its address:

```
let b1 = true;
let b2 = true;
let b3 = false;
print!("{} {} {}",
    &b1 as *const bool as usize,
    &b2 as *const bool as usize,
    &b3 as *const bool as usize);
```

In a 64-bit system, this will print three huge numbers, resembling 140727116566237 140727116566238 140727116566239. Instead, in a 32-bit system, it will print three numbers smaller than 5 billion.

Also the constructs to get such numbers will not be explained here.

Here is a representation of the location of the three objects above:

Absolute address	Binary value	Variable name	Type
140727116566237	0000_0000	b3	bool
140727116566238	0000_0001	b2	bool
140727116566239	0000_0001	b1	bool

Each one of the three objects occupies just one byte. The first printed number is the address of the b1 variable; the second the address of the b2 variable; and the third the address of the b3 variable. As it appears, the three numbers are consecutive, and that means that the three objects are allocated in contiguous virtual memory locations.

You should have noted also that the three numbers form a decreasing sequence. That means that as objects are allocated, they are located in lower and lower addresses. These objects are stack allocated, and therefore here we see that the stack grows downward.

The first number contains the true Boolean value, which is represented by the 1 byte, which in turn consists of seven bits having zero value and one bit having one value. Also the second object contains the true value. Instead, the third object contains the false value, represented by eight bits having zero value.

When allocating single bytes, the Rust compiler usually lays them out sequentially and contiguously, but when allocating larger objects, their position in memory is not easily predictable.

Almost all modern processors require that elementary data have particular memory locations, and so Rust places its objects so that they are easily accessible by the processors.

The typical alignment rule is this: "Every object of a primitive type must have an address that is a multiple of its own size".

So, while the objects occupying just one byte can be placed anywhere, the objects occupying two bytes can be placed only at even addresses, the objects occupying four bytes can be placed only at addresses that are divisible by four, and the objects occupying eight bytes can be places only at addresses that are a multiple of eight.

In addition, larger objects often have addresses that are a multiple of sixteen.

Therefore, such alignment requirements can create unused spaces, the so-called "padding".

Sizes of Composite Data Types

The effect of padding appears when there is a sequence of composite objects:

```
enum E1 { E1a, E1b };
enum E2 { E2a, E2b(f64) };
use std::mem::*;
print!("{} {} {} {} {} {}",
    size_of_val(&[0i16; 80]),
    size_of_val(&(0i16, 0i64)),
    size_of_val(&[(0i16, 0i64); 100]),
    size_of_val(&E1::E1a),
    size_of_val(&E2::E2a),
    size_of_val(&vec![(0i16, 0i64); 100]));
```

This will print: "160 16 1600 1 16 24".
This means that:

- an array of 80 16-bit numbers occupies 160 bytes, that is 80 * 2, and so there is no waste;

- a tuple of a 16-bit number and a 64-bit number occupies 16 bytes, like if both numbers would occupy 8 bytes, and so a padding of 6 bytes has been added.

- an array of 100 16-byte tuples occupies 1600 bytes, and so there is no padding between array items, but the padding of every item is multiplied by the length of the array;

- an enum having all its variants without data fields occupies always just one byte;

- an enum whose largest variant contains an 8-byte number occupies 16 bytes, even if the current value has no data, because there are 7 bytes of padding;

- a vector of 100 16-byte tuples looks like to occupy just 24 bytes, but of course something is missing from this measure.

Let's see just the case of the vector.

The data placed in the stack must have a size known at compile time, and so arrays can be fully allocated in the stack, while for vectors only a fixed-size header can be placed in the stack, while the remaining data must be allocated in the heap.

Vector Allocation

We saw that vectors must be implemented as a two-object structure: a stack-allocated fixed-size header, and a heap-allocated variable-length buffer.

There are theoretically several possible ways to implement a vector data structure.

One way would be to keep in the header only a pointer to the buffer.

That has the disadvantage that every time the length of the array is desired, an indirection level would be required. The length of arrays is needed quite often, implicitly or explicitly, and so it is better to keep such information in the header.

A naive way to implement the buffer would be to size it just large enough to keep the desired data. For example, if a vector of 9 i32 items is requested, a buffer of 9 * 4 bytes is allocated in the heap.

As long as such vector does not grow, this is good. But if another item is pushed into such vector, the buffer must be reallocated, and heap allocations and deallocation are costly. In addition, the old buffer contents must be copied to the new buffer.

If a 1000-item vector is constructed an item at a time by creating an empty vector and calling 1000 times the push function, there shall be 1000 heap allocations, 999 heap deallocations, and 1000 * 999 / 2 == 499_500 copies of items.

To improve such awful performance, a larger buffer may be allocated, so that a reallocation is performed only when such buffer is not enough.

Therefore there is the need to track both the number of places in the allocated buffer, and the number of used places in such buffer.

The number of places in the allocated buffer is usually named `capacity`, and that is also the name of the function used to access such number.

```
let mut v = vec![0; 0];
println!("{} {}", v.len(), v.capacity());
v.push(11);
println!("{} {}", v.len(), v.capacity());
v.push(22);
println!("{} {}", v.len(), v.capacity());
```

```
v.push(33);
println!("{} {}", v.len(), v.capacity());
v.push(44);
println!("{} {}", v.len(), v.capacity());
v.push(55);
println!("{} {}", v.len(), v.capacity());
```

This will print:

```
0 0
1 4
2 4
3 4
4 4
5 8
```

When an empty vector is created, it contains zero items, and it hasn't even allocated a heap-buffer, and so its capacity is also zero.

When the first item is added, the vector object allocates in the heap a buffer capable of containing four 32-bit numbers (i.e., a 16-byte buffer), and so its capacity is 4, but it effectively contains just one item, and so its length is 1.

When three other items are added to the vector, there is no need to allocate memory, as the pre-allocated buffer is large enough to contain them.

But when the fifth item is added to the vector, a larger buffer must be allocated. The new buffer has a capacity of 8 items.

Therefore, the vec object stores three subobjects in the stack: a pointer to the heap-allocated buffer, which is a memory address; the capacity of such buffer as a number of items, which is a usize number; and the length of the vector as a number of items, which is a usize number that is less than or equal to the capacity.

For this reason, the header of any vector occupies 3 * 8 == 24 bytes in any 64-bit system, and 3 * 4 == 12 bytes in any 32-bit system.

Let's see what happens if we add one thousand items to a vector of 32-bit numbers.

```
let mut v = vec![0; 0];
let mut prev_capacity = std::usize::MAX;
for i in 0..1_000 {
    let cap = v.capacity();
```

```
    if cap != prev_capacity {
        println!("{} {} {}", i, v.len(), cap);
        prev_capacity = cap;
    }
    v.push(1);
}
```

This (probably) will print:

```
0 0 0
1 1 4
5 5 8
9 9 16
17 17 32
33 33 64
65 65 128
129 129 256
257 257 512
513 513 1024
```

Well, it will print the same also for a vector of any type of items.

The variable `cap` stores the current capacity of the vector; the variable `prev_capacity` stores the previous capacity of the vector, and it is initialized to a huge value.

At each iteration, before adding an item to the vector, it is checked to see if the capacity has changed. Each time the capacity changes, both the number of inserted items and the current capacity are printed.

It appears that the capacity is always a power of two, and all the powers of two are passed, just skipping the value 2. In this way, there are just 9 allocations, 8 deallocations, and 4 + 8 + 16 + 32 + 64 + 128 + 256 + 512 == 1020 copies, and so the real algorithm is much more efficient than the naive version described at the beginning of this section.

CHAPTER 13

Defining Closures

In this chapter, you will learn:

- Why there is a need for anonymous inline functions, with type inference for the arguments and the return value type, without having to write braces, and which can access the variables that are alive at the function definition point

- How such lightweight functions, named "closures", can be declared and invoked

The Need for "Disposable" Functions

The Rust way to sort an array in ascending order is this:

```
let mut arr = [4, 8, 1, 10, 0, 45, 12, 7];
arr.sort();
print!("{:?}", arr);
```

This will print: `"[0, 1, 4, 7, 8, 10, 12, 45]"`;

But if you want to sort it in descending order, or using some other criterion, there are no prepackaged functions; you must invoke the sort_by function, passing to it a reference to a comparison function. Such function receives two items, and it returns an indication of which of them must precede the other one:

```
let mut arr = [4, 8, 1, 10, 0, 45, 12, 7];
use std::cmp::Ordering;
fn desc(a: &i32, b: &i32) -> Ordering {
    if a < b { Ordering::Greater }
```

© Carlo Milanesi 2018
C. Milanesi, *Beginning Rust*, https://doi.org/10.1007/978-1-4842-3468-6_13

```
    else if a > b { Ordering::Less }
    else { Ordering::Equal }
}
arr.sort_by(desc);
print!("{:?}", arr);
```

This will print: "[45, 12, 10, 8, 7, 4, 1, 0]".

The desc function returns a value whose type is defined by the standard library in the following way:

```
enum Ordering { Less, Equal, Greater }
```

This works, but it has several drawbacks.

First, the desc function is defined only to be used just in one point, in the following statement. Usually a function is not created to be used only in one point; rather, the body of the function is expanded where it is needed. However, the library function sort_by requires a function. What is needed is an inline anonymous function, which is a function that is declared in the same point where it is used.

Moreover, while the type specification is optional for variable declarations, it is required for the arguments and the return value for function declarations. These specifications, like the name of the function, are convenient when such function is invoked from faraway statements, and possibly by other programmers. But when you have to write a function to be invoked just where it has been declared, such type specifications are mostly annoying. So it would be a convenient feature to declare and invoke inline an anonymous function with type inference of its arguments and return value.

Another drawback regards the need to enclose the function body in braces. Usual functions, typically, contain several statements, and so it is not at all annoying having to enclose such statements in braces. Instead, anonymous functions often consist of a single expression, which would be convenient to be able to write without having to enclose it in braces. Given that a block is still an expression, it would be nice to have an inline anonymous function with type inference and a single expression as body.

Capturing the Environment

All that we said so far in this chapter is valid also in many other languages, C included. But Rust functions have an additional unusual limitation: they cannot access any variable that is declared outside of them. You can access `static` items, and also `constants`, but you cannot access stack-allocated (that is "let-declared") variables. For example, this program is illegal:

```
let two = 2.;
fn print_double(x: f64) {
    print!("{}", x * two);
}
print_double(17.2);
```

Its compilation generates the error: `can't capture dynamic environment in an fn item`. By "dynamic environment" it means the set of the variables that happen to be valid where the function is invoked. In a way, it is "dynamic," as a given function may be invoked in several statements, and the variables that are valid in one of those statements may not be valid in another statement. To "capture the environment" means to be able to access those variables.

Instead, this is valid:

```
const TWO: f64 = 2.;
fn print_double(x: f64) {
    print!("{}", x * TWO);
}
print_double(17.2);
```

and this too:

```
static TWO: f64 = 2.;
fn print_double(x: f64) {
    print!("{}", x * TWO);
}
print_double(17.2);
```

Such a limitation has a good reason: external variables effectively get into the programming interface of the function, but they are not apparent from the function signature, and so they are misleading for understanding code.

167

But when a function can be invoked only where it has been defined, the fact that it accesses external variables does not cause it to be less understandable, because those external variables are already available to the declaration statement.

Therefore, the requirements of our feature are the following: an inline anonymous function, with type inference; a single expression as body; and the capture of any valid variable.

Closures

Because of its great usefulness, in Rust there is such a feature, which is named "closure".

A closure is just a handier kind of function, fit to define small anonymous functions, and to invoke them just where they have been defined.

In fact, you can also define a closure, assign it to a variable, so giving it a name, and then invoke it later using its name. This not the most typical usage of closures, though. Even type specification is possible. Here is the above descending order sorting example, performed using a closure instead of the desc function:

```
let mut arr = [4, 8, 1, 10, 0, 45, 12, 7];
use std::cmp::Ordering;
let desc = |a: &i32, b: &i32| -> Ordering {
    if a < b { Ordering::Greater }
    else if a > b { Ordering::Less }
    else { Ordering::Equal }
};
arr.sort_by(desc);
print!("{:?}", arr);
```

The only differences with respect to the previous example are:

- The let keyword was used instead of fn.

- The = symbol has been added after the name of the closure.

- The (and) symbols, which enclose the function arguments, have been replaced by the | (pipe) symbol.

- A semicolon has been added after the closure declaration.

So far, there are no advantages, but we said that the closure can be defined where it has to be used, and that the types and the braces are optional. Therefore, we can transform the previous code into this one:

```
let mut arr = [4, 8, 1, 10, 0, 45, 12, 7];
use std::cmp::Ordering;
arr.sort_by(|a, b|
    if a < b { Ordering::Greater }
    else if a > b { Ordering::Less }
    else { Ordering::Equal });
print!("{:?}", arr);
```

This is already a nice simplification. But there is more.

The standard library already contains the cmp function (shorthand for "compare"); this function returns an Ordering value according to which of its two arguments is greater. The two following statements are equivalent:

```
arr.sort();
arr.sort_by(|a, b| a.cmp(b));
```

Therefore, to obtain the inverted order, you can use, indifferently, each one of the following statements:

```
arr.sort_by(|a, b| (&-*a).cmp(&-*b));
arr.sort_by(|a, b| b.cmp(a));
```

Here is a complete example:

```
let mut arr = [4, 8, 1, 10, 0, 45, 12, 7];
arr.sort_by(|a, b| b.cmp(a));
print!("{:?}", arr);
```

Also the use directive has been removed because it is not required anymore.

Other Examples

Here is another example that shows six ways to invoke a closure:

```
let factor = 2;
let multiply = |a| a * factor;
print!("{}", multiply(13));
let multiply_ref: &(Fn(i32) -> i32) = &multiply;
print!(
    " {} {} {} {} {}",
    (*multiply_ref)(13),
    multiply_ref(13),
    (|a| a * factor)(13),
    (|a: i32| a * factor)(13),
    |a| -> i32 { a * factor }(13));
```

This will print: "26 26 26 26 26 26".

This program contains six identical closure invocations. Each of them takes an i32 argument named a; multiplies it by the captured variable factor, whose value is 2; and returns the result of such multiplication. The argument is always 13, and so the result is always 26.

In the second line, the first closure is declared, using a type inference both for the argument a and for the return value. The body of the closure accesses the external variable factor, declared by the previous statement, and so such variable is captured inside the closure, with its current value. The closure is then used to initialize the variable multiply, whose type is inferred.

In the third line, the closure assigned to the multiply variable is invoked just like any function.

In the fourth line, the address of the just declared closure is used to initialize the multiply_ref variable. The type of this variable could be inferred too, but it has been specified explicitly. The word Fn is used to specify the type of a function. Every function has a type determined by the types of its arguments and its return value. The expression Fn(i32) -> i32 means "the type of a function that takes an i32 as argument and returns an i32". Such a type expression is preceded by an & symbol, because what we have is a "reference to a function", not "a function".

In the seventh line, the reference to a function is dereferenced, obtaining a function, and that function is invoked.

In the eighth line, that function is invoked without dereferencing the reference, as such dereference operation is implicit for a function invocation.

In the last three statements, three anonymous closures are declared and invoked. The first one infers both the type of the argument and the type of the return value; the second one specifies the type of the argument and infers the type of the return value; and the third one infers the type of the argument and specifies the type of the return value.

Notice that the argument 13 is passed to the closure always enclosed in parentheses. To avoid confusing such expression (13) with the previous expression that specifies the closure, in some cases such closure expression must be enclosed in parentheses too. In the last case, instead, the body of the closure had to be enclosed in braces to separate it from the return value type specification.

The braces are required also when the closure contains several statements, like in this case:

```rust
print!(
    "{}",
    (|v: &Vec<i32>| {
        let mut sum = 0;
        for i in 0..v.len() {
            sum += v[i];
        }
        sum
    })(&vec![11, 22, 34]));
```

This will print "67" which is the sum of the numbers contained in the vector.

In this case, it was required to specify the type of the argument, as otherwise the compiler couldn't infer it, and it would emit the error message "the type of this value must be known in this context", regarding the expression v.len().

CHAPTER 14

Using Changeable Strings

In this chapter, you will learn:

- How static strings are implemented

- How dynamic strings are implemented

- How you can add characters to or remove characters from a
  dynamic string

- How to convert a static string to a dynamic string, and conversely

- How to concatenate strings

Static Strings

Are the strings that we have used so far changeable?

They may be mutable and so, in a sense, we can change them:

```
let mut a = "Hel";
print!("{}", a);
a = "lo";
print!("{}", a);
```

This will print "Hello". But in what sense did we change it? We changed abruptly all the content of the string, not just some characters. In fact, so far we changed strings only by assigning to a string variable a string literal or another string variable.

But if we wanted to create a string either algorithmically, or by reading it from a file, or by letting the user type it in, how could we do it? Simply stated, using the kind of strings we have used so far, we cannot do that. Indeed, although these string objects can be changed to refer to other string content, they have an immutable *content*, that is,

© Carlo Milanesi 2018
C. Milanesi, *Beginning Rust*, https://doi.org/10.1007/978-1-4842-3468-6_14

it is not possible to overwrite some characters or to add or remove characters. Because of this, they are called *static* strings. The following example helps to clarify:

```rust
use std::mem::*;
let a: &str = "";
let b: &str = "0123456789";
let c: &str = "abcdè";
print!("{} {} {}",
    size_of_val(a),
    size_of_val(b),
    size_of_val(c));
```

This program will print 0 10 6.

First, notice that we specified the type of the three variables. Such type is &str, which is "reference to str."

The str word is defined in the standard library as the type of an unmodifiable array of bytes representing a UTF-8 string. Each time the compiler parses a literal string, it stores in a static program area the characters of that string, and such area is of str type. Then the compiler uses a reference to such area as the value of such literal string expression, and so any string literal is of type &str.

In the example, the size_of_val generic function is invoked on the three string variables. Remember that such a function returns the size of the object referenced by its argument. If the argument is a, that is of type &str, this function returns the size of the string buffer referenced by a, which is of type str.

So the sizes of the three buffers referred to by the variables a, b, and c are printed. Such sizes are respectively 0, 10, and 6 bytes. Indeed, the first string was empty, and the second one contained exactly ten digits; instead, the third string contained only five characters, but the number six was printed as its length. This is because of the UTF-8 notation. In such notation, every character is represented by one or more bytes, depending on the character. The ASCII characters are represented by a single byte, while the "grave e" character, that is, è, is represented by two bytes. So, the whole string of five characters is represented by six bytes.

Notice that the buffers referred to by the a, b, and c variables are of the same type, which is str, but they have different lengths: 0, 10, and 6. So here, for the first time, we see a type that hasn't an associated length.

Such types are not very common, but they have some limitations. One is that you cannot declare a variable or a function argument of such type. Another obvious limitation is that you cannot ask the size of such type.

```
let a: str;
fn f(a: str) {}
print!("{}", std::mem::size_of::<str>());
```

All the three previous statements are illegal.

But then, how can the previous program get the sizes of the buffers? In C language, string terminators are used to mark the end of strings, but Rust has no string terminators.

Actually the &str type is not a normal Rust reference, containing just a pointer, but it is a pair of a pointer and a length. The pointer value is the address of the beginning of the string buffer, and the length value is the number of bytes of the string buffer.

Let's explore this strange type in more depth.

```
use std::mem::*;
let a: &str = "";
let b: &str = "0123456789";
let c: &str = "abcdè";
print!("{} {} {}; ",
    size_of_val(&a),
    size_of_val(&b),
    size_of_val(&c));
print!("{} {} {}",
    size_of_val(&&a),
    size_of_val(&&b),
    size_of_val(&&c));
```

This program in a 64-bit system will print "16 16 16; 8 8 8", while in a 32-bit system it will print "8 8 8; 4 4 4".

The first print statement prints the sizes of the variables themselves, which are of type &str. Such variables result in sizes that are twice as large as that of a normal reference, as they contain a pointer object and a usize object. So, when we invoke the len function on a static string, we just read the second field of that pair.

The second print statement prints the sizes of references to the variables themselves, which are of type &&str. They are normal references.

Dynamic Strings

So if we want to create or change the contents of a string at runtime, the `&str` type, which we always used so far, is unfit.

But Rust provides also another kind of strings, the *dynamic strings*, whose content can be changed:

```
let mut a: String = "He".to_string();
a.push('l');
a.push('l');
a.push('o');
print!("{}", a);
```

This will print `"Hello"`.

The a variable is of type String, which is the type Rust uses for dynamic strings.

In Rust there are no literal dynamic strings; literal strings are always static. But a dynamic string may be constructed from a static string in several ways. One is to invoke the `to_string` function on a static string. The name of this function should be thought as it were `to_dynamic_string` or `to_String`. But the first alternative would be too long, and the second one would violate the convention of never using uppercase letters in the name of functions.

A dynamic string can be printed like any static string, as shown by the last statement of the example. But it is capable of something a static string cannot do: to grow.

Each of the second, third, and fourth statements add a character at the end of the string.

It is possible also to add characters in other positions inside a dynamic string, or to remove any character.

```
let mut a: String = "Xy".to_string(); // "Xy"
a.remove(0); // "y"
a.insert(0, 'H'); // "Hy"
a.pop(); // "H"
a.push('i'); // "Hi"
print!("{}", a);
```

This prints `"Hi"`.

The a variable is initialized to contain `"Xy"`. Then the character at position 0 is removed, leaving `"y"`. Then an `"H"` is inserted at position 0, obtaining a `"Hy"`. Then the last character is popped from the end, leaving "H". Then an "i" is pushed at the end, obtaining the final "Hi".

Implementation of String

While a Rust static string is somewhat similar to a C language string, with an additional counter, a Rust dynamic string is quite similar to a C++ std::string object. The main difference between Rust and C++ dynamic string types is that while any C++ string contains an array of characters, any Rust dynamic string, like any Rust static string, contains an array of bytes that represent a UTF-8 string; it does not contain an array of characters.

Remaining in the Rust language, there are other similarities. While static string buffers are similar to arrays, that is, the str type is similar to the generic [u8; N] type, dynamic strings are similar to vectors of bytes, that is, the String type is similar to the Vec<u8> type.

Indeed, the functions we saw above – push, pop, insert, and remove, and also the len function have the same name of the corresponding functions of the Vector generic type.

In addition, both dynamic strings and vectors have the same implementation. Both are structures consisting of three fields:

- the address of the beginning of the heap-allocated buffer containing the data items;

- the number of items that may be contained in the allocated buffer;

- the number of items presently used in the allocated buffer.

However, notice that for the strings, such "items" are bytes, not characters:

```
let mut s1 = "".to_string();
s1.push('e');
let mut s2 = "".to_string();
s2.push('è');
let mut s3 = "".to_string();
s3.push('€');
print!("{} {}; ", s1.capacity(), s1.len());
print!("{} {}; ", s2.capacity(), s2.len());
print!("{} {}", s3.capacity(), s3.len());
```

This may print: "4 1; 2 2; 3 3". That means that the ASCII character e occupies just one byte in a four-byte buffer, the accented character è occupies two bytes in a two-byte buffer, and the currency symbol € occupies three bytes in a three-byte buffer. The number of bytes occupied is because of the UTF-8 standard, while the size of the buffer is dependent on the implementation of the Rust standard library, and it may change in future versions.

Let's see what happens when several characters are added to a dynamic string, one at a time:

```
let mut s = "".to_string();
for _ in 0..10 {
    println!("{:?} {} {}",
        s.as_ptr(), s.capacity(), s.len());
    s.push('a');
}
println!("{:?} {} {}: {}",
    s.as_ptr(), s.capacity(), s.len(), s);
```

This, in a 64-bit system, may print:

```
0x1 0 0
0x7fbf95e20020 4 1
0x7fbf95e20020 4 2
0x7fbf95e20020 4 3
0x7fbf95e20020 4 4
0x7fbf95e20020 8 5
0x7fbf95e20020 8 6
0x7fbf95e20020 8 7
0x7fbf95e20020 8 8
0x7fbf95e2a000 16 9
0x7fbf95e2a000 16 10: aaaaaaaaaa
```

The as_ptr function (to be read "as pointer") returns the address of the heap-allocated buffer containing the characters of the string.

Notice that when the string is empty, such address is simply 1, which is an invalid memory address, because no buffer is allocated for a string just created as empty.

When one ASCII character is added, a 4-byte buffer is allocated at an address represented by the hexadecimal number 7fbf95e20020.

Adding three other characters, no reallocations are required because the buffer is large enough.

When the fifth character is added, a reallocation is required, but, as the memory immediately following the buffer is still free, the buffer may be simply extended to 8 bytes, so avoiding the overhead of allocating a new buffer, copying the four used bytes, and deallocating the previous buffer.

Again, adding 3 other characters, no reallocations are required, but when the ninth character is added, not only the buffer is to be extended to 16 bytes, but it has to be relocated, as, presumably, not every one of the 8 next bytes is free.

At the end, the string uses 10 bytes.

Creating Strings

There are several ways to create an empty dynamic string.

```
let s1 = String::new();
let s2 = String::from("");
let s3 = "".to_string();
let s4 = "".to_owned();
let s5 = format!("");
print!("({}{}{}{}{})", s1, s2, s3, s4, s5);
```

This will print "()".

The new function of the String type is the basic constructor, similar to a "default constructor" in C++.

The from function of the String type is the converter constructor, similar to a "non-default constructor" in C++.

The functions to_string and to_owned are now interchangeable. There are both because historically they were somewhat different.

The format macro is identical to the print macro, with the only difference that while the latter sends its result to the console, the former returns a String object containing the result.

Except for the new function, all the previous ways to create a dynamic string can be used also to convert a non-empty static string to a dynamic string.

```
let s = "a,";
let s1 = String::from(s);
let s2 = s.to_string();
let s3 = s.to_owned();
//let s4 = format!(s);
//let s5 = format!("a,{}");
let s6 = format!("{}", s);
print!("({}{}{}{})", s1, s2, s3, s6);
```

This will print "(a,a,a,a,)".

Instead, the statements in the fifth and sixth lines would generate compilation errors. Indeed, the format macro, like the print and println macros, require that their first argument is a literal, and that such literal contains as many placeholders as the successive arguments to the macro.

Concatenating Strings

A dynamic string can be obtained also by concatenating two static strings, two dynamic strings, or a dynamic string and a static string.

```
let ss1 = "He";
let ss2 = "llo ";
let ds1 = ss1.to_string();
let ds2 = ss2.to_string();
let ds3 = format!("{}{}", ss1, ss2);
print!("{}", ds3);
let ds3 = format!("{}{}", ss1, ds2);
print!("{}", ds3);
let ds3 = format!("{}{}", ds1, ss2);
print!("{}", ds3);
let ds3 = format!("{}{}", ds1, ds2);
print!("{}", ds3);
```

This will print Hello Hello Hello Hello.

Often, it is desired to append a string to another string, which of course must be mutable. This is possible using the format macro, but it is verbose and inefficient:

```
let mut dyn_str = "Hello".to_string();
dyn_str = format!("{}{}", dyn_str, ", ");
dyn_str = format!("{}{}", dyn_str, "world");
dyn_str = format!("{}{}", dyn_str, "!");
print!("{}", dyn_str);
```

This is a better way:

```
let mut dyn_str = "Hello".to_string();
dyn_str.push_str(", ");
dyn_str.push_str("world");
dyn_str.push_str("!");
print!("{}", dyn_str);
```

The function push_str takes a static string and pushes all its characters to the end of the receiving string. Both programs print "Hello, world!".

There is also a more compact form for the function push_str.

```
let mut dyn_str = "Hello".to_string();
dyn_str += ", ";
dyn_str += "world";
dyn_str += "!";
print!("{}", dyn_str);
```

The += operator, when applied to a String object, is equivalent to the push_str function.

It's possible also to append String objects or single characters.

```
let comma = ", ".to_string();
let world = "world".to_string();
let excl_point = '!';
let mut dyn_str = "Hello".to_string();
dyn_str += &comma;
dyn_str.push_str(&world);
dyn_str.push(excl_point);
print!("{}", dyn_str);
```

This program is equivalent to the previous ones. Notice that to pass a dynamic string as an argument of push_str or +=, it has to be converted to a static string beforehand. Such effect is obtained using the & operator. Actually, with such an operator, a reference to a String is obtained, but any reference to a String can be implicitly converted to a reference to str.

```
let word = "bye".to_string();
let w1: &str = &word;
let w2: &String = &word;
print!("{} {}", w1, w2);
```

This will print: "bye bye".

CHAPTER 15

Ranges and Slices

In this chapter, you will learn:

- How to use closed ranges, and open-ended ranges

- How to process portions of arrays or vectors using slices

The Ranges

We already saw a way to write a `for` loop:

```
for i in 0..12 { println!("{}", i); }
```

But there is another possible way to write it:

```
let dozen = 0..12;
for i in dozen { println!("{}", i); }
```

This shows that the `0..12` clause is not a part of the `for` statement syntax, but it is an expression, whose value can be assigned to a variable. And that value can be used in `for` statements. The type of such value is named "range".

Here is some more code using a range:

```
let range: std::ops::Range<usize> = 3..8;
println!("{:?}, {}, {}, {}",
    range, range.start, range.end, range.len());
for i in range { print!("{}, ", i); }
```

This will print:

```
3..8, 3, 8, 5
3, 4, 5, 6, 7,
```

183

© Carlo Milanesi 2018
C. Milanesi, *Beginning Rust*, https://doi.org/10.1007/978-1-4842-3468-6_15

In the first line, we see that any range is a concretization of the Range<T> generic type, where T must be an integer type able to represent both extremes of the range.

The second statement prints some value about the variable range. First the variable itself is printed for debugging and obtaining 3..8; then the values of the two fields' start and end of ranges are printed, obtaining respectively 3 and 8. This shows that the type Range contains these two fields. Indeed, it does not contain anything else.

Then the len function is invoked, which simply evaluates the expression end - start, and so it evaluates 8 - 3, and prints 5.

At last, that range is used in a for loop to scan the values from start *included* to end *excluded*. Notice that the iterated values are as many as the value returned by the invocation of len.

The parametric type T of the type Range<T> can be inferred by the two arguments:

```
let r1 = 3u8..12u8;
let r2 = 3u8..12;
let r3 = 3..12u8;
let r4 = 3..12;
let r5 = -3..12;
let r6 = 3..12 as i64;
print!(
    "{} {} {} {} {} {}",
    std::mem::size_of_val(&r1),
    std::mem::size_of_val(&r2),
    std::mem::size_of_val(&r3),
    std::mem::size_of_val(&r4),
    std::mem::size_of_val(&r5),
    std::mem::size_of_val(&r6));
```

This will print: "2 2 2 8 8 16".

The r1 variable has both extremes declared as u8, and so they have that type, which occupies one byte, and so the whole range occupies two bytes.

The r2 and r3 variables have one extreme declared as u8 and the other left unspecified. Therefore it is forced to be u8 too.

The r4 and r5 variables have both extremes of type unspecified, and there is no further constraint on such variables, and so their T parameters get the default i32 type.

The r6 variable has an extreme of type i64 and the other unconstrained, and so T must be i64.

Notice that all the following statements are illegal:

```
let r1 = 3u8..12i8;
let r2: std::ops::Range<u32> = -3..12;
let r3: std::ops::Range<i32> = 3i16..12;
```

In the first statement, the two extremes have different types. In the second statement, -3 is not a value of type u32. In the third statement, 3i16 is not a value of type i32.

The following statements are allowed but probably wrong, and so they generate compilation warnings:

```
let _r1 = 3u8..1200;
let _r2 = 3..5_000_000_000;
```

They both generate an integer overflow warning, because the first range will be of type Range<u8> and the second one of type Range<i32>.

The following statements are allowed without warning, even if they are probably nonsensical:

```
let _r1 = false .. true;
let _r2 = "hello" .. "world";
let _r3 = 4.2 .. 7.9;
```

Indeed, such absurd ranges cannot be used in a for loop.

Passing a Sequence to a Function

Let's assume you need to create a function that gets as argument an 8-number array, and that returns the smallest number in this array. For such a purpose, you could write this program:

```
fn min(arr: [i32; 8]) -> i32 {
    let mut minimum = arr[0];
    for i in 1..arr.len() {
        if arr[i] < minimum { minimum = arr[i]; }
    }
    minimum
}
print!("{}", min([23, 17, 12, 16, 15, 28, 17, 30]));
```

This program will correctly print 12. Though, such `min` function has some drawbacks:

1. It gets as argument a *copy* of the whole array, requiring a significant time to transfer it, and occupying a significant stack space and cache space.

2. It cannot receive the request to process just a portion of the array.

3. It can receive only 8-number arrays. If we would pass an array of seven or nine items, we would get a compilation error.

4. It cannot receive a vector as argument.

To overcome the first drawback, you can pass the array *by reference*, instead of *by value*, using the following code:

```
fn min(arr: &[i32; 8]) -> i32 {
    let mut minimum = arr[0];
    for i in 1..arr.len() {
        if arr[i] < minimum { minimum = arr[i]; }
    }
    minimum
}
print!("{}", min(&[23, 17, 12, 16, 15, 28, 17, 30]));
```

Two "&" characters have been added, one where the argument is declared, in the first line; and one where the function is invoked, in the last line. As we have already seen, it is not required to change the body of the function, as the `arr` reference is implicitly dereferenced.

To overcome the second drawback, you could add an argument to specify from which item to start processing, and another argument to specify how many arguments to process:

```
fn min(arr: &[i32; 8], start: usize, count: usize) -> i32 {
    // Let's assume 'start' is between 0 and 7,
    // and 'count' is between 1 and 8 - start.
    let mut minimum = arr[start];
    for i in start + 1..start + count {
```

```
    if arr[i] < minimum { minimum = arr[i]; }
    }
    minimum
}
print!("{}", min(&[23, 17, 12, 16, 15, 28, 17, 30], 3, 2));
```

This will print 15. Indeed, it is specified to process two items starting from the one in position 3 (counting from 0). Therefore, only the two items having values 16 and 15 are processed.

However, two drawbacks remain.

Consider that our function needs to know only from which memory address to start processing, how many items to process, and which is the type of the items of the sequence. It is not required to know whether such sequence is a part of a larger sequence, and even less where such larger sequence starts and ends.

In addition, consider that any vector keeps its data in heap-allocated array, and so such a function could process it, once it knew where are the items to process.

The Slices

Considering all this, and to overcome all the cited drawbacks, the concept of "slice" has been introduced in the language. Its syntax is that of references:

```
fn min(arr: &[i32]) -> i32 {
    // Let's assume 'arr' is not empty.
    let mut minimum = arr[0];
    for i in 1..arr.len() {
        if arr[i] < minimum { minimum = arr[i]; }
    }
    minimum
}
print!("{}", min(&[23, 17, 12, 16, 15, 28, 17, 30]));
```

Also this program will print 12, but it has the following single difference from the second program in this chapter: in the type of the argument, the "; 8" clause has disappeared. Now the type of the arr argument looks like a reference to an array, but without specifying the size of the array.

This kind of type is a *reference to a slice*, or *slice reference*. Its generic form is `"&[T]"`, where `"T"` represents any type that can be contained in an array. Here, "slice" means a sub-sequence of items inside a sequence of items, like an array or a vector buffer. For this purpose, the implementation of a slice reference is a pair of values: the address of the first item of the sequence, and the number of items.

Notice that usually we have variables whose type is "slice reference" and rarely "slice". A slice would have type `"[T]"`, but such type cannot be passed as argument to a function, as it has a size not defined at compilation time, and a requirement of the arguments of functions is that they have a compile-time defined size. Therefore, we can pass to a function only *references to slices*, not *slices*. Such objects are a pair of a pointer and a length, and so their memory occupation is exactly twice that of normal references.

Using a slice reference is quite similar to using an array. The main implementation difference is that an invocation of the `len` function on an array can be optimized away, replacing it by the constant length defined by the type of the array, while an invocation of the `len` function on a reference to a slice is implemented as an access to the second field of such object.

Actually, in previous chapters we already saw something very similar to slices and to slice references: strings buffers, and static strings.

We can build this table of similarities:

undefined-length sequence of bytes	(address of beginning, length in bytes)	(address of beginning, length in bytes, number of bytes used)
String buffer: `str`	Static string: `&str`	Dynamic string: `String`
Slice of bytes: `[u8]`	Reference to slice of bytes: `&[u8]`	Vector or bytes: `Vec<u8>`

In the first column there are the types having undefined length. The *string buffers*, whose type is `str`, are undefined-length sequences of bytes interpreted as sequences of UTF-8 characters. The *slices* of unsigned 8-bit numbers, whose type is `[u8]`, are undefined-length sequences of bytes.

In the second column there are the references to the types of the first column. The *static strings*, whose type is `&str`, are structs of two fields: the memory address of the beginning of a string buffer, and the length of that buffer in bytes. The *references to slices* of unsigned 8-bit numbers, whose type is `&[u8]`, are structs of two fields: the memory address of the beginning of a slice of unsigned 8-bit numbers, and the length of that slice.

In the third column there are the dynamically allocated heap-allocated objects. The *dynamic strings*, whose type is String, are structs of three fields: the memory address of the beginning of a string buffer allocated in the heap, the length of that buffer in bytes, and the number of bytes presently used in that buffer. The *vectors* of unsigned 8-bit numbers, whose type is Vec<u8>, are structs of three fields: the memory address of the beginning of a slice of unsigned 8-bit numbers allocated in the heap, the length of that slice, and the number of bytes presently used in that slice.

Going back to the last example program, notice that the invocation of the min function hasn't changed. A reference to an array is still passed as argument. In fact, such an array reference is implicitly converted into a slice reference, using the array address as slice address, and the array length as slice length.

Therefore, the last statement of the program passes to the function a structure of two fields: the first is the memory address of the array item containing the number 23, and the second is the number 8.

Using slices, flexibility is much increased. Indeed, it's now possible to write:

```
fn min(arr: &[i32]) -> i32 {
    // Let's assume 'arr' is not empty.
    let mut minimum = arr[0];
    for i in 1..arr.len() {
        if arr[i] < minimum { minimum = arr[i]; }
    }
    minimum
}
print!("{} ", min(&[23, 17]));
print!("{}", min(&vec![55, 22, 33, 44]));
```

This will print: "17 22".

The first invocation passes only two arguments, and 17 is the lesser of them. So, the min function is not limited anymore to process 8-item arrays, but it can process arrays and slices having any positive length.

The second invocation of min shows how our function can process also the data contained in a vector, with no need to copy them. The value passed to the function is a simple reference to a vector, but, because the function argument is of type "reference to slice", the argument becomes a reference to a slice representing the whole contents of the vector.

So, we have overcome all the drawbacks of the first solution.

Slicing

But, having these handy slices, a new possible use of them emerges.

Let's say we have an array or a vector, for example, the vector [23, 17, 12, 16, 15, 2], and a function that gets a slice as argument, for example, the min function seen above, and we want to use such a function to process just a portion of our array or vector. For example, we want to find the minimum value among the third, fourth, and fifth items of that array.

What we need is a way to forge a slice as a portion of an array or vector, not necessarily the entire array or vector.

The syntax comes quite naturally. To get the item of index 2 of an array arr or of a vector v, you'd write, respectively, arr[2] or v[2]. Well, to get all the items of index between 2 and 5 of such containers, you'll write, respectively, arr[2..5] or v[2..5].

Here is another use of our ranges!

So the program would be:

```
fn min(arr: &[i32]) -> i32 {
    // Let's assume 'arr' is not empty.
    let mut minimum = arr[0];
    for i in 1..arr.len() {
        if arr[i] < minimum { minimum = arr[i]; }
    }
    minimum
}
let arr = [23, 17, 12, 16, 15, 2];
let range = 2..5;
let slice_ref = &arr[range];
print!("{}", min(slice_ref));
```

This will print 12, which is the minimum among 12, 16, and 15. The last four lines can be merged in:

```
fn min(arr: &[i32]) -> i32 {
    // Let's assume 'arr' is not empty.
    let mut minimum = arr[0];
    for i in 1..arr.len() {
```

```
        if arr[i] < minimum { minimum = arr[i]; }
    }
    minimum
}
print!("{} ", min(&[23, 17, 12, 16, 15, 2][2..5]));
```

The operation of taking a slice from an array or a vector is named "slicing".

Notice that, like in the for loop, the upper extreme of the range is excluded for slicing too. Indeed, specifying the range 2..5, the items included in the range are those in positions 2, 3, and 4, counting from zero.

The slicing operator can be applied to both arrays and vectors, but also to other slices:

```
let arr = [55, 22, 33, 44, 66, 7, 8];
let v = vec![55, 22, 33, 44, 66, 7, 8];
let sr1 = &arr[2..5];
let sr2 = &v[2..5];
print!("{:?} {:?} {:?} {:?}", sr1, sr2, &sr1[1..2], &sr1[1]);
```

This will print: "[33, 44, 66] [33, 44, 66] [44] 44".

The sr1 variable is a reference to a slice, which refers to the third, the fourth, and the fifth items of the arr array.

The sr2 variable is a similar reference to a slice, but it refers to items in the v vector.

After having printed the items referred to by these slice references, a slice of the first slice is taken. It refers to the second item of that slice, which is the fourth item of the underlying array.

At last, the second item of sr1 is taken, by simple indexing.

Out-of-Range Slicing

In addition to normal slicing, one could do something even weirder:

```
let arr = [55, 22, 33, 44, 66];
let _r1 = 4..4; let _a1 = &arr[_r1];
let _r2 = 4..3; //let _a2 = &arr[_r2];
let _r3 = -3i32..2; //let _a3 = &arr[_r3];
let _r4 = 3..8; //let _a4 = &arr[_r4];
```

In this program, except for the first line, every line declares a range, and then tries to use it to slice the array declared in the first line.

All the ranges are valid, but not all the slicing operations are valid, and so some statements have been commented out.

The second line is perfectly valid. It gets a slice starting from the position 4 and ending before position 4. So it is an empty slice, but empty slices are allowed.

The third line uses a backward slice that ends before starting. That is allowed by the compiler, but it causes a panic at runtime, like an out-of-range array access. The runtime error message, printed on the console, is a `slice index that starts at 4 but ends at 3`. Try removing the comment symbol `//`, compile, and run to see this error, and then rewrite the comment symbol.

The fourth line uses a range whose limits are of type `i32`. That causes a compilation error, because slicing, like sequence indexing, requires the `usize` type.

The fifth line uses a range exceeding the size of the sequence. It can be compiled, but causes a panic with the message `index 8 out of range for slice of length 5`.

Notice that all this has been shown when slicing an array, but it holds true also for slicing vectors and for slicing slices.

Mutable Slicing

What does it mean to change the contents of a slice? A slice is a portion of another sequence, and so changing its contents means changing the value of one or more items in the underlying sequence.

```
let mut arr = [11, 22, 33, 44];
{
    let sl_ref = &mut arr[1..3];
    print!("{:?}", sl_ref);
    sl_ref[1] = 0;
    print!(" {:?}", sl_ref);
}
print!(" {:?}", arr);
```

This will print: `"[22, 33] [22, 0] [11, 22, 0, 44]"`.

The `sl_ref` variable is an *immutable* reference to a *mutable* slice. Therefore, the reference cannot be changed, but the slice can be changed, and that means you can change the value of its items. And so it is done two lines below, by assigning zero to the second item of the slice, which is the third item of the underlying array.

To be able to get a reference to a mutable slice, the underlying sequence must be mutable. And this requires the mut clause in the first line.

And what does it mean to change a slice reference? A slice reference is a kind of reference, and so changing it means to cause it to refer to another portion of sequence, that is, to another portion of the same sequence, or to a portion of another sequence.

```
let arr = [11, 22, 33, 44];
{
    let mut sl_ref = &arr[1..3];
    print!("{:?}", sl_ref);
    sl_ref = &arr[0..1];
    print!(" {:?}", sl_ref);
}
print!(" {:?}", arr);
```

This will print: "[22, 33] [11] [11, 22, 33, 44]".

In this program the arr variable is an immutable array, and indeed it will not be changed. The sl_ref variable is a *mutable* reference to an *immutable* slice. It is initialized to refer to the second and third items of the array, and then it is changed to refer to the first item of the array.

Open-Ended Ranges and Slicing

Sometimes it is desired to get all the items from the beginning of a sequence to a given position n, or all the items from a given position n to the end of a sequence.

It could be done in this way:

```
let arr = [11, 22, 33, 44];
let n = 2;
let sr1 = &arr[0..n];
let sr2 = &arr[n..arr.len()];
print!("{:?} {:?}", sr1, sr2);
```

This will print: "[11, 22] [33, 44]".

But it is simpler to write in this way:

```
let arr = [11, 22, 33, 44];
let n = 2;
let sr1 = &arr[..n];
let sr2 = &arr[n..];
print!("{:?} {:?}", sr1, sr2);
```

In the third line, the range has no lower limit; and in the fourth line, the range has no upper limit.

Actually, these ranges are distinct types:

```
let r1: std::ops::RangeFrom<i32> = 3..;
let r2: std::ops::RangeTo<i32> = ..12;
println!("{:?} {:?} {} {}", r1, r2,
    std::mem::size_of_val(&r1),
    std::mem::size_of_val(&r2));
```

This will print: "3.. ..12 4 4". The r1 variable is of type RangeFrom, meaning that it has a lower limit, but not an upper limit. The r2 variable is of type RangeTo, meaning that it has an upper limit, but not a lower limit. Both occupy only 4 bytes, because they need to store only one i32 object.

RangeTo values are useful only for open-ended slicing, but RangeFrom values may be used also to specify for loops.

```
for i in 3.. {
    if i * i > 40 { break; }
    print!("{} ", i);
}
```

This will print: "3 4 5 6". The loop starts by assigning to i the value 3, and keeps incrementing it indefinitely, or until some other statement breaks the loop.

There is one last generic type of ranges:

```
let range: std::ops::RangeFull = ..;
let a1 = [11, 22, 33, 44];
let a2 = &a1[range];
print!("{} {:?} {:?}", std::mem::size_of_val(&range), a1, a2);
```

This will print: "0 [11, 22, 33, 44] [11, 22, 33, 44]".

Any RangeFull stores no information, and so its size is zero. It is used to specify a range exactly as large as the underlying sequence.

CHAPTER 16

Using Iterators

In this chapter, you will learn:

- How characters are stored in Rust strings, and why they do not allow direct access

- How to read string characters or string bytes using iterators

- How to read items from slices, arrays, and vectors using iterators

- How to modify items from slices, arrays, and vectors using mutating iterators

- How to use some iterator adapters: `filter`, `map`, and `enumerate`

- How to use some iterator consumers: `any`, `all`, `count`, `sum`, `min`, `max`, and `collect`

- The concept of lazy processing in iterator chains

String Characters

We already saw that Rust has both static strings and dynamic strings, and that both types share the same character coding, which is UTF-8. Such coding uses sequences of one to six bytes to represent each Unicode character, and so a string is not simply an array of characters, but it is an array of bytes that represents a sequence of characters.

But if `s` is a string, what's the meaning of the expression `s[0]`? Is it the first character or the first byte of `s`?

Any choice could be surprising for someone, and so in Rust such an expression is not allowed for strings. To get the first byte, it is necessary to first convert the string to a slice of bytes.

© Carlo Milanesi 2018
C. Milanesi, *Beginning Rust*, https://doi.org/10.1007/978-1-4842-3468-6_16

```
let s = "abc012è€";
for i in 0..s.len() {
    println!("{}: {}", i, s.as_bytes()[i]);
}
```

This will print:

```
0: 97
1: 98
2: 99
3: 48
4: 49
5: 50
6: 195
7: 168
8: 226
9: 130
10: 172
```

The function as_bytes converts the string to which it is applied into an immutable slice of u8 numbers. Such conversion has zero runtime cost, because the representation of a string buffer is already that sequence of bytes.

The UTF-8 representation of any ASCII character is just the ASCII code of that character. And so, for the characters a, b, c, 0, 1, and 2, their ASCII value is printed.

The è character is represented by a pair of bytes, having values 195 and 168. And the € character is represented by a sequence of three bytes, having values 226, 130, and 172. Therefore, to get to a character in a given position, it is necessary to scan all the previous characters.

This situation is similar to that of text files, compared to fixed-record-length files. Using a fixed-record-length file, it is possible to read a record in any n position by "seeking" that position, without previously reading all the preceding lines. Instead, using a variable-line-length file, to read the n-th line, it is required to read all the preceding lines.

Scanning a String

Therefore, to process the characters of a string, it is necessary to scan them.

Say that, given the string "€èe", we want to print the third character. First we must scan three bytes to get the first character, because the "€" character is represented by a sequence of three bytes; then we must scan two further bytes to get the second character, because the "è" character is represented by a sequence of two bytes; then we must scan one further byte to get the third character, because the "e" character is represented by a sequence of just one byte.

So, we need a way to get the next character of a string, given the current position, and to advance the current position, at the end of the read character.

In computer science, the objects that perform such behavior of extracting an item at the current position in a sequence, and then advance that position, are named "iterators" (or sometimes "cursors"). Therefore, we need a *string iterator*.

Here is a program that uses a string iterator:

```
fn print_nth_char(s: &str, mut n: u32) {
    let mut iter: std::str::Chars = s.chars();
    loop {
        let item: Option<char> = iter.next();
        match item {
            Some(c) => if n == 1 { print!("{}", c); },
            None => { break; },
        }
        n -= 1;
    }
}
print_nth_char("€èe", 3);
```

This program first defines a function whose purpose is to get a string s, a number n, and then to print the character of s at position n (counting from 1), if there is a character at such position, or else to do nothing. The last line of the program invokes such a function to print the third character of "€èe", and so the program prints e.

The Rust standard library provides a string iterator type named "Chars". Given a string "s," you get an iterator over "s" by evaluating s.chars(), as it is done in the second line of the program above.

Any iterator has the next function. Such a function returns the next item of the underlying sequence at the current position, and advances the current position. However, most sequences have an end. And so, iterators can return the next value only if they haven't yet reached the end of the sequence. To consider the possibility of having finished the sequence, the next function of Rust iterators returns a value of Option<T> type. Such value is None if the sequence has no more items.

Using the match statement, the Some case causes the processing of the next character of the string, and the None case causes the exit from the otherwise infinite loop.

If the argument n was 1, it was requiring it to print the first character of the string, and so the value of the c variable would be printed. Otherwise, nothing is done with that character. After the match statement, the n counter, which was mutable, is decremented, so that when it reaches 1 we have reached the required character to print.

Given a string, it is easy to print the numeric codes of its characters.

```rust
fn print_codes(s: &str) {
    let mut iter = s.chars();
    loop {
        match iter.next() {
            Some(c) => { println!("{}: {}", c, c as u32); },
            None => { break; },
        }
    }
}
print_codes("€èe");
```

This will print:

```
€: 8364
è: 232
e: 101
```

For every character, the character itself is printed, along with its numeric code.

Using Iterators in `for` Loops

The previous example is somewhat cumbersome, and so, it should undergo a drastic syntactic simplification.

```
fn print_codes(s: &str) {
    for c in s.chars() {
        println!("{}: {}", c, c as u32);
    }
}
print_codes("€èe");
```

This program generates the same machine code of the previous one, but it is much clearer for a human reader.

It appears that the expression after the `in` keyword in a `for` loop can be an iterator.

But what is exactly an *iterator?* It is not a type, but a type specification. An iterator is considered to be any expression that has a `next` method returning an `Option<T>` value.

So far, we used ranges in for loops. Well, all ranges with a starting limit are iterators, as they have a `next` function.

```
// OK: std::ops::Range<u32> is an iterator
let _v1 = (0u32..10).next();

// OK: std::ops::RangeFrom<u32> is an iterator
let _v2 = (5u32..).next();

// Illegal: std::ops::RangeTo<u32> is not an iterator
// let _v3 = (..8u32).next();

// Illegal: std::ops::RangeFull is not an iterator
// let _v4 = (..).next();
```

It is possible also to iterate over the bytes of a string:

```
for byte in "€èe".bytes() {
    print!("{} ", byte);
}
```

This will print: "226 130 172 195 168 101". The first three numbers represent the € character; the next two numbers represent the è character; and the last byte, 101, is the ASCII code of the e character.

This program can be broken down into the following code.

```
let string: &str = "€èe";
let string_it: std::str::Bytes = string.bytes();
for byte in string_it {
    print!("{} ", byte);
}
```

While the chars function, seen above, returns a value whose type is std::str::Chars, the bytes function, used here, returns a value whose type is std::str::Bytes.

Both Chars and Bytes are string iterator types, but while the next function of Chars returns the next character of the string, the next function of Bytes returns the next byte of the string.

These string functions are both different from the as_bytes function, which returns a slice reference on the bytes of the string.

It is also quite typical to iterate over a slice, an array, or a vector. Strings are not iterators, slices, arrays, nor vectors. But, just like a string iterator is obtained by invoking the chars function, so a slice, array, or vector iterator is obtained by invoking the iter function.

```
for item_ref in (&[11u8, 22, 33]).iter() {
    // *item_ref += 1;
    print!("{} ", *item_ref);
}
for item_ref in [44, 55, 66].iter() {
    // *item_ref += 1;
    print!("{} ", *item_ref);
}
for item_ref in vec!['a', 'b', 'c'].iter() {
    // *item_ref = if *item_ref == 'b' { 'B' } else { '-' };
    print!("{} ", *item_ref);
}
```

This will print: "11 22 33 44 55 66 a b c".

This program can be broken down into the following code.

```
let slice: &[u8] = &[11u8, 22, 33];
let slice_it: std::slice::Iter<u8> = slice.iter();
for item_ref in slice_it {
    // *item_ref += 1;
    print!("{} ", *item_ref);
}
let arr: [i32; 3] = [44, 55, 66];
let arr_it: std::slice::Iter<i32> = arr.iter();
for item_ref in arr_it {
    // *item_ref += 1;
    print!("{} ", *item_ref);
}
let vec: Vec<char> = vec!['a', 'b', 'c'];
let vec_it: std::slice::Iter<char> = vec.iter();
for item_ref in vec_it {
    // *item_ref = if *item_ref == 'b' { 'B' } else { '-' };
    print!("{} ", *item_ref);
}
```

The iter function, applied to a slice of items of type T, or to an array of items of type T, or to a vector of items of type T, returns a value of type std::slice::Iter<T>. As its name suggests, such type of returned values is an iterator type, and so it can be used in a for loop.

When iterating over a range of numbers of T type, the loop variable is of T type, and when iterating over a string iterator, the loop variable is of char type; instead, when iterating over a sequence of T type, the loop variable is of &T type, that is, it is a reference.

Therefore, to access its value, a dereference operator (*) can (and sometimes must) be applied.

The first statement inside the bodies of the three loops has been commented out, because it is illegal. In fact, the loop variable is immutable. And such immutability was understandable even from the declaration of slice, arr, and vec as immutable variables.

We saw that the string iterator on the bytes of a string is created using the `bytes` function.

```
for byte in "€èe".bytes() {
    print!("{} ", byte);
}
```

Another way to iterate over the bytes of a string is first to create the slice reference over the bytes of the string, using the `as_bytes` function, and then iterate over such slice reference.

```
for byte in "€èe".as_bytes().iter() {
    print!("{} ", byte);
}
```

This program is equivalent to the previous one.

Iterations *Without* Mutation

So far we used iterators only to read sequences, and this is quite typical.

When iterating over the characters of a string, it is unreasonable to try to change them, as the new character may be represented by a different number of bytes than the existing character. For example, if an è character is replaced by an e character, two bytes must be replaced by just one byte. Therefore, the Rust standard library has no way to change a string character-by-character using a character string iterator.

When iterating over the bytes of a string, it is unsafe to try to change them, as the new byte may be creating an invalid UTF-8 string. Therefore, the Rust standard library has no way to change a string byte-by-byte using a byte string iterator.

When iterating over a range, as we have already seen, the range value used by the loop is the one at the beginning of the loop, even if it is changed inside the loop:

```
let mut r = "abc".chars();
for i in r {
    r = "XY".chars();
    print!("{} {}; ", i, r.next().unwrap());
}
```

This will print: "a X; b X; c X;". The assignment inside the loop is applied, but the loop still uses the initial value.

The loop variable is initialized at any iteration:

```
let r = 0..5;
for mut i in r {
    i += 10;
    print!("{} ", i);
}
```

This will print: "10 11 12 13 14". The increment inside the loop is possible because i has the mut clause, but i is reinitialized at the next iteration.

Therefore, for strings and for ranges there is no need of iterators that allow changes to the items of the sequence.

Iterations *with* Mutation

Sometimes, when iterating over a sequence, there is the need to mutate the items of that sequence. The iterators we saw so far cannot do that, and not even a mutable iterator can.

In fact, a mutable iterator is something that can and may be made to iterate over another sequence, not that can be used to mutate the sequence that it iterates over.

A possible use of a mutable iterator is this.

```
let slice1 = &[3, 4, 5];
let slice2 = &[7, 8];
let mut iterator = slice1.iter();
for item_ref in iterator {
    print!("[{}] ", *item_ref);
}
iterator = slice2.iter();
for item_ref in iterator {
    print!("({}) ", *item_ref);
}
```

This will print: "[3] [4] [5] (7) (8)".

The variable iterator first refers to the sequence slice1 and then to the sequence slice2.

An iterator is similar to a reference, in that a mutable reference is not the same concept of a reference to a mutable object.

But if you want to change the values in a sequence through an iterator over such a sequence, you cannot use a normal (mutable or immutable) iterator, even if :

```
let mut slice = &mut [3, 4, 5];
{
    let mut iterator = slice.iter();
    for mut item_ref in iterator {
        *item_ref += 1;
    }
}
print!("{:?}", slice);
```

Although this program contains several mut clauses, it generates a compiler error at the line in the body of the loop, because *item_ref is still immutable.

For such a purpose, you need another type of iterator, a *mutating* iterator, which, of course, must be initialized over a mutable sequence.

```
let slice = &mut [3, 4, 5];
{
    let iterator = slice.iter_mut();
    for item_ref in iterator {
        *item_ref += 1;
    }
}
print!("{:?}", slice);
```

This will print: "[4, 5, 6]".

Apart from removing some unnecessary mut clauses, the only change with respect to the previous program is that the invocation of iter has been replaced by an invocation of iter_mut. Think to these functions, respectively, like "get an iterator to read it", and "get an iterator to mutate it".

This program can also be changed by making explicit the type of the iterator.

```
let slice = &mut [3, 4, 5];
{
    let iterator: std::slice::IterMut<i32> =
        slice.iter_mut();
```

```
    for item_ref in iterator {
        *item_ref += 1;
    }
}
print!("{:?}", slice);
```

While `iter` returns a value of `Iter<T>` type, `iter_mut` returns a value of `IterMut<T>` type.

Getting back to the program above that iterated over a slice, an array, and a vector without changing the values of such sequences, here is the same program in which the values of the sequences are changed.

```
for item_ref in (&mut [11u8, 22, 33]).iter_mut() {
    *item_ref += 1;
    print!("{} ", *item_ref);
}
for item_ref in [44, 55, 66].iter_mut() {
    *item_ref += 1;
    print!("{} ", *item_ref);
}
for item_ref in vec!['a', 'b', 'c'].iter_mut() {
    *item_ref = if *item_ref == 'b' { 'B' } else { '-' };
    print!("{} ", *item_ref);
}
```

This will print: "12 23 34 45 56 67 - B -".
This program can be broken down in the following code.

```
let slice: &mut [u8] = &mut [11u8, 22, 33];
let slice_it: std::slice::IterMut<u8> = slice.iter_mut();
for item_ref in slice_it {
    *item_ref += 1;
    print!("{} ", *item_ref);
}
let mut arr: [i32; 3] = [44, 55, 66];
let arr_it: std::slice::IterMut<i32> = arr.iter_mut();
for item_ref in arr_it {
    *item_ref += 1;
```

```
        print!("{} ", *item_ref);
    }
    let mut vec: Vec<char> = vec!['a', 'b', 'c'];
    let vec_it: std::slice::IterMut<char> = vec.iter_mut();
    for item_ref in vec_it {
        *item_ref = if *item_ref == 'b' { 'B' } else { '-' };
        print!("{} ", *item_ref);
    }
```

The differences with the similar program in which the first statement of every loop body was commented out are the following ones:

- The slice variable is a slice reference on *mutable* bytes.

- The arr and vec variables are *mutable*.

- Each of the three invocations of the iter function has been replaced by invocations of the iter_mut function.

- The iter_mut function returns a value of IterMut generic type, and so the three iterators have this type, instead of the Iter generic type.

- The items referenced by the loop variable item_ref are actually changed, because the relative statements have been un-commented in.

Here is a program that demonstrates that the changes to the underlying data are effective.

```
let slice = &mut [11u8, 22, 33];
for item_ref in slice.iter_mut() {
    *item_ref += 1;
}
print!("{:?} ", slice);

let mut arr = [44, 55, 66];
for item_ref in arr.iter_mut() {
    *item_ref += 1;
}
print!("{:?} ", arr);
```

```
let mut vec = vec!['a', 'b', 'c'];
for item_ref in vec.iter_mut() {
    *item_ref = if *item_ref == 'b' { 'B' } else { '-' };
}
print!("{:?} ", vec);
```

This will print: "[12, 23, 34] [45, 56, 67] ['-', 'B', '-']".

So far we have encountered four functions that get a sequence and return an iterator: chars, bytes, iter, and iter_mut. Functions that don't get iterators but return iterators are named "*iterator generators*".

An Iterator Adapter: `filter`

Let's see some other uses of iterators.

For example, given an array of numbers, how can I print all the negative numbers of such an array?

A possible way is this:

```
let arr = [66, -8, 43, 19, 0, -31];
for n in arr.iter() {
    if *n < 0 { print!("{} ", n); }
}
```

This will print: "-8 -31".

But another possible way is this:

```
let arr = [66, -8, 43, 19, 0, -31];
for n in arr.iter().filter(|x| **x < 0) {
    print!("{} ", n);
}
```

The `filter` function is in the standard library. It is to be applied to an iterator, and it takes a closure as argument. As its name suggests, the purpose of this function is "filtering" the iterated sequence, that is, to discard the items that do not satisfy the criterion implemented by the closure, and let pass only the items that satisfy such criterion.

The `filter` function gets an item at a time from the iterator, and invokes the closure once for every item, passing such item as argument. In our example, the current item, which is an integer number, is assigned to the x local variable.

The closure must return a Boolean that indicates whether the item is accepted (`true`) or rejected (`false`) by the filtering. The rejected items are destroyed, while the accepted ones are passed to the surrounding expression.

In fact, the `filter` function returns an iterator that (when its `next` function is invoked) produces just the items for which the closure returned `true`.

As we were interested in accepting only the negative numbers, the condition inside the closure is x < 0. But there are also two asterisks; how come?

We already said that the iterator returned by the `iter` function produces *references* to the items of the sequence, not the items themselves, and so an asterisk is required to get the item.

In addition, the `filter` function, when it receives an item from the iterator, passes to the closure a reference to such item, and so another asterisk is required. Therefore x is a reference to a reference to an integer number. The two asterisks are required to get that number and to compare it with zero.

We said that the `filter` function returns another iterator. And so we can use it inside a `for` loop, where we used to use iterators.

Because the `filter` function gets an iterator and returns an iterator, it can be seen that it "transforms" an iterator into another. Such iterator "transformers" are usually named "iterator adapters". The term "adapter" recalls that of electrical connectors: if a plug does not fit a socket, you use an adapter.

The `map` Iterator Adapter

Given an array of numbers, how can you print the double of each number of that array?

You can do it in this way:

```
let arr = [66, -8, 43, 19, 0, -31];
for n in arr.iter() {
    print!("{} ", n * 2);
}
```

This will print: "132 -16 86 38 0 -62".

But you can also do it in this way:

```
let arr = [66, -8, 43, 19, 0, -31];
for n in arr.iter().map(|x| *x * 2) {
    print!("{} ", n);
}
```

The map function is another iterator adapter in the standard library. Its purpose is to "transform" the values produced by an iterator into other values. Differing from the filter function, the value returned by the closure can be of any type. Such value represents the transformed value.

Actually, the map function returns a newly created iterator that produces all the items returned by the closure received as an argument.

While the filter adapter removes some items of the iterated sequence, and it keeps the others unchanged, the map adapter does not remove any items, but it transforms them.

Another difference between them is that while filter passes a reference as the argument of its closure, map passes a value.

The **enumerate** Iterator Adapter

Traditionally, to iterate over a sequence you used to increment an integer counter, and then access the items of the sequence using that counter, in this way:

```
let arr = ['a', 'b', 'c'];
for i in 0..arr.len() {
    print!("{} {}, ", i, arr[i]);
}
```

This will print: "0 a, 1 b, 2 c,".

Using an iterator over the sequence, it is possible to avoid using the integer counter.

```
let arr = ['a', 'b', 'c'];
for ch in arr.iter() {
    print!("{}, ", ch);
}
```

This will print: "a, b, c,".

211

But if you need also a counter, you should get to the old technique, or add another variable and increment it explicitly:

```
let arr = ['a', 'b', 'c'];
let mut i = 0;
for ch in arr.iter() {
    print!("{} {}, ", i, *ch);
    i += 1;
}
```

But there is another possibility:

```
let arr = ['a', 'b', 'c'];
for (i, ch) in arr.iter().enumerate() {
    print!("{} {}, ", i, *ch);
}
```

In the second line, the loop variable is actually a tuple of a variable integer and a reference to a character. At the first iteration, the i variable gets 0 as a value, while the ch value gets as a value the address of the first character of the array. At every iteration, both i and ch are incremented.

This works because the enumerate function takes an iterator and returns another iterator. This returned iterator, at each iteration, returns a value of type (usize, &char). This tuple has at its first field a counter, and as its second field a copy of the item received from the first iterator.

An Iterator Consumer: any

Given a string, how can you determine if it contains a given character?

You could do it in this way:

```
let s = "Hello, world!";
let ch = 'R';
let mut contains = false;
for c in s.chars() {
```

```
    if c == ch {
        contains = true;
    }
}
print!("\"{}\" {} '{}'.",
    s,
    if contains {
        "contains"
    } else {
        "does not contain"
    },
    ch);
```

This will print: "Hello, world!" does not contain 'R'.

It does so because character equality comparison is case sensitive. But if you replace the uppercase R in the second line with a lowercase r, it will print: "Hello, world!" contains 'r'.

You could do it also in this way:

```
let s = "Hello, world!";
let ch = 'R';
print!("\"{}\" {} '{}'.",
    s,
    if s.chars().any(|c| c == ch) {
        "contains"
    } else {
        "does not contain"
    },
    ch);
```

Here, the contains variable, and the loop that possibly sets it to true have been removed; and the only other use of such a variable has been replaced by the expression s.chars().any(|c| c == ch).

As the only purpose of the contains variable was to indicate if the s string contained the ch character, of course also the expression that replaces it must have the same value.

We know that the s.chars() expression is evaluated to an iterator over the characters of the s string. Then the any function, which is in the standard library, is applied to such iterator. Its purpose is determining if a Boolean function (aka "predicate") is true for any item produced by the iterator.

The any function must be applied to an iterator and must receive a closure as an argument. It applies that closure to every item received from the iterator, and it returns true as soon as the closure returns true on an item, or returns false if the closure returns false for all the items.

Therefore, such a function tells us if "any" item satisfies the condition specified by the closure.

You can also use the any function to determine if an array contains any negative number:

```
print!("{} ",
    [45, 8, 2, 6].iter().any(|n| *n < 0));
print!("{} ",
    [45, 8, -2, 6].iter().any(|n| *n < 0));
```

This will print: "false true".

To clarify, you can annotate the closures with types:

```
print!("{} ", [45, 8, 2, 6].iter()
    .any(|n: &i32| -> bool { *n < 0 }));
print!("{} ", [45, 8, -2, 6].iter()
    .any(|n: &i32| -> bool { *n < 0 }));
```

Omitting the & symbols would generate type errors.

Notice that while the iterator adapters seen above returned iterators, the any function is applied to an iterator, but it returns a value that is a Boolean, not an iterator.

Every function that is applied to an iterator but does not return an iterator is called "iterator consumer", because it gets data from an iterator but does not put them into another iterator, and so it "consumes" data, instead of "adapting" data.

The all Iterator Consumer

With the any function you can determine if *at least* one iterated item satisfies a condition. And how can you determine if *all* iterated items satisfy a condition?

For example, to determine if all the numbers in an array are positive, you can write:

```
print!("{} ", [45, 8, 2, 6].iter()
    .all(|n: &i32| -> bool { *n > 0 }));
print!("{} ", [45, 8, -2, 6].iter()
    .all(|n: &i32| -> bool { *n > 0 }));
```

This will print: "true false".

Notice that while the any function means a repeated application of the or logical operator, the all function means a repeated application of the and logical operator. Notice also that, following logical rules, if the iterator produces no items, the any function returns false for any closure, and the all function returns true for any closure.

The **count** Iterator Consumer

Given an iterator, how do you know how many items it will produce?

Well, if you are iterating a slice, an array, or a vector, you better use the len function of such objects, as it is the simplest and fastest way to get their lengths. But if you want to know how many characters there are in a string, you must scan it all, because the number of chars comprising a string is not stored anywhere, unless you did it.

So you need to use the simplest iterator consumer.

```
let s = "€èe";
print!("{} {}", s.chars().count(), s.len());
```

This will print "3 6", meaning that this string contains three characters represented by six bytes.

The count iterator consumer does not get any argument, and it always returns a usize value.

The **sum** Iterator Consumer

If, instead of counting the iterated items, you want to add them, it is almost as simple.

```
print!("{}", [45, 8, -2, 6].iter().sum::<i32>());
```

This will print: 57. Also the sum iterator consumer does not get arguments. Yet, it requires a type parameter in angle brackets. It is the type of the returned number. Here, it is required, because otherwise the compiler could not infer such a type. But in other cases, like the following one, it is optional.

```
let s: i32 = [45, 8, -2, 6].iter().sum();
print!("{}", s);
```

It is possible also to add the items of an empty sequence.

```
let s: u32 = [].iter().sum();
print!("{}", s);
```

It will print 0.

Notice that while the count function was applicable to any iterator, the sum function is applicable only to iterators that produce addable items. The statement [3.4].iter().sum::<f64>(); is valid, while the statement [true].iter().sum::<bool>() is illegal, because it is not allowed to sum Booleans.

The min and max Iterator Consumers

If an iterator produces values that can be compared with one another, it is possible to get the minimum or the maximum of those values. But there is a problem: the empty sequences. If our iterator produces no items, we can count them, and this count is zero; we can add them, and their sum is zero; but we cannot get the maximum nor the minimum of an empty sequence. Therefore, the min and the max iterator consumers produce an Option value, which is Some number if they are applied to a non-empty sequence of numbers, but it is None if it is applied to an empty sequence.

```
let arr = [45, 8, -2, 6];
match arr.iter().min() {
    Some(n) => print!("{} ", n),
    _ => (),
}
match arr.iter().max() {
    Some(n) => print!("{} ", n),
    _ => (),
}
```

```
match [0; 0].iter().min() {
    Some(n) => print!("{} ", n),
    _ => print!("---"),
}
```

This will print -2 45 ---.

The min and max consumers can also be applied to iterators that produce non-numeric objects, provided they are comparable.

```
let arr = ["hello", "brave", "new", "world"];
match arr.iter().min() {
    Some(n) => print!("{} ", n),
    _ => (),
}
match arr.iter().max() {
    Some(n) => print!("{} ", n),
    _ => (),
}
```

This will print: "brave world".

The collect Consumer

The any, all, count, sum, min, and max iterator consumers return simple information regarding a possibly long sequence of items.

But we could wish to put all the consumed items into a Vector.

```
let arr = [36, 1, 15, 9, 4];
let v = arr.iter().collect::<Vec<&i32>>();
print!("{:?}", v);
```

This will print: "[36, 1, 15, 9, 4]".

The collect function has created a new Vec<&i32> object, and it has pushed into it all the items produced by the iterator.

This function is parameterized by the type of the resulting collection, because such function can be used to put items in various kinds of collections, and it wasn't clear from the environment that a Vec was needed. In fact, Rust is able to infer the type &i32, and so it can be replaced by the placeholder _.

```
let arr = [36, 1, 15, 9, 4];
let v = arr.iter().collect::<Vec<_>>();
print!("{:?}", v);
```

But if the type of the resulting collection can be inferred, then it can be omitted from the parameterization of collect. So, even this program is equivalent to the previous one:

```
let arr = [36, 1, 15, 9, 4];
let v: Vec<_> = arr.iter().collect();
print!("{:?}", v);
```

Also, string characters or strings bytes can be collected into a string or into a vector:

```
let s = "Hello";
println!("{:?}", s.chars().collect::<String>());
println!("{:?}", s.chars().collect::<Vec<char>>());
println!("{:?}", s.bytes().collect::<Vec<u8>>());
println!("{:?}", s.as_bytes().iter().collect::<Vec<&u8>>());
```

This will print:

```
"Hello"
['H', 'e', 'l', 'l', 'o']
[72, 101, 108, 108, 111]
[72, 101, 108, 108, 111]
```

The second and third statements apply the chars function to a string, obtaining an iterator producing characters. But the second statement collects those characters into a String object, while the third statement collects them into a vector of characters.

The fourth statement uses the bytes function to obtain an iterator producing bytes. Then those bytes, which are the ASCII representation of the characters, are collected into a vector.

The fifth statement uses the as_bytes function to see the string as a slice of bytes. Then the iter function is used to obtain an iterator over such slice, producing references to bytes. Then such references to bytes are collected into a vector.

Notice that the collect function cannot be used to put the iterated items into a static string, an array, or a slice, because it needs to allocate the needed space at runtime.

Iterator Chains

Assume you have an array of numbers, and you want to create a vector containing only the positive numbers of such array, multiplied by two.

You could write it without using iterators:

```
let arr = [66, -8, 43, 19, 0, -31];
let mut v = vec![];
for i in 0..arr.len() {
    if arr[i] > 0 { v.push(arr[i] * 2); }
}
print!("{:?}", v);
```

This will print [132, 86, 38].

Or equivalently you could use an iterator, without using iterator adapters:

```
let arr = [66, -8, 43, 19, 0, -31];
let mut v = vec![];
for n in arr.iter() {
    if *n > 0 { v.push(*n * 2); }
}
print!("{:?}", v);
```

Or equivalently you could use an iterator and two iterator adapters, without using an iterator consumer:

```
let arr = [66, -8, 43, 19, 0, -31];
let mut v = vec![];
for n in arr
    .iter()
    .filter(|x| **x > 0)
    .map(|x| *x * 2)
{
    v.push(n);
}
print!("{:?}", v);
```

Or equivalently you could use an iterator, two iterator adapters, and an iterator consumer:

```
let arr = [66, -8, 43, 19, 0, -31];
let v = arr
    .iter()
    .filter(|x| **x > 0)
    .map(|x| *x * 2)
    .collect::<Vec<_>>();
print!("{:?}", v);
```

This last version shows a programming pattern that is typical of functional languages: the iterator chain.

From a sequence, an iterator is created, then zero or more iterator adapters are chained, then an iterator consumer closes the chain.

Such chains begin with an iterator or with a function that is not applied to an iterator but creates an iterator, aka *iterator generator*; they proceed with zero or more functions that are applied to an iterator and create another iterator, aka *iterator adapters*; they end with an iterator as result, or with a function that is applied to an iterator but does not create another iterator, aka *iterator consumer*.

We saw several iterator generators: iter, iter_mut, chars, bytes; and we saw ranges, which are iterators with no need to be created by a generator.

We saw several iterator adapters: filter, map, enumerate.

And we saw several iterator consumers: any, all, count, sum, min, max, collect.

Iterators Are "Lazy"

Let's change the last example by adding some debug prints:

```
let v = [66, -8, 43, 19, 0, -31]
    .iter()
    .filter(|x| { print!("F{} ", x); **x > 0 })
    .map(|x| { print!("M{} ", x); *x * 2 })
    .collect::<Vec<_>>();
print!("{:?}", v);
```

This will print F66 M66 F-8 F43 M43 F19 M19 F0 F-31 [132, 86, 38].

The runtime operations are the following ones.

The invocation of `iter` prepares an iterator, but it does not access the array. Let's name "I" such iterator.

The invocation of `filter` prepares an iterator, but it does not manage data. Let's name "F" such iterator.

The invocation of `map` prepares an iterator, but it does not manage data. Let's name "M" such iterator.

The invocation of `collect` asks "M" for an item; "M" asks "F" for an item; "F" asks "I" for an item; "I" takes the number 66 from the array and passes it to "F", which prints it, checks whether it is positive, and so passes it to "M", which prints it, doubles it, passes it to `collect`, which then pushes it to the vector.

Then, `collect`, because it has just received Some item and not None, asks "M" for another item, and the trip is repeated until the number -8 arrives to "F", which rejects it as non-positive. Indeed -8 is not printed by "M". At this point, "F," because before it has just received Some item, asks "I" for another item.

The algorithm proceeds in this way until the array is finished. When "I" cannot find other items in the array, it sends a None to "F" to indicate there are no more items. When "F" receives a None, it sends it to "M", which sends it to `collect`, which stops asking items, and the whole statement is finished.

Similarly, if this whole expression except for the `collect` invocation is in the header of a `for` loop, this mechanism is activated just as well.

But let's omit both the `for` loop and any iterator consumer.

```
[66, -8, 43, 19, 0, -31]
    .iter()
    .filter(|x| { print!("F{} ", x); **x > 0 })
    .map(|x| { print!("M{} ", x); *x * 2 });
```

This does print nothing, because it does nothing. Even the compiler reports the warning unused `` `std::iter::Map` `` `which must be used: iterator adapters are lazy and do nothing unless consumed.`

In computer science, to be "lazy" means trying to do some processing as late as possible. Iterator adapters are lazy, as they process data only when another function asks them for an item: it can be another iterator adapter, or an iterator consumer, or a `for` loop, which acts as a consumer. If there is no data sink, there is no data access.

CHAPTER 17

Input/Output and Error Handling

In this chapter, you will learn:

- How to get the arguments from the command line used to launch the program

- How to return a status code to the operating system when exiting the program

- How to get and set the process environment variables

- Techniques and best practices to handle runtime errors

- How to read from the console keyboard and how to write to the console screen

- How primitive types are converted to string

- How to read or write a binary file

- How to read a text file a line at a time

Command-Line Arguments

The most basic form of input of a program is through the command line.

```
let command_line: std::env::Args = std::env::args();
for argument in command_line {
    println!("[{}]", argument);
}
```

© Carlo Milanesi 2018
C. Milanesi, *Beginning Rust*, https://doi.org/10.1007/978-1-4842-3468-6_17

If this program is compiled to create a file named, say, main, and such file is launched writing the command line "./main   first   second", it will print:

```
[./main]
[first]
[second]
```

The args standard library function returns an iterator over the command-line arguments. Such an iterator has type Args, and it produces String values. The first value produced is the program name, with the path used to reach it. The others are the program arguments.

Any blank is usually removed; to keep blanks, you have to enclose arguments in quotation marks, which will be removed. If you launch ./main " first argument" "second argument   ", it will print:

```
[./main]
[ first argument]
[second argument   ]
```

This program can be abbreviated in this:

```
for a in std::env::args() {
    println!("[{}]", a);
}
```

Process Return Code

The most basic form of output of a program is its return code.

```
std::process::exit(107);
```

This program will terminate immediately when it invokes the "exit" function, and it will return to the launching process the number 107.

If this program is launched from a console of Unix, Linux, or MacOS, probably, if afterward you write the command "echo $?", you will get 107 printed on the console. The corresponding Windows command is "echo %errorlevel%".

Environment Variables

Another form of input/output is through environment variables.

```
for var in std::env::vars() {
    println!("[{}]=[{}]", var.0, var.1);
}
```

This program will print one line for every environment variable. However, to read or write a specific environment variable, this code is better:

```
print!("[{:?}]", std::env::var("abcd"));
std::env::set_var("abcd", "This is the value");
print!(" [{:?}]", std::env::var("abcd"));
```

Probably, this will print: "[Err(NotPresent)] [Ok("This is the value")]". First, probably, the "abcd" environment variable is not yet defined, and so the invocation of the "var" function returns the "Err" variant of a "Result" value. The specific kind of error is the enum "NotPresent". Then, such an environment variable is set for the current process, using an invocation of the "set_var" function. And so, at the next try to get it, it is found, and its string value is returned inside an "Ok" variant.

A similar program is this one:

```
print!("{}",
    if std::env::var("abcd").is_ok() {
        "Already defined"
    } else {
        "Undefined"
    });
std::env::set_var("abcd", "This is the value");
print!(", {}.", match std::env::var("abcd") {
    Ok(value) => value,
    Err(err) => format!("Still undefined: {}", err),
});
```

It will print: "Undefined, This is the value.".

Reading from the Console

For command-line oriented programs, a typical way to get input is to read a line from the keyboard until the user presses Enter. Such input may be redirected to read from a file or from the output of another process.

```
let mut line = String::new();
println!("{:?}", std::io::stdin().read_line(&mut line));
println!("[{}]", line);
```

As this program starts, it waits for your input from the keyboard, until you press some keys and then Enter. If, for example, you type "Hello", and then you press Enter, it will print:

```
Ok(6)
[Hello
]
```

The "stdin" function returns a handle to the standard input stream of the current process. On that handle, the "read_line" function can be applied. It waits for an end-of-line or an end-of-file character from the standard input stream, and then it tries to read all the characters present in the input buffer. That read may fail, because another thread is reading it at the same time.

If that read is successful, the characters read are put in a string object, assigned to the "line" variable, received as argument by reference to a mutable object, and the "read_line" function returns an "Ok" result object, whose data is the number of bytes read. Notice that such number is "6", because in addition to the five bytes of the string "Hello", there is the end-of-line control character. In fact, when the "line" variable is printed, the terminating closed bracket is printed in a separate line, because the end-of-line character is printed too.

If the "read_line" function cannot read characters from the standard input stream, it returns an "Err" result object, and it does not change the value of the "line" variable.

Let's see what happens when several lines are read from the standard input stream.

```
let mut text = format!("First: ");
let inp = std::io::stdin();
inp.read_line(&mut text).unwrap();
text.push_str("Second: ");
```

```
inp.read_line(&mut text).unwrap();
println!("{}: {} bytes", text, text.len());
```

If when you run this program, you type "eè€", then you hit Enter, then you type "Hello", and then you hit Enter again, it will print:

```
First: eè€
Second: Hello
: 28 bytes
```

If your keyboard does not allow you to type those characters, try to type any non-ASCII character.

First, notice that the string printed in the last line spans three lines as it contains two end-of-line characters. In addition, it contains the 7-byte ASCII string "First: ", and the 8-byte ASCII string "Second: ". Also "Hello" is an ASCII string, and it contains 5 bytes. As we saw in another chapter, the "eè€" string contains 6 bytes, so we have 7 + 6 + 1 + 8 + 5 + 1 = 28 bytes.

Second, let's see how the contents of the "text" variable are built up. Notice that the "read_line" function appends the typed line to the object specified by its argument, instead of overwriting it. The "text" variable is initialized to contain "First:". Then, in the third line, the first typed line is appended to those contents. Then, in the fourth line, the literal string "Second:" is appended to it. Finally, in the fifth line, the second typed line is appended.

Third, notice that when the "read_line" function reads the input buffer, it clears it, as the original buffer contents are not read again when the function is invoked for the second time.

Fourth, notice that after every invocation of "read_line", there is an invocation of "unwrap", but its return value is ignored.

Such invocation could be omitted.

```
let mut text = format!("First: ");
let inp = std::io::stdin();
inp.read_line(&mut text);
text.push_str("Second: ");
inp.read_line(&mut text);
println!("{}: {} bytes", text, text.len());
```

However, when this program is compiled, the compiler emits, for both invocations of "read_line", the warning "unused `std::result::Result` which must be used". It means that "read_line" returns a value of type "Result" and that value is ignored or not used. Rust considers it dangerous to ignore a return value of type "Result", because such a type could represent a runtime error, and so the program logic does not take into account such a kind of error. This is dangerous in production code, but it is not appropriate in debug code either, as it hides the errors that you are looking for.

Therefore, in debug code, it is appropriate to write always at least an ".unwrap()" clause.

But in production code, matters are not so simple.

Proper Runtime Error Handling

In real-world software, often it happens to make many invocations of functions that return a "Result" type value. Let's call "fallible" such functions. A fallible function normally returns an "Ok," but in exceptional cases it returns an "Err"

In C++, Java, and other object-oriented languages, the standard error handling technique is based on the so-called "exceptions", and the "throw" "try", and "catch" keywords. In Rust, there are no such things; all error-handling is based on the "Result" type, its functions, and the "match" statement.

Assume, as it is typical, that you are writing a function "f," which, to accomplish its task, has to invoke several fallible functions, "f1", "f2", "f3", and "f4". Each of them returns an error message if it fails, or a result if it is successful. If a function fails, that error message should be immediately returned by the "f" function as its error message. If a function is successful, its result should be passed as an argument to the next function. The result of the last function is passed as result of the "f" function.

One possibility is to write this:

```
fn f1(x: i32) -> Result<i32, String> {
    if x == 1 {
        Err(format!("Err. 1"))
    } else {
        Ok(x)
    }
}
```

```rust
fn f2(x: i32) -> Result<i32, String> {
    if x == 2 {
        Err(format!("Err. 2"))
    } else {
        Ok(x)
    }
}
fn f3(x: i32) -> Result<i32, String> {
    if x == 3 {
        Err(format!("Err. 3"))
    } else {
        Ok(x)
    }
}
fn f4(x: i32) -> Result<i32, String> {
    if x == 4 {
        Err(format!("Err. 4"))
    } else {
        Ok(x)
    }
}
fn f(x: i32) -> Result<i32, String> {
    match f1(x) {
        Ok(result) => {
            match f2(result) {
                Ok(result) => {
                    match f3(result) {
                        Ok(result) => f4(result),
                        Err(err_msg) => Err(err_msg),
                    }
                }
                Err(err_msg) => Err(err_msg),
            }
        }
```

```
            Err(err_msg) => Err(err_msg),
    }
}
match f(2) {
    Ok(y) => println!("{}", y),
    Err(e) => println!("Error: {}", e),
}
match f(4) {
    Ok(y) => println!("{}", y),
    Err(e) => println!("Error: {}", e),
}
match f(5) {
    Ok(y) => println!("{}", y),
    Err(e) => println!("Error: {}", e),
}
```

This will print:

```
Error: Err. 2
Error: Err. 4
5
```

It is quite obvious that such a pattern becomes unwieldy as the number of invocations increases, because the indentation level increases by two at every invocation added.

This code can be made linear by replacing the "f" function with the following one:

```
fn f(x: i32) -> Result<i32, String> {
    let result1 = f1(x);
    if result1.is_err() { return result1; }
    let result2 = f2(result1.unwrap());
    if result2.is_err() { return result2; }
    let result3 = f3(result2.unwrap());
    if result3.is_err() { return result3; }
    f4(result3.unwrap())
}
```

Every intermediate result is stored in a temporary variable, and then such variable is checked using the "is_err" function. In case of failure, it is returned; in case of success, the "unwrap" function is used to extract the actual result.

This pattern is so typical that a language feature has been introduced in the language. Here is an equivalent version of the "f" function:

```
fn f(x: i32) -> Result<i32, String> {
    f4(f3(f2(f1(x)?)?)?)
}
```

The question mark is a special macro such that, when applied to an expression like in "e?", if "e" is of generic type "Result<T,E>", it is expanded as the expression "match e { Some(v) => v, _ => return e }"; instead, if "e" is of a generic type "Option<T>", it is expanded as the expression "match e { Ok(v) => v, _ => return e }". In other words, such macro examines if its argument is "Some" or "Ok", and in such case unwraps it, or otherwise returns it as a return value of the containing function.

It can be applied only to expressions of type "Result<T,E>" or "Option<T>", and, of course, if can be used only inside a function with a proper return value type. If the enclosing function return value type is "Result<T1,E>", the question mark macro can be applied only to an expression of "Result<T2,E>" type, where "T2" can be different from "T1", but "E" must be the same; instead, if the enclosing function return value type is "Option<T1>", the question mark macro can be applied only to an expression of "Option<T2>" type.

So, the right pattern to build a robust error handling is the following. Every function that contains an invocation to a fallible function should be a fallible function or should handle the "Result" value in a "match" statement, or similar handling. In the first case, every invocation of a fallible function should be followed by a question mark to propagate the error condition. The "main" function (or the starting functions of a secondary thread) cannot be a fallible function, and so, at some point in the invocation chain, there should be a "match" statement for a "Result" value.

Writing to the Console

We already wrote to the console in almost every program snippet we wrote, but we always used the "print" or "println" macros, which are implemented using a standard library function. However, you can also directly use library functions to print some text to the console.

```
use std::io::Write;
//ILLEGAL: std::io::stdout().write("Hi").unwrap();
//ILLEGAL: std::io::stdout().write(String::from("Hi")).unwrap();
std::io::stdout().write("Hello ".as_bytes()).unwrap();
std::io::stdout().write(String::from("world").as_bytes()).unwrap();
```

This will print: "Hello world".

The "stdout" standard library function returns a handle to the standard output stream of the current process. On that handle, the "write" function can be applied.

Though, the "write" function cannot directly print static nor dynamic strings, and of course neither numbers or general composite objects.

The "write" function gets an argument of "&[u8]" type, which is a reference to a slice of bytes. Such bytes are printed to the console as an UTF-8 string. So, if you want to print an object that is not a slice of bytes in UTF-8 format, first you have to translate it to such a thing.

To convert both a static string and a dynamic string to a reference to a slice of bytes, you can use the "as_bytes" function. This function just returns the address of the first byte of the string, and the number of bytes used by the string object. Such values are already contained in the header of the string object, and so this function is extremely efficient.

Finally, notice that the "write" function returns a "Result" type value, that is, it is a fallible function. If you are quite sure it is not going to fail, you'd best invoke the "unwrap" function on its return value.

Converting a Value to a String

If you want to print the textual representation of another kind of value, you can try to use the "to_string" function, defined for all primitive types.

```
let int_str: String = 45.to_string();
let float_str: String = 4.5.to_string();
let bool_str: String = true.to_string();
print!("{} {} {}", int_str, float_str, bool_str);
```

This will print: "45 4.5 true".

The "to_string" function allocates a String object, whose header is in the stack and whose contents are in the heap. Therefore, it is not extremely efficient.

File Input/Output

In addition to reading and writing to the console, in Rust it is rather easy also to read and write both binary and text sequential files.

```
use std::io::Write;
let mut file = std::fs::File::create("data.txt").unwrap();
file.write_all("eè€".as_bytes()).unwrap();
```

The second line invokes the "create" function to create a file named "data.txt" in the current folder of the file system. This function is fallible, and, if it is successful in creating a file, it returns a file handle to the file just created.

The last line invokes the "write_all" function to write some bytes in the newly create file. The saved bytes are the six bytes representing the string "eè€".

Assuming in the current directory there is the text file named "data.txt" you just created by running the previous program, you can read that file by running the following program.

```
use std::io::Read;
let mut file = std::fs::File::open("data.txt").unwrap();
let mut contents = String::new();
file.read_to_string(&mut contents).unwrap();
print!("{}", contents);
```

This program will print: "eè€".

The second line invokes the "open" function to open an existing file named "data. txt" in the current folder. This function fails if the file does not exist, or if it is not accessible for whatever reason. If it succeeds, a file handle to such file is assigned to the "file" variable.

The fourth line invokes the "read_to_string" function on the "file" handle to read all the contents of that file into a string variable, passed by reference to a mutable object.

The last line prints to the console the contents just read from the file.

So now you can copy a file into another one. But if a file is huge, it is impossible to load it all into a string before writing it. It is required to read and write a portion at a time. However, it is inefficient to read and write small portions.

Here is a rather efficient program to copy a file.

```
use std::io::Read;
use std::io::Write;
let mut command_line: std::env::Args = std::env::args();
command_line.next().unwrap();
let source = command_line.next().unwrap();
let destination = command_line.next().unwrap();
let mut file_in = std::fs::File::open(source).unwrap();
let mut file_out = std::fs::File::create(destination).unwrap();
let mut buffer = [0u8; 4096];
loop {
    let nbytes = file_in.read(&mut buffer).unwrap();
    file_out.write(&buffer[..nbytes]).unwrap();
    if nbytes < buffer.len() { break; }
}
```

This program must be launched passing two command-line arguments. The first one is the path of the source file, and the second one is the path of the destination file.

The lines from the third to the sixth one assign to the "source" variable the contents of the first argument, and to the "destination" variable the contents of the second argument.

The next two lines open the two files. First the source file is opened, and the new handle is assigned to the "file_in" variable. Then the destination file is created (or truncated, if already existing), and the new handle is assigned to the "file_out" variable.

Then a 4096-byte buffer is allocated in the stack.

At last, a loop repeatedly reads a 4096-byte chunk from the source file and writes it to the output file. The number of bytes read is automatically as many as the length of the buffer. But if the remaining portion of the file is not long enough, the read bytes are less than 4096, or even zero.

So, the number of bytes read is put into the "nbytes" variable.

For a file larger than 4096 bytes, at the first iteration the number of bytes read will be 4096, and so some other iterations will be required. For a smaller file, one iteration will be enough.

In any case, the buffer is written to the file up to the number of bytes read. So, a slice of the buffer is taken from the beginning to the number of read bytes.

Then, if the number of bytes read was less than the length of the buffer, the loop is terminated, as the end of the input file has been reached. Otherwise the loop continues with other iterations.

Notice that there is no need to close explicitly the files. As soon as the file handles exit their scopes, the files are automatically closed, saving and releasing all internal temporary buffers.

Processing Text Files

We saw how to read or write sequentially a file of arbitrary data.

But when a file contains raw text, like a program source file, it is more convenient to process it a line at a time.

For example, if we want to compute how many lines there are in a text file, and how many of them are empty or contain only blanks, you can write this program:

```
let mut command_line = std::env::args();
command_line.next();
let pathname = command_line.next().unwrap();
let counts = count_lines(&pathname).unwrap();
println!("file: {}", pathname);
println!("n. of lines: {}", counts.0);
println!("n. of empty lines: {}", counts.1);

fn count_lines(pathname: &str)
-> Result<(u32, u32), std::io::Error> {
    use std::io::BufRead;

    let f = std::fs::File::open(pathname)?;
    let f = std::io::BufReader::new(f);
```

```
    let mut n_lines = 0;
    let mut n_empty_lines = 0;
    for line in f.lines() {
        n_lines += 1;
        if line?.trim().len() == 0 {
            n_empty_lines += 1;
        }
    }
    Ok((n_lines, n_empty_lines))
}
```

If this program, enclosed in the usual "main" function, is saved in a file named "countlines.rs", and then it is compiled, and it is run with the argument "countlines. rs", it will print:

```
file: countlines.rs
n. of lines: 26
n. of empty lines: 2
```

In the first line, the invocation of "args" gets the command-line iterator and stores it in the "command_line" variable.

In the second line, the zeroth command-line argument is discarded.

In the third line, the first command-line argument is consumed and assigned to the "pathname" variable. If there is no such argument, the program panics.

In the fourth line, the "count_lines" function, defined later, is invoked passing to it a reference to the path name of the file to read. It is a fallible function. If it is successful, it returns a tuple of two values: the total number of lines counted in the read file, and the number of those lines that are empty or that contain only blanks. That pair is assigned to the "counts" variable.

The fifth, sixth, and seventh lines are print statements.

From the ninth line, there is the declaration of the "count_lines" function. It gets a string slice as an argument, and returns a "Result" that in case of success is a pair of "u32" numbers, and in case of failure is a standard I/O error.

The "open" function is invoked to get a handle for the file indicated by the pathname received as an argument. The question mark following it means that if the open function fails, the "count_lines" function returns immediately the same error code returned by the "open" function.

The operations performed on a file are not buffered by default. That is optimal if you don't need buffering, or if you prefer to apply your own buffering. But if you prefer a buffered stream, you can create a "BufReader" object from a "raw" file handle. As text lines are usually much shorter than the optimal I/O buffer size, it is more efficient to use a buffered input stream, when reading a text file. After having created a "BufReader" object, there is no more need to use explicitly the "File" object, and so the newly created object can be assigned to another variable named "f", so that it will shadow the preexisting variable.

Then, the two counters "n_lines" and "n_empty_lines" are declared and initialized.

Then, there is the loop over the file contents. The "BufReader" type provides the "lines" function that returns an iterator over the lines contained in the file. Notice that Rust iterators are lazy; that is, there is never a memory structure containing all the lines, but every time the iterator is asked for a line, it asks the file buffered reader for a line, and then provides the obtained line. So, at each iteration, the "for" loop puts the next line in the "line" variable and executes the loop block.

But any file read can fail, and so "line" is not a simple string; its type is "Result<String, std::io::Error>". Therefore, when it is used, "line" is followed by a question mark, to get its string value or to return the I/O error.

In the loop body, the "n_lines" counter is incremented by one at any line, while the "n_empty_lines" is incremented by one only when the line, after having removed from it any leading or trailing blanks by invoking "trim", has zero length.

The last statement returns a successful value: "Ok". The data of such value are the two counters.

Using Traits

In this chapter, you will learn:

- How traits can avoid incomprehensible compiler error messages when invoking generic functions

- How the bounding of a generic parameter can be monolithic, or it can be broken up in several traits

- How traits create a scope for the functions they contain

- How to use the "self" keyword to create functions that can be invoked using the "dot notation", with a simpler syntax

- How to use the standard library traits, like the "Display" trait

- How iterating is just a trait

- How to define type aliases

- How to define generic iterators

- How to use associated types to simplify generic iterators use

- How to define your own iterators

The Need for Traits

Let's say we need a function to compute the mathematical fourth root, named "quartic root". Exploiting the sqrt standard library function, which computes the square root of the number to which it is applied, we could write:

```
fn quartic_root(x: f64) -> f64 { x.sqrt().sqrt() }
let qr = quartic_root(100f64);
print!("{} {}", qr * qr * qr * qr, qr);
```

© Carlo Milanesi 2018
C. Milanesi, *Beginning Rust*, https://doi.org/10.1007/978-1-4842-3468-6_18

This will print: "100.00000000000003 3.1622776601683795".

But we could need also a function to compute the quartic root of 32-bit floating-point numbers, without casting them to the f64 type. Exploiting the fact that also f32 has a sqrt function, we could write:

```
fn quartic_root_f64(x: f64) -> f64 { x.sqrt().sqrt() }
fn quartic_root_f32(x: f32) -> f32 { x.sqrt().sqrt() }
print!("{} {}",
    quartic_root_f64(100f64),
    quartic_root_f32(100f32));
```

This will print: "3.1622776601683795 3.1622777".

But instead of writing similar functions differing only in the types of their arguments and variables, we could try to write a generic function, like this one:

```
fn quartic_root<Number>(x: Number) -> Number {
    x.sqrt().sqrt()
}
print!("{} {}",
    quartic_root(100f64),
    quartic_root(100f32));
```

But this code is illegal, generating the compilation error "no method named `sqrt` found for type `Number` in the current scope". That means that in the expression "x.sqrt()", the expression "x" is of the "Number" generic type, and such type doesn't have the sqrt applicable function. Actually, the type Number has just been defined, and so it has pretty much *no* applicable function.

In this aspect, Rust differs from C++. In this latter language, we can write the following code, in which a function template is corresponding to our generic function:

```
#include <iostream>
#include <cmath>

template <typename Number>
Number quartic_root(Number x) {
    return sqrt(sqrt(x));
}
```

CHAPTER 18   USING TRAITS

```
int main() {
    std::cout << quartic_root((float)100)
        << " " << quartic_root((double)100);
}
```

Even in C++ code, the "Number" generic type has no applicable function when the compiler first encounters the invocation of "sqrt", and so the compiler cannot know if such statement is allowed. But when the two invocations of the "quartic_root" function are encountered, the two concrete functions "quartic_root<float>" and "quartic_root<double>" are generated by the compiler. This is called "generic function instantiation", or "function monomorphization". Such instantiation checks that, for the "float" and "double" concrete types, the "sqrt" function is applicable.

The drawback of the C++ solution appears when there is a programming error, like this one:

```
#include <iostream>
#include <cmath>

template <typename Number>
Number quartic_root(Number x) {
    return sqrt(sqrt(x));
}

int main() {
    std::cout << quartic_root("Hello");
}
```

When the C++ compiler tries to instantiate the "quartic_root" function for the "const char*" type, which is the type of the expression "Hello", it needs to generate the invocation of the function whose signature is "sqrt(const char*)". But there is no such function declaration, and so the compiler emits a compilation error complaining about that missing function.

The drawback is that typically the "quartic_root" function declaration is written by one developer (or developer organization), and the invocation of that function is written by another developer (or developer organization). The developer who invokes the function passing a string instead of a number would like to get an error message like "in the invocation of quartic_root at line 10, you cannot pass a string", instead, in C++, you necessarily get an error message like "at line 6, you cannot apply sqrt on a Number, where Number is a string, when this function is called from line 10".

The C++ message is somewhat obscure if you don't know how quartic_root is implemented. And this is a very simple example. In real-world C++ code, error messages for type errors in generic function invocation tend to be really very obscure, because they talk about variables, functions, and types that belong to the implementation of the library, not to its interface. To understand them, it is not enough to know the API well; it is required to know the whole library implementation.

Traits to the Rescue

The Rust technique to avoid this drawback for simple cases like this one is more complicated than the C++ technique, but it creates much clearer error messages for more complex cases, like those of real-world software.

```rust
trait HasSquareRoot {
    fn sq_root(self) -> Self;
}
impl HasSquareRoot for f32 {
    fn sq_root(self) -> Self { f32::sqrt(self) }
}
impl HasSquareRoot for f64 {
    fn sq_root(self) -> Self { f64::sqrt(self) }
}
fn quartic_root<Number>(x: Number) -> Number
where Number: HasSquareRoot {
    x.sq_root().sq_root()
}
print!("{} {}",
    quartic_root(100f64),
    quartic_root(100f32));
```

This will print: "3.1622776601683795 3.1622777".

The first statement is a declaration of a "trait" named "HasSquareRoot", containing the signature of a function named "sq_root". A Rust trait is a container of function signatures; in this case it contains just one signature. The meaning of a trait is the *capability* to use some functions. The meaning of the "HasSquareRoot" trait is that the "sq_root" function can be invoked on every type having the "HasSquareRoot" capability, or, as it is usually said, every type that *satisfies* the "HasSquareRoot" trait.

But which types satisfy the "HasSquareRoot" trait? Well, no one does, because we just defined that trait, and any trait is not satisfied by any type, except the ones that have been declared to satisfy it.

So, the next two statements in the example above make the "f32" and "f64" types satisfy that trait. In other words, with these "impl" statements, the capability to invoke the "sq_root" function is given to the "f32" and "f64" types. For such purpose, another kind of statement is introduced, where the "impl" keyword is shorthand for "implementation".

Those "impl" statements mean that the "HasSquareRoot" trait, which is just a programming interface, or API, is implemented here for the specified types by the specified code. Of course, the signatures of the functions contained in the "impl" statements are the same as the signature contained in the previous "trait" statement; but they have also a body, because they are implementations of such signature. Speaking in C++ terms, they are *definitions* of the previous function *declaration*.

Rust traits are similar to Java or C# *interfaces*, or to abstract classes without data members.

Because of the first three statements, we have a new trait and two existing types that now implement such a trait.

The fourth statement is the declaration of the "quartic_root" generic function, parameterized by the "Number" generic type. However, such a declaration has a new portion: at the end of the signature, there is the clause "where Number: HasSquareRoot". Such clause is named "trait bound", and it is a part of the signature of the function. It literally means that the "Number" generic type must implement the "HasSquareRoot" trait.

Function signatures are a kind of contract between the code that invokes the functions and the code in the body of the functions, and so their "where" clauses are part of that contract.

For the code that invokes the function, such "where" clause means "when invoking this function, you must ensure that the type you pass for the Number type parameter implements the HasSquareRoot trait". For example, the "100f32" and "100f64" expressions are of the "f32" and "f64" type, respectively, and both such types implement the "HasSquareRoot" trait, and so they are valid arguments. But if you replace the last line of the program with "quartic_root("Hello"));", you have that the type of the expression "Hello", that is "&str", does not implement the "HasSquareRoot" trait, and so you violate the contract. Actually, you get the compilation error "the trait bound `&str: main::HasSquareRoot` is not satisfied".

Trying to compute the quartic root of a string is nonsensical, but even if you replace the last line of the program with "quartic_root(81i32));", you get a compilation error. Its message is "the trait bound `i32: main::HasSquareRoot` is not satisfied". This is because the "HasSquareRoot" trait has not been implemented for the i32 type, regardless of the reasonableness of such operation. If you think that such a trait is worthwhile for other types, you can implement it for them.

Instead, if the contract is seen by the code in the body of the function, that "where" clause means "when this function is invoked, the type passed for the "Number" type parameter is ensured to implement the "HasSquareRoot" trait, and so you can use every function belonging to such trait, but no other function". For example, in the body of the function, the "x.sq_root()" expression is valid, because the "x" expression is of the "Number" generic type, and such a type is declared to implement the "HasSquareRoot" trait, and that trait contains the "sq_root" function, and so such a function is available to the "x" variable. But if you replace that body with "x.abs()", that would be a valid statement if "x" were of "f64" or "f32" type, you get the compilation error: "no method named `abs` found for type `Number` in the current scope". It means that the "x" expression, which is of the "Number" generic type, is not able to invoke the "abs" function. In fact, inside the function body, it is not known that "x" will be an "f64" or an "f32"; it is just a "Number", and all that a "Number" is able to do is what is contained in the "HasSquareRoot" trait, which is the "sq_root" function.

Generic Functions with No Trait Bounds

In the declaration of a generic function, if there is no "where" clause, or if a type parameter is not cited in the "where" clause, no trait is associated to that type, and so you can do very little with an object of that generic type. You can do only this:

```
fn _f1<T>(a: T) -> T { a }
fn _f2<T>(a: T) -> T {
    let b: T = a;
    let mut c = b;
```

```
    c = _f1(c);
    c
}
fn _f3<T>(a: &T) -> &T { a }
```

With a value of an unbounded type parameter "T", you can only:

- pass it as function argument, by value or by reference;

- return it from a function, by value or by reference;

- declare, initialize, or assign a local variable.

Instead, even the trivial following code causes compilation errors:

```
fn g(a: i32) { }
fn f<T>(a: T) -> bool {
    g(a);
    a == a
}
```

The third line is illegal, because "g" requires a value having "i32" type, while "a" could have any type. And the fourth line is illegal because the "T" type could be unable to be compared for equality.

Therefore, trait bounds on the type parameters of generic functions are almost always used.

A very rare case of an important generic standard library function that does not need trait bounds is used in this program:

```
let mut a = 'A';
let mut b = 'B';
print!("{}, {}; ", a, b);
std::mem::swap(&mut a, &mut b);
print!("{}, {}", a, b);
```

It will print: "A, B; B, A".

The "swap" generic function can exchange the values of any two objects having the same type. Its signature is: "fn swap<T>(x: &mut T, y: &mut T)".

Scope of Traits

Our trait contained a function named "sq_root", to make it clear it was not the same thing as the "sqrt" standard library function. The two implementations of the "sq_root" function *use* the standard library "sqrt" functions, but they are other functions. However, we could also name that function "sqrt", obtaining this equivalent valid program:

```
fn sqrt() {}
trait HasSquareRoot {
    fn sqrt(self) -> Self;
}
impl HasSquareRoot for f32 {
    fn sqrt(self) -> Self { f32::sqrt(self) }
}
impl HasSquareRoot for f64 {
    fn sqrt(self) -> Self { f64::sqrt(self) }
}
fn quartic_root<Number>(x: Number) -> Number
where Number: HasSquareRoot {
    x.sqrt().sqrt()
}
sqrt();
print!("{} {}",
    quartic_root(100f64),
    quartic_root(100f32));
```

Notice that now we have four distinct uses of the name "sqrt":

- "f32::sqrt", used in the sixth line, refers to a function declared in the standard library, where it is associated to the "f32" type. It computes the square root of a value having "f32" type, and returns a value having "f32" type.

- "f64::sqrt", used in the ninth line, refers to a function declared in the standard library, where it is associated to the "f64" type. It computes the square root of a value having "f64" type, and returns a value having "f64" type.

- "fn sqrt(self) -> Self" is a method of the "HasSquareRoot" trait, and all the types that implement such trait must have a method with that same signature. Its signature is declared in the third line, and it is implemented in the sixth and ninth lines.

- "fn sqrt()" is a local function outside the "HasSquareRoot" trait, and it has nothing to do with it. It is declared in the first line, and invoked in the fifteenth line. By the way, it does nothing.

You know Rust does not allow two functions with the same name in the same scope. Nevertheless the code above is valid; that means that these four functions with the same name belong to four different scopes.

Traits with Multiple Functions

If in the previous example we replace the expressions "100f64" and "100f32" with "-100f64" and "-100f32", the program will print "NaN NaN". The "NaN" text means "Not a Number", and it is a standard result of the attempt to compute the square root of a negative floating-point number.

Let's assume we need a function that computes the quartic root of the absolute value of floating-point numbers. We could choose to use the "abs" function of the standard library to compute the absolute value, or to check if the argument is negative, and in such case use its opposite.

In the first case, our "Number" generic type needs also the "abs" function. So we can write this program:

```
trait HasSqrtAndAbs {
    fn sqrt(self) -> Self;
    fn abs(self) -> Self;
}
impl HasSqrtAndAbs for f32 {
    fn sqrt(self) -> Self { f32::sqrt(self) }
    fn abs(self) -> Self { f32::abs(self) }
}
```

```
impl HasSqrtAndAbs for f64 {
    fn sqrt(self) -> Self { f64::sqrt(self) }
    fn abs(self) -> Self { f64::abs(self) }
}
fn abs_quartic_root<Number>(x: Number) -> Number
where Number: HasSqrtAndAbs {
    x.abs().sqrt().sqrt()
}
print!("{} {}",
    abs_quartic_root(-100f64),
    abs_quartic_root(-100f32));
```

This will print: "3.1622776601683795 3.1622777".

The changes with respect to the previous program are the following ones.

First, the useless standalone "sqrt" function has been removed.

Then, in the trait declaration, the signature of an "abs" function has been added.

Then, that "abs" function has been implemented for the "f32" and "f64" types. Such implementations invoke the "abs" function of "f32" and "f64" types.

Then, the four occurrences of the trait name have been changed to "HasSqrtAndAbs", to clarify their new purpose.

Then, in the generic function, the "abs" function is applied to the x argument, before the two invocations of "sqrt".

Then, the three occurrences of the name of the generic function have been changed to "abs_quartic_root", to clarify their new purpose.

Then, the arguments of the two invocations of "abs_quartic_root" have become negative.

This solution allows you to easily add functions invocations to your generic functions definitions, but it has one drawback.

If you omit the implementation of "abs" for "f64", you get the compilation error "not all trait items implemented, missing: `abs`". On the other hand, If you add the implementation of a function named, say, "exp", you get the compilation error "method `exp` is not a member of trait `HasSqrtAndAbs`". Therefore, every "impl" block must have the same signatures of the trait it is implementing: not one more, not one less, not one different.

Sometimes, a few functions are strictly coupled, and so, every time one of them is needed, all of them should be implemented anyway. But what if in some generic functions you want to use a type that has a "sqrt" function, but not an "abs" function, or conversely? You are forced to implement even the functions you don't need.

To avoid this, you can declare a new trait, obtaining the following equivalent program:

```
trait HasSquareRoot {
    fn sqrt(self) -> Self;
}
impl HasSquareRoot for f32 {
    fn sqrt(self) -> Self { f32::sqrt(self) }
}
impl HasSquareRoot for f64 {
    fn sqrt(self) -> Self { f64::sqrt(self) }
}
trait HasAbsoluteValue {
    fn abs(self) -> Self;
}
impl HasAbsoluteValue for f32 {
    fn abs(self) -> Self { f32::abs(self) }
}
impl HasAbsoluteValue for f64 {
    fn abs(self) -> Self { f64::abs(self) }
}
fn abs_quartic_root<Number>(x: Number) -> Number
where Number: HasSquareRoot + HasAbsoluteValue {
    x.abs().sqrt().sqrt()
}
print!("{} {}",
    abs_quartic_root(-100f64),
    abs_quartic_root(-100f32));
```

Here, the trait "HasSquareRoot" is the original one, but the new "HasAbsoluteValue" trait has been declared and implemented for "f32" and "f64".

Moreover, the "where" clause of the declaration of the "abs_quartic_root" function has one more trait bound for the "Number" type parameter: in addition to the "HasSquareRoot" trait, the "HasAbsoluteValue" has been added. The two traits are separated by a *plus* symbol.

This trait bound adds to the capabilities of "Number" the capabilities of both traits. In this way, you can pick the traits you need for your generic type.

Methods

We already saw that there are two possible syntaxes to invoke a function: "f(x, y)" and "x.f(y)". The first one is the "functional" syntax, and the second one is the "object-oriented" syntax. Previously, we invoked some functions of the standard library using the functional syntax, like String::new() or String::from(""), and other functions using the "object-oriented" syntax, like "abcd".to_string(), "abcd".len(), vec![0u8; 0].push(7u8). The "object-oriented" syntax is usually named "dot notation", and it is similar to the syntax to access the fields of tuples, tuple-structs, and structs.

However, any function that may be invoked using the dot notation may also be invoked using the functional notation.

```
print!("{},", "abcd".to_string());
print!("{},", [1, 2, 3].len());
let mut v1 = vec![0u8; 0];
v1.push(7u8);
print!("{:?}; ", v1);

print!("{},", std::string::ToString::to_string("abcd"));
print!("{:?},", <[i32]>::len(&[1, 2, 3]));
let mut v2 = vec![0u8; 0];
Vec::push(&mut v2, 7u8);
print!("{:?}", v2);
```

This will print: "abcd,3,[7]; abcd,3,[7]". First, three functions are invoked using the dot notation: to_string, len and push. Then, the same functions are invoked using the functional notation.

Notice that, when transforming the dot notation into the functional notation, the object to which the function is applied becomes an additional first argument. Such first argument must be decorated by the possibly required dereference symbol (&), or mutation keyword (mut) or both, which are implicit in the dot notation.

In addition, there is a problem of scoping. In the standard library, there are several functions named to_string, len, or push. Using the dot notation, the proper function is automatically chosen. Instead, using the functional notation, the scope of the function must be written explicitly. In the example, the to_string function is in the std::string::ToString scope, the len function is in the <[i32]> scope, and the push function is in the Vec scope.

The dot notation appears to be so good in simplifying code, that you may wish to use it for the functions you declare. If you want to declare a function that returns the double of a given number, you can write:

```
fn double(x: i32) -> i32 {
    x * 2
}
print!("{}", double(7i32));
```

This will print: "14".

So, you may wish to write:

```
fn double(x: i32) -> i32 {
    x * 2
}
print!("{}", 7i32.double());
```

But this code generates the compilation error "no method named `double` found for type `i32` in the current scope".

This is because the functions we declared before this chapter could be invoked only using the functional syntax. The dot notation can be used to invoke only functions declared as implementation of a trait. Such functions are named "methods", following the "object-oriented" terminology.

To allow the dot notation, you can write:

```
trait CanBeDoubled {
    fn double(self) -> Self;
}
```

```
impl CanBeDoubled for i32 {
    fn double(self) -> Self {
        self * 2
    }
}
print!("{}", 7i32.double());
```

This will print: "14".

The name of the trait (CanBeDoubled) is arbitrary. Usually, if a trait contains only one function, the trait has just that name put into Pascal-case. Following this convention, it had to be named Double.

The meaning of this code is this.

A new capability has been declared to be given to some types. It is the ability to compute the double of the objects of such types, and so it is named CanBeDoubled. For a type, to have such a capability means that there is a function named double that can get a value of such type (self), and it can return a value of that same type (Self). There is no guarantee that such return value is in any way the "double" of the argument.

After having introduced this trait, no type still has such capability.

Then, it was declared that the i32 type has such capability, that is, it has such double function, and a body for such function was provided.

Now, while the expressions 7u32.double() and 7i64.double() are still invalid, the expression 7i32.double() means a shorthand for the expression i32::double(7i32). When compiling such an expression, the compiler searches the operations supported by the type i32 for the operation double, and it finds such an operation with the appropriate signature.

The "self" and "Self" Keywords

In the preceding section, we found two new keywords: "self" and "Self" (remember that Rust is case sensitive).

In the statement "trait CanBeDoubled { fn double(self) -> Self; }", "self" means the value on which the "double" method will be applied, whichever it will be, and "Self" means the type of "self".

So, the "self" word is a pseudo-argument of a method, and the "Self" word represents the type of such an argument. Therefore, "self" and "Self" can be used only inside a "trait or impl block. And "self", if present, must be the first argument of a method.

Inside the "impl CanBeDoubled for i32" block, the following six lines are equivalent:

```
fn double(self) -> Self {
fn double(self: Self) -> Self {
fn double(self: i32) -> Self {
fn double(self) -> i32 {
fn double(self: Self) -> i32 {
fn double(self: i32) -> i32 {
```

The first three lines return a value of type "Self"; but we are implementing a trait for the "i32" type, and so "Self" is "i32", and so we can replace "Self" with "i32" in the last three lines, with the same meaning.

The first and fourth lines get an argument "self" with an implicit type; but, by definition, the type of "self" is "Self", and so we can make it explicit in the second and fifth lines; but in this "impl" block, "Self" is "i32", and so we can replace "Self" with "i32" in the third and sixth lines, with the same meaning.

Of those six versions, the one commonly used is the first one, because it is the most compact and generic.

In the body of the "double" function, both the "self" and "Self" keywords are allowed. There was no need to use "Self", but "self" was used to take the value to be multiplied by two.

Let's see another example.

We want to be able to write the expression "foobarbaz".letters_count('a') that counts how many characters are in the string, and therefore returns 2. We can do it in this way:

```
trait LettersCount {
    fn letters_count(&self, ch: char) -> usize;
}
impl LettersCount for str {
    fn letters_count(&self, ch: char) -> usize {
        let mut count = 0;
        for c in self.chars() {
            if c == ch {
                count += 1;
            }
        }
```

```
        count
    }
}
print!("{} ", "".letters_count('a'));
print!("{} ", "ddd".letters_count('a'));
print!("{} ", "ddd".letters_count('d'));
print!("{} ", "foobarbaz".letters_count('a'));
```

This will print: "0 0 3 2".

Because we want to use a dot notation, first we declare a trait, whose name is derived from the function name. Our function will need two arguments: the string slice to search, and the character to look for. But we don't want to pass as an argument a copy of the string slice; we want to pass just a string slice reference, and so we declare the argument as "&self", so that "self" is a string slice, having arbitrary length, and "&self" is a string slice reference, having the size of a pair of pointers.

The return value is "usize" representing a non-negative large-but-efficient unsigned integer number.

Then we implement that trait for our type "str", which is the string slice type. Here we have no need of the "Self" keyword. The body uses the imperative style. It scans all characters provided by the iterator returned by the "chars" function, and every time a character equal to our looked-for character is encountered, a counter is incremented. The resulting value of the counter is the desired result.

Notice that if we had opted for a functional style, we would get a much shorter program. In fact, the whole body of the function can be equivalently replaced by the following line.

```
self.chars().filter(|c| *c == ch).count()
```

Standard Traits

We saw from the first chapters of this book that when using the "print", "println", and "format" macros, you can use the "{}" placeholder only for the types that support it, and for the other types you should use the "{:?}" placeholder, which is meant for debugging purposes.

But how come some types support the "{}" placeholder and others don't? And how could you make your own type support that placeholder?

Actually, internally, those macros use the "fmt" function specified by the "std::fmt::Display" standard library trait. All the primitive types implement that trait, and if you do it for your types, you can obtain the same results.

```rust
struct Complex {
    re: f64,
    im: f64,
}
impl std::fmt::Display for Complex {
    fn fmt(&self, f: &mut std::fmt::Formatter) -> std::fmt::Result {
        write!(
            f,
            "{} {} {}i",
            self.re,
            if self.im >= 0. { '+' } else { '-' },
            self.im.abs()
        )
    }
}
let c1 = Complex { re: -2.3, im: 0. };
let c2 = Complex { re: -2.1, im: -5.2 };
let c3 = Complex { re: -2.2, im: 5.2 };
print!("{}, {}, {}", c1, c2, c3);
```

This will print: "-2.3 + 0i, -2.1 - 5.2i, -2.2 + 5.2i".

In the standard library there are many traits, and many implementations of them for the primitive types.

The "Iterator" Trait

One particularly interesting standard library trait is "Iterator". Let's see which problems it solves.

You can write a function that, given a *range*, returns its third item, if it has at least three items, or nothing, if it has not enough items.

```
fn get_third(r: std::ops::Range<u32>) -> Option<u32> {
    if r.len() >= 3 {
        Some(r.start + 2)
    } else {
        None
    }
}
print!("{:?} {:?}", get_third(10..12), get_third(20..23));
```

This will print: "None Some(22)".

You can also write a function that, given a *slice*, returns its third item, if it has at least three items, or nothing, if it has not enough items.

```
fn get_third(s: &[f64]) -> Option<f64> {
    if s.len() >= 3 {
        Some(s[2])
    } else {
        None
    }
}
print!("{:?} {:?}",
        get_third(&[1.0, 2.0]),
        get_third(&[1.1, 2.1, 3.1]));
```

This will print: "None Some(3.1)".

These two programs are quite similar. But using iterators, it should be possible to write a generic function that, given an iterator, returns its third produced item, if it can produce at least three items, or nothing, if it cannot produce enough items. Then, you can apply this function to replace the two previous programs, because a range is just an iterator and a slice can be iterated over.

Yet, if you try to compile the following program,

```
fn get_third<Iter, Item>(mut iterator: Iter) -> Option<Item> {
    iterator.next();
    iterator.next();
    iterator.next()
}
```

```
print!("{:?} {:?}",
    get_third(0..9),
    get_third([11, 22, 33, 44].iter()));
```

you get several compilation errors.

The idea seemed good. We want to write a function that is parameterized both on the type of iterator, "Iter", and on the type of the items produced by such iterator, "Item". The argument is an iterator, and the return value is an optional produced item.

The function body invokes three times the iterator "next" function to produce three items; it discards the first two items, and it returns the value returned by the third invocation.

Then, the "get_third" function is invoked two times: one with a range, and one with an array iterator.

The compilation errors for this code are of two kinds:

- The "iterator" variable is unbound, and so it has no "next" function. When we see the invocations of the "get_third" function, we see that its arguments are iterators, and so they have a "next" function. However, Rust needs to know which functions can be invoked on an object of a generic parameter by examining only the function declaration, not also the function invocation.

- Looking at the invocations of "get_third", the type of the generic parameter "Item" cannot be inferred, because no expression with that type is passed as an argument.

Regarding the first kind of errors, it should be noted that the "iterator" concept is not defined by the Rust language. This concept is defined by the Rust standard library through a standard trait, the "Iterator" trait. When, in the chapter on iterators, we said that an iterator is everything that has a "next" function, we meant that an iterator is every type that implements the "Iterator" standard library trait. Such a trait contains the "next" function, and so every iterator must have that function.

Moreover, it is not required to implement such a trait for your iterator, because every iterator, by definition, implements the "Iterator" trait. It is enough to bound the function parameter type to the "Iterator" trait.

So, the first line becomes:

```
fn get_third<Iter, Item>(mut iterator: Iter) -> Option<Item>
    where Iter: std::iter::Iterator {
```

But there is still the second kind of errors: how to determine the concrete type of the "Item" type parameter. To solve that problem, the "type" Rust keyword must be introduced.

The "type" Keyword

Say you want to write a portion of code that now uses the "f32" type, but in the future could use the "f64" type or some other type. If you intersperse your code with the "f32" keyword, when you want to switch to the "f64" type you should search and replace all those occurrences, and that is laborious and error prone.

You could encapsulate your code in a generic function, but if that code is just a portion of a function or, conversely, spans several functions, that solution is inconvenient.

This situation is similar to the use of literals. It is well known that instead of writing "magic" literals inside your code, it is better to define named constants, and use those constants inside your code. In this way, the purpose of your code becomes clearer, and when you want to change the value of a constant, you change only one line.

Similarly, instead of writing:

```
fn f1(x: f32) -> f32 { x }
fn f2(x: f32) -> f32 { x }
let a: f32 = 2.3;
let b: f32 = 3.4;
print!("{} {}", f1(a), f2(b));
```

it is better to write

```
type Number = f32;
fn f1(x: Number) -> Number { x }
fn f2(x: Number) -> Number { x }
let a: Number = 2.3;
let b: Number = 3.4;
print!("{} {}", f1(a), f2(b));
```

Both source programs generate the same executable program that will print: "2.3 3.4". But the second one begins with an additional statement. The "type" keyword introduces a type alias. It simply means that whenever the word "Number" is used as a type, it means the "f32" type. Indeed, in the rest of the program every one of the six occurrences of the word "f32" has been replaced by the "Number" word, which has just the same meaning.

The corresponding construct in C language is that using the "typedef" keyword.

Such constructs do not introduce a distinct type; they introduce just a new name for the same type. This implies that the following code is valid:

```
type Number = f32;
let a: Number = 2.3;
let _b: f32 = a;
```

The variable "_b" is of "f32" type and it is initialized by the value of the variable "a", and so they must be of the same type. But "a" is declared to be of the "Number" type, and so "Number" and "f32" must be the same type.

Using the "type" construct has at least two advantages:

- The purpose of a type may become clearer, if you use a meaningful name instead of a primitive type.

- If, in the previous program, you later decide to use everywhere the "f64" type instead of the "f32" type, you need to change only one occurrence, instead of six occurrences.

But the "type" keyword has another important use.

Generic Traits

In a previous chapter, we saw generic functions and generic structs. Well, even a trait can be parameterized by one or more types, if some of its functions need a generic parameter. And type parameterization of a trait can be done in two non-equivalent ways.

Suppose, like shown in the following pseudo-code, that we would like to write a generic function named "is_present", which takes as arguments a generic collection and a numeric search key, and returns whether that key has been found in that collection. To accomplish such function, a generic method named "contains" is invoked on the collection. Such a method is declared as part of the "Searchable" trait, and so, the generic `Collection` type must be bounded to such a trait. But such a trait allows us to perform searches using different types of keys, and so also the trait is generic, having the type of the search key as a generic parameter. In the `"is_present"` function, the trait bound specifies the `"u32"` type as the value of the trait type parameter, because that type will be the one used to search the collection.

```
trait Searchable<Key> {
    fn contains(&self, key: Key) -> bool;
}
fn is_present<Collection>(coll: &Collection, id: u32) -> bool
where Collection: Searchable<u32>
{
    coll.contains(id)
}
```

Here is a complete valid program that uses that algorithm:

```
trait Searchable<Key> {
    fn contains(&self, key: Key) -> bool;
}
struct RecordWithId {
    id: u32,
    _descr: String,
}
struct NameSetWithId {
    data: Vec<RecordWithId>,
}
impl Searchable<u32> for NameSetWithId {
    fn contains(&self, key: u32) -> bool {
        for record in self.data.iter() {
            if record.id == key {
                return true;
            }
        }
        false
    }
}
```

```rust
fn is_present<Collection>(coll: &Collection, id: u32) -> bool
where
    Collection: Searchable<u32>,
{
    coll.contains(id)
}
let names = NameSetWithId {
    data: vec![
        RecordWithId {
            id: 34,
            _descr: "John".to_string(),
        },
        RecordWithId {
            id: 49,
            _descr: "Jane".to_string(),
        },
    ],
};
print!("{} {}", is_present(&names, 48), is_present(&names, 49));
```

It will print: "false true".

After the declaration of the "Searchable" generic trait, two structs are declared: "RecordWithId", representing a data item identified by a unique number; and "NameSetWithId", representing a collection of items having "RecordWithId" type.

Then, the trait is implemented for this collection type. There are two possible ways to implement a generic trait: to keep it generic, by writing something like "impl<T> Searchable<T> for NameSetWithId {"; or to concretize it, by writing something like "impl Searchable<u32> for NameSetWithId {". Here the second way has been chosen, because the following implementation of the "contains" had to be specific not only for the "NameSetWithId" collection type, but also for the "u32" search key type.

After the declaration of the "is_present" function, the collection object is constructed, and at last the "is_present" function is invoked twice; the key 48 is not found in the "names" collection, but the key 49 is found.

This solution works, but is has some drawbacks.

One is this. The needed implementation of the "Searchable" trait had to be specific for the search key type "u32", and so it had to specify it as type parameter value, but in the "where" clause of the "is_present" function declaration, such a type was specified again as a type parameter value. It seems a useless repetition, and a future type change requires a double edit.

But now consider a more complex situation.

```
trait Searchable<Key, Count> {
    fn contains(&self, key: Key) -> bool;
    fn count(&self, key: Key) -> Count;
}
struct RecordWithId {
    id: u32,
    _descr: String,
}
struct NameSetWithId {
    data: Vec<RecordWithId>,
}
impl Searchable<u32, usize> for NameSetWithId {
    fn contains(&self, key: u32) -> bool {
        for record in self.data.iter() {
            if record.id == key {
                return true;
            }
        }
        false
    }
    fn count(&self, key: u32) -> usize {
        let mut c = 0;
        for record in self.data.iter() {
            if record.id == key {
                c += 1;
            }
        }
        c
    }
}
```

```
fn is_present<Collection>(coll: &Collection, id: u32) -> bool
where
    Collection: Searchable<u32, usize>,
{
    coll.contains(id)
}
let names = NameSetWithId {
    data: vec![
        RecordWithId {
            id: 34,
            _descr: "John".to_string(),
        },
        RecordWithId {
            id: 49,
            _descr: "Jane".to_string(),
        },
    ],
};
print!(
    "{}, {}; {} {}",
    names.count(48),
    names.count(49),
    is_present(&names, 48),
    is_present(&names, 49)
);
```

This will print: "0, 1; false true".

Here the "Searchable" generic trait has a new function signature, a new type parameter, needed by such function. Of course, the implementation of such trait for the "NameSetWithId" type must implement also the new function.

What is not so obvious is that the signature of the "is_present" generic function must also specify a type for the new trait parameter. Well, this function does not use at all that type, and so this information is useless here, but required.

Using Associated Types to Simplify Generic Traits Use

Actually, it is typical to write a generic trait and then only a few implementations for it, and to have those implementations that bind some or all the generic parameters for that trait, and then to write many generic functions that bound their generic parameters to that trait. With the above syntax, all those functions are forced to depend on all the generic parameter types that they are not interested in.

A better solution for those cases is shown by the following program, which is equivalent to the previous one:

```
trait Searchable { //1
    type Key; //2
    type Count; //3
    fn contains(&self, key: Self::Key) -> bool; //4
    fn count(&self, key: Self::Key) -> Self::Count; //5
}
struct RecordWithId {
    id: u32,
    _descr: String,
}
struct NameSetWithId {
    data: Vec<RecordWithId>,
}
impl Searchable for NameSetWithId { //6
    type Key = u32; //7
    type Count = usize; //8
    fn contains(&self, key: Self::Key) -> bool { //9
        for record in self.data.iter() {
            if record.id == key {
                return true;
            }
        }
        false
    }
```

```
    fn count(&self, key: Self::Key) -> usize { //10
        let mut c = 0;
        for record in self.data.iter() {
            if record.id == key {
                c += 1;
            }
        }
        c
    }
}
fn is_present<Collection>(
    coll: &Collection,
    id: <Collection as Searchable>::Key,//11
) -> bool
Where
    Collection: Searchable, //12
{
    coll.contains(id)
}
let names = NameSetWithId {
    data: vec![
        RecordWithId {
            id: 34,
            _descr: "John".to_string(),
        },
        RecordWithId {
            id: 49,
            _descr: "Jane".to_string(),
        },
    ],
};
print!(
    "{}, {}; {} {}",
    names.count(48),
    names.count(49),
```

```
    is_present(&names, 48),
    is_present(&names, 49)
);
```

The lines changed with respect to the previous version are marked by a "//" marker.

First (at markers 1, 2, and 3), the "Searchable" trait is no more generic. Its two generic parameters have become associated types, using the "type" keyword, but without a value for such types.

As a consequence, every use of the "Key" and "Count" type parameters inside the trait declaration (at markers 4 and 5) has to be prefixed by "Self::".

Of course, the implementation also has to be changed. It is no more generic (at marker 6), and it has to specify values for the associated types (at markers 7 and 8). Then, optionally, the concrete type "u32" can and should be made more generic, replacing it with an associated type (at markers 9 and 10).

The advantages of all these changes are in the signature of the "is_present" function. First (at marker 11), instead of specifying a concrete type, a reference to the associated type "Key" is specified, and then (at marker 12), there is no more need to specify type parameters for the "Searchable" trait, because it is no more generic.

Let examine deeper the type specification at marker 11. Here, we want to refer to the type name "Key", declared at marker 2 and specified at marker 7. That type name definition was inside a trait block and an implementation block, and so a scope specification is needed. We want to access the "Searchable" trait, when used to bound the "Collection" type, as it is specified at marker 12. To specify such a scope, the syntax is "<type1 as type2>", which in this case is not to be read as "type1 converted to type2", but "type1 restricted to type2".

You can better understand all this if you consider that a data type is in essence the set of operations you can apply on such data. Bounding (or restricting) a type means considering only some of the operations available for that type. So the expression "Collection as Searchable" means "get all the features of the Collection type and consider only those that come from the Searchable trait". Actually the "Collection" type could be bounded to several traits, and several of them could have a "Key" type name. The type expression "<Collection as Searchable>::Key" means "the Key type defined for the Collection type when implementing the Searchable trait".

In this case, all of this mechanism does not seem to give big advantages, but the larger the software base, the bigger the advantages are.

The "**Iterator**" Standard Trait Declaration

About the "Iterator" standard library trait, we said that it contains only one item: the "next" function signature. That's not really true. Think of this: there are iterators that produce numbers, others that produce characters, and others that produce other types. Of course, the "Iterator" trait must be, in some way, generic in the type of the items it produces.

But instead of being a generic trait, it has a "type" item signature. You can think of the "Iterator" standard library trait as defined in this way:

```
trait Iterator {
    type Item;
    fn next(&mut self) -> Option<Self::Item>;
}
```

That definition forces any concrete iterator to define a type for "Item" that represents the type of the produced items, and a function body for "next", that returns the next item, if possible, or "None", if there are no more items to return.

Here is a possible implementation for an iterator over a range of numbers:

```
trait MyIterator {
    type Item;
    fn next(&mut self) -> Option<Self::Item>;
}
struct MyRangeIterator<T> {
    current: T,
    limit: T,
}
impl MyIterator for MyRangeIterator<u32> {
    type Item = u32;
    fn next(&mut self) -> Option<Self::Item> {
        if self.current == self.limit {
            None
        } else {
            self.current += 1;
            Some(self.current - 1)
        }
    }
}
```

```
let mut range_it = MyRangeIterator {
    current: 10,
    limit: 13,
};
print!("{:?}, ", range_it.next());
print!("{:?}, ", range_it.next());
print!("{:?}, ", range_it.next());
print!("{:?}, ", range_it.next());
print!("{:?}, ", range_it.next());
```

This will print: "Some(10), Some(11), Some(12), None, None,".

The "My" prefixes are used to make clear that here the standard library is not used.

First, a trait similar to the "Iterator" standard library trait is defined.

Then, there is a definition of the data structure needed to implement an iterator over a range of numbers.

An iterator should have a current position that will be initialized to point to the first item of a sequence, and that will be incremented at every invocation of "next". This current position is stored in the "current" field.

Moreover, an iterator should be able to detect if there is another item to produce, or if there are no more items. For that purpose, the iterator should be able to query an underlying sequence data structure or should keep a limit inside itself. Our "MyRangeIterator" iterator has no underlying sequence, and therefore it keeps a "limit" field to check if the end of the sequence has been reached.

Then, there is the implementation of the "MyIterator" trait for the "MyRangeIterator<u32>" type. This is a concrete type, and therefore also the implementation is concrete, not generic. As required, the "type" item is specified, and the "next" method has a valid body. This body does what is reasonable: if the current item has reached the limit, "None" is returned; otherwise the current number is incremented, and the value before the increment is returned.

Then, the "range_it" variable is declared. It is an iterator, and like any iterator, it is mutable. It has no sense having an immutable iterator, as we don't want every invocation of "next" to always return the same value or a random value. The state of the iterator must change every time "next" returns a non-None value, and so the iterator must be mutable.

Finally, "next" is invoked five times on our iterator. The first three times, "next" can produce a value, and then, because the iterator has reached its limit, "None" is always produced.

Actually, there is no need to define the "MyIterator" trait, because we can use the "Iterator" standard library trait. Using this standard library trait has the big advantage of being able to use all the iterator adapters and iterator consumers provided by the Rust standard library.

```rust
struct MyRangeIterator<T> {
    current: T,
    limit: T,
}
impl Iterator for MyRangeIterator<u32> {
    type Item = u32;
    fn next(&mut self) -> Option<Self::Item> {
        if self.current == self.limit {
            None
        } else {
            self.current += 1;
            Some(self.current - 1)
        }
    }
}
print!(
    "{:?}; ",
    MyRangeIterator {
        current: 10,
        limit: 13,
    }.collect::<Vec<_>>()
);
for i in (MyRangeIterator {
    current: 20,
    limit: 24,
}) {
    print!("{} ", i);
}
```

This will print: "[10, 11, 12]; 20 21 22 23".

Because our "MyRangeIterator" objects have a type that implements the "Iterator" trait, they can be used with the "collect" iterator consumer, and also in the "for" statement.

Using Generic Iterators

Now, we can go back to the problem presented in the "Standard traits" section of this chapter. We wanted to write a generic function named "get_third", which gets any iterator and returns the third item produced by such iterator, if possible, or otherwise "None".

This problem is solved by this code:

```
fn get_third<Iter>(mut iterator: Iter) -> Option<Iter::Item>
where
    Iter: std::iter::Iterator,
{
    iterator.next();
    iterator.next();
    iterator.next()
}
print!(
    "{:?} {:?} {:?} {:?}",
    get_third(10..12),
    get_third(20..29),
    get_third([31, 32].iter()),
    get_third([41, 42, 43, 44].iter())
);
```

This will print: "None Some(22) None Some(43)".

The "get_third" function gets any mutable iterator as an argument, and so it is a generic function parameterized by the type of such iterator. By getting an iterator type, it is allowed to access its "Item" associated type, and its "next" method. So, we can declare that the value returned by our function has the same type of the value returned by the iterator, which is "Option<Iter::Item>", which inside the iterator implementation is "Option<Self::Item>".

This example was useful to demonstrate how to write a function that gets an iterator as an argument. Yet, actually there is no need for this specific function, as the standard library already contains a function even more generic than that: the "nth" iterator consumer. The following program is equivalent to the previous one:

```
print!(
    "{:?} {:?} {:?} {:?}",
    (10..12).nth(2),
    (20..29).nth(2),
    ([31, 32].iter()).nth(2),
    ([41, 42, 43, 44].iter()).nth(2)
);
```

CHAPTER 19

Object-Oriented Programming

In this chapter, you will learn:

- How to associate functions to types without using traits, with inherent implementations

- How Rust object-orientation differs from C++ object-orientation

- Which traits can be implemented on which types, and which cannot

- How to specify that a method can mutate the object on which it is applied

- Some conventions regarding the methods that construct objects

- Why Rust does not use data inheritance

- What are static dispatch and dynamic dispatch, how they are implemented, and when to use them

Inherent Implementations

In the previous chapter, we saw how to solve the following problem. You have a struct named "Stru", that you want to use for two purposes: as a namespace containing the function f1, to be invoked by the expression "Stru::f1(500_000)"; and for creating an instance of Stru, named "s", on which to invoke the method f2, for example, in the expression "s.f2(456).x".

© Carlo Milanesi 2018
C. Milanesi, *Beginning Rust*, https://doi.org/10.1007/978-1-4842-3468-6_19

A possible solution is this:

```
trait Tr {
    fn f1(a: u32) -> bool;
    fn f2(&self, b: u16) -> Self;
}
struct Stru {
    x: u16,
    y: u16,
}
impl Tr for Stru {
    fn f1(a: u32) -> bool {
        a == 0
    }
    fn f2(&self, b: u16) -> Self {
        if b == self.x || b == self.y {
            Stru {
                x: self.x + 1,
                y: self.y + 1,
            }
        } else {
            Stru {
                x: self.x - 1,
                y: self.y - 1,
            }
        }
    }
}
let s = Stru { x: 23, y: 456 };
print!("{} {}", Stru::f1(500_000), s.f2(456).x);
```

This program will print: false 24.

First, the trait "Tr" is declared, with its two functions' signatures, f1 and f2, and the struct "Stru" is declared; then, the trait Tr is implemented for such struct, by declaring the two functions with their bodies; and finally, the struct is instantiated and the two functions are invoked.

This pattern is so common, that there is a shorthand way to write it. You can equivalently write:

```
struct Stru {
    x: u16,
    y: u16,
}
impl Stru {
    fn f1(a: u32) -> bool {
        a == 0
    }
    fn f2(&self, b: u16) -> Self {
        if b == self.x || b == self.y {
            Stru {
                x: self.x + 1,
                y: self.y + 1,
            }
        } else {
            Stru {
                x: self.x - 1,
                y: self.y - 1,
            }
        }
    }
}
let s = Stru { x: 23, y: 456 };
print!("{} {}", Stru::f1(500_000), s.f2(456).x);
```

In this second program, the trait definition has been removed, and with it the need to invent a trait name; consequently, from the impl statement, the Tr for clause has been removed. Now the impl statement is applied directly to a type, with no need to have a trait. Instead of implementing a trait for a type, now that type has a so-called "inherent" implementation.

For those of you who know the object-oriented programming paradigm, this is that: we have a user-defined type, Stru, with some data members, x and y; and some methods, f1 and f2.

275

The C++ program corresponding to the previous example is this:

```cpp
#include <iostream>
int main() {
    struct Stru {
        unsigned short x;
        unsigned short y;
        static bool f1(unsigned long a) {
            return a == 0;
        }
        Stru f2(unsigned short b) const {
            return b == x || b == y ?
                Stru {
                    (unsigned short)(x + 1),
                    (unsigned short)(y + 1)
                }
                :
                Stru {
                    (unsigned short)(x - 1),
                    (unsigned short)(y - 1)
                }
            ;
        }
    };
    Stru s = { 23, 456 };
    std::cout << std::boolalpha << Stru::f1(500000)
        << " " << s.f2(456).x;
}
```

The corresponding features are the following ones.

Class definitions in object-oriented programming languages contain data definitions and function definitions. Rust separates them. The data definitions are in a `struct` construct, and the function declarations are in an `impl` construct. The `struct` and `impl` constructs combined correspond to a class definition of languages like C++ or Java. The fields of the struct are the data members of the class, and the methods of the `impl` statement are the methods of the class.

In particular, the Rust methods whose argument list begins with a self pseudo-argument are the so-called "object methods" in object-oriented programming, which in C++ are named "non-static member functions", while the Rust methods whose argument list does not begin with a self pseudo-argument are the so-called "class methods" in object-oriented programming, which in C++ are named "static member functions".

Inside an object method, the "self" keyword refers to the current object, like the "self" or "this" keyword of object-oriented languages.

To invoke a method having the self argument, dot notation is used, like in s.f2(456), while to invoke a method without the self argument, the syntax is like Stru::f1(500_000), that is, it requires the name of the type followed by a double-colon, followed by the name of the function.

A difference between Rust and C++ is that when referring to a field of the current object, say x, in Rust you must write self.x, while in C++ and other languages the corresponding expression is this->x, but, if there is no ambiguity, you may write simply x, with the same meaning.

Another difference between Rust and most other object oriented languages is that in those languages the reference to the current object (named self, this, or Me) is always a pointer or a reference. In Rust, if you write &self in the method signature, you get a *reference*, while if you write simply self you get a *copy* of the current object.

Peculiarities of Rust Object-Orientation

But there are other differences between Rust object-oriented programming and other object-oriented languages.

```
S::f2();
impl S { fn f1() { print!("1"); } }
impl S { }
S::f1();
impl S { fn f2() { print!("2"); } fn _f3() {} }
struct S {}
```

This will print: "21".

This code contains some declarations mixed with some executable statements.

The executable statements are in the first and fourth lines. They are executed in the order they appear. First, the f2 function is invoked, and then the f1 function.

The `struct` and `impl` construct can be placed in any point and in any order, provided they are in the same scope. The struct and the function can be defined after they are used. However, usually traits, structs, and functions are used only after their declaration.

In a given scope, there can be only one `struct` S statement. You cannot add other fields to an already-defined struct. Instead, there can be several `impl` S statements. You can "reopen" a struct and add some more methods. In the example, the first `impl` block adds the f1 method, the second block adds nothing, and the third block adds the f2 and _f3 methods.

```
struct S1 {}
struct S2 {}
impl S1 {
    fn f() {}
    //ILLEGAL: fn f(a: i32) {}
}
impl S2 {
    fn f() {}
}
S1::f();
S2::f();
```

In Rust you cannot have several functions having the same name in the same scope. A type creates a scope. Therefore, you cannot have two methods named f for the same type S1, even if such methods have different arguments. Yet, you can declare two methods having the same name for two distinct types, like S1::f and S2::f.

```
enum Continent {
    Africa,
    America,
    Asia,
    Europe,
    Oceania,
}
impl Continent {
    fn name(&self) -> &str {
        match *self {
            Continent::Africa => "Africa",
            Continent::America => "America",
```

```
            Continent::Asia => "Asia",
            Continent::Europe => "Europe",
            Continent::Oceania => "Oceania",
        }
    }
}
print!("{}", Continent::Asia.name());
```

This will print: "Asia".

In Rust, you can add methods not only to structs, but also to any type defined in your code, like enums and tuple-structs.

Regarding primitive types, you cannot directly add methods to them.

```
impl i32 {}
```

For this code, which tries to add something to the i32 primitive type, even if the list of methods is empty, the compiler emits the message: only a single inherent implementation marked with `#[lang = "i32"]` is allowed for the `i32` primitive. That means that the i32 primitive type allows only one implementation of its methods, which is the one provided by the language and the standard library.

And you cannot directly add methods to non-primitive types that are defined in the standard library or in another library.

```
impl Vec<i32> {}
```

For this code, the compiler emits the message cannot define inherent `impl` for a type outside of the crate where the type is defined. A "crate" is a program or a library. The Vec generic type is defined in the standard library. So that error message means that you cannot add methods to Vec in an inherent implementation, that is, without implementing a trait, if your code is outside of the library in which Vec is defined, which is outside of the standard library.

Regarding traits, you cannot implement a trait declared in the standard library or in another library for a type declared in the standard library or in another library.

```
impl std::iter::Iterator for i32 {}
```

For this code, the compiler emits the message only traits defined in the current crate can be implemented for arbitrary types. It means that because the "Iterator" trait has not been declared in your code, and the "i32" type has not been declared in your code, that trait cannot be implemented for that type.

However, any trait defined in your code can be implemented for any type.

```
trait Tr {
    fn f1();
    fn f2(&self);
}
impl Tr for bool {
    fn f1() { print!("Tr::f1 "); }
    fn f2(&self) { print!("Tr::f2 "); }
}
bool::f1();
true.f2();
```

This will print: "Tr::f1 Tr::f2".

And any trait can be implemented for any type defined in your code.

```
struct Pair(u32, u32);
impl std::iter::Iterator for Pair {
    type Item = u32;
    fn next(&mut self) -> Option<Self::Item> {
        None
    }
}
let mut a = Pair(23u32, 34u32);
print!("{:?}", a.next());
```

This will print: "None".

First the "Pair" type is defined. Then, the "Iterator" trait, declared in the standard library, is implemented for the "Pair" type. Such implementation is extremely simple: its "next" method returns always "None".

Then, an object of "Pair" type is allocated. And finally, the "next" function is invoked on this object that qualifies as an iterator, even if we know it does not iterate in any sense.

Summarizing, if "Ty" is a type, the clause "impl Ty" is allowed only if "Ty" is declared in the current crate; and, as shown by the following table, if "Tr" is a trait, the clause "impl Tr for Ty" is allowed if "Tr" *or* "Ty" is declared in the current crate, and it is not allowed only if both "Tr" *and* "Ty" are part of the language, the standard library or another library.

	The "Tr" trait is declared in THE CURRENT crate	The "Tr" trait is declared in ANOTHER crate
The "Ty" type is declared in THE CURRENT crate	"impl Tr for Ty" is allowed	"impl Tr for Ty" is allowed
The "Ty" type is declared in ANOTHER crate	"impl Tr for Ty" is allowed	"impl Tr for Ty" is ILLEGAL

Mutating Methods

In Rust, everything that does not contain the mut keyword is immutable. That holds also for the self pseudo-argument. If you want to change the object to which a method is applied, you have to add a mut keyword.

```
struct S { x: u32 }
impl S {
    fn get_x(&self) -> u32 { self.x }
    fn set_x(&mut self, x: u32) { self.x = x; }
}
let mut s = S { x: 12 };
print!("{} ", s.get_x());
s.set_x(17);
print!("{} ", s.get_x());
```

This will print: "12 17".

The equivalent C++ program is the following one:

```
#include <iostream>
int main() {
    struct S {
        unsigned long x;
        unsigned long get_x() const { return x; }
        void set_x(unsigned long x) { this->x = x; }
    };
```

```
    S s = { 12 };
    std::cout << s.get_x() << " ";
    s.set_x(17);
    std::cout << s.get_x() << " ";
}
```

Notice that for the get_x method, where in Rust self has no mut keyword, C++ has a const keyword at the end of the signature; and for the set_x method, where in Rust self has a mut keyword, C++ has no const keyword.

Constructors

Every time we needed a struct object, we had to specify the values of all its fields.

This is contrary to data abstraction principles, according to which any type should have an interface independent of its implementation.

To allow the handling of an object in a way independent of its implementation, some languages provide specific features named "constructors". Instead, in Rust, it is enough to provide one or more methods that don't take "self" as an argument and having "Self" as the return value type. Therefore, such methods are commonly named *constructors*. There isn't a specific syntax for Rust constructors, but there are some conventions.

```
struct Number {
    x: f64,
}
impl Number {
    fn new() -> Number { Number { x: 0. } }
    fn from(x: f64) -> Number { Number { x: x } }
    fn value(&self) -> f64 { self.x }
}
let a = Number::new();
let b = Number::from(2.3);
print!("{} {}", a.value(), b.value());
```

This will print: "0 2.3". The "new" and "from" methods are constructors. By convention, a constructor without arguments is named "new", and a constructor with one argument is named "from". However, often there are several constructors with one argument; in such case, only one of them, or none at all, is named "from".

You can find instances of this convention in the standard library:

```
let a = String::new();
let b = String::from("abcd");
print!("({}) ({});", a, b);
let c = Vec::<i32>::new();
let d = Vec::<u8>::from("abcd");
print!(" {:?} {:?}", c, d);
```

This will print: `"() (abcd); [] [97, 98, 99, 100]"`. The `"a"` variable is initialized by a dynamic empty string; the `"b"` variable is initialized by a dynamic string created by copying a static string; the `"c"` variable is an empty vector of integers; and the `"d"` variable is a byte vector created by copying the contents of a static string.

Composition Instead of Inheritance

At the beginning of the object-oriented programming era, inheritance appeared as a panacea, which is a technique that could be applied to any problem. In fact, there are three kinds of inheritance: data inheritance, method implementation inheritance, and method interface inheritance. As years went by, it was realized that data inheritance created more problems than the ones it solved, and so Rust does not support it. In place of data inheritance, Rust uses composition.

Let's assume we already have a type representing a text to draw on the graphical screen, and we want to create a type representing a text surrounded by a rectangle. For simplicity, instead of drawing the text, we will print it on the console, and instead of drawing the rectangle, we will surround the text in brackets:

```
struct Text { characters: String }
impl Text {
    fn from(text: &str) -> Text {
        Text { characters: text.to_string() }
    }
    fn draw(&self) {
        print!("{}", self.characters);
    }
}
```

```
let greeting = Text::from("Hello");
greeting.draw();

struct BoxedText {
    text: Text,
    first: char,
    last: char,
}
impl BoxedText {
    fn with_text_and_borders(
        text: &str, first: char, last: char)
        -> BoxedText
    {
        BoxedText {
            text: Text::from(text),
            first: first,
            last: last,
        }
    }
    fn draw(&self) {
        print!("{}", self.first);
        self.text.draw();
        print!("{}", self.last);
    }
}
let boxed_greeting =
    BoxedText::with_text_and_borders("Hi", '[', ']');
print!(", ");
boxed_greeting.draw();
```

This will print: "Hello [Hi]".

The first statement defines a struct representing a text, characterized only by the string that contains its characters.

The second statement defines two methods for this struct: "from", which is a constructor; and "draw", which prints the string contained in the object. Having only this, we can create a Text object, and we can draw it using such a method.

Now assume that you want to capitalize on this struct and its associated methods to create a text enclosed in a box, represented by a struct named "BoxedText". That is what inheritance usually is touted for.

In Rust, instead of using inheritance, you create a "BoxedText" struct that *contains* an object of "Text" type, and some additional fields. In this case, there are two fields representing the character to print before and after the base text.

Then, you declare the implementation of the methods you want to encapsulate in the "BoxedText" type, or to apply to objects of "BoxedText" type. They are a constructor, named "with_text_and_borders"; and a function to draw the current object, named "draw".

The constructor gets all the information it needs and initializes a new object with that information. In particular, the field having type "Text" is initialized by invoking the "from" constructor of "Text".

The method to draw the current object has the same signature of the similar method associated to "Text" objects, but this is just a coincidence, due to the fact that such methods do similar things. They could have different names, different argument types, or different return value types. The body of this "draw" function, though, contains an invocation of the "draw" function of "Text".

Finally, an object having type "BoxedText" is created, and its method "draw" is invoked, having as a result that the string "[Hi]" is printed.

In this program, re-use happens in the following places:

- The first field of "struct BoxedText" is "text: Text". It re-uses that data structure.

- The constructor of "BoxedText" contains the expression "Text::from(text)". It re-uses the constructor of the "Text" type.

- The body of the "draw" method of the "BoxedText" type contains the statement "self.text.draw();". It re-uses the "draw" method associated to the "Text" type.

Memory Usage of Composition

There is no difference between the memory usage of composition and that of inheritance. They both use just the needed memory:

```
struct Base1 {
    _x: f64
}
struct Base2 {}
struct Derived1 {
    _b1: Base1,
    _b2: Base2,
}
struct Derived2 {
    _d1: Derived1,
    _other: f64,
}
use std::mem::size_of;
print!("{} {} {} {}",
    size_of::<Base1>(), size_of::<Base2>(),
    size_of::<Derived1>(), size_of::<Derived2>());
```

This will print: "8 0 8 16". "Base1" is a struct containing only an 8-byte number, and it occupies 8 bytes; "Base2" is a struct containing nothing, and it occupies 0 bytes; "Derived1" is a struct containing two structs, one large 8 bytes and the other large 0 bytes, and it occupies 8 bytes; finally, "Derived2" is a struct containing a struct large 8 bytes and an 8-byte number, and it occupies 16 bytes. We can say that memory is used as efficiently as possible.

Static Dispatch

Two sections ago, we saw how to define the "Text" and "BoxedText" types so that the latter re-uses some data and code written for the former.

Now assume you need to write a function capable of drawing several kinds of text objects. In particular, if it receives as an argument an object of "Text" type, it should invoke the "draw" method associated with the "Text" type, while if it receives as argument an object of "BoxedText" type, it should invoke the "draw" method associated to the "BoxedText" type.

If Rust were a dynamically typed language, this function would be:

```
fn draw_text(txt) {
    txt.draw();
}
```

Of course, this is not allowed in Rust, because the type of the txt argument must be specified explicitly.

Rust allows two non-equivalent solutions for this problem. One is this:

```
trait Draw {
    fn draw(&self);
}

struct Text { characters: String }
impl Text {
    fn from(text: &str) -> Text {
        Text { characters: text.to_string() }
    }
}
impl Draw for Text {
    fn draw(&self) {
        print!("{}", self.characters);
    }
}

struct BoxedText {
    text: Text,
    first: char,
    last: char,
}
impl BoxedText {
    fn with_text_and_borders(
        text: &str, first: char, last: char)
        -> BoxedText
```

```
        {
            BoxedText {
                text: Text::from(text),
                first: first,
                last: last,
            }
        }
    }
}
impl Draw for BoxedText {
    fn draw(&self) {
        print!("{}", self.first);
        self.text.draw();
        print!("{}", self.last);
    }
}

let greeting = Text::from("Hello");
let boxed_greeting =
    BoxedText::with_text_and_borders("Hi", '[', ']');

// SOLUTION 1 //
fn draw_text<T>(txt: T) where T: Draw {
    txt.draw();
}
draw_text(greeting);
print!(", ");
draw_text(boxed_greeting);
```

This will print: "Hello, [Hi]".

The last three lines are the ones that print the resulting text. The "draw_text(greeting)" statement receives an object having type "Text" and prints "Hello"; and the "draw_text(boxed_greeting)" statement receives an object having type "BoxedText" and prints "[Hi]". Such a generic function is defined just before. These last six lines are the first solution to the problem. The preceding part of the program is in common with the second solution.

But let's start to examine this program from the beginning.

First, the "Draw" trait is declared, as the capability of an object to be drawn.

Then the "Text" and "BoxedText" types are declared, with their associated methods, similarly to the example of the "Composition instead of inheritance" section, but only the two constructors "Text::from" and "BoxedText::with_text_and_borders" are kept as inherent implementations; the two "draw" functions, instead, now are implementations of the Draw trait.

Regarding the previous example, we said that the two "draw" methods had the same signature by coincidence, and they could have different signatures just as well. In this last example, instead, this equality is no more a coincidence; such functions are now used to implement the Draw trait, and so they must have the same signature of the function contained in such a trait.

After having declared the struct types, with their associated functions, the two variables "greeting" and "boxed_greeting" are created and initialized, one for each of those types.

And then there is the first solution. The "draw_text" generic function receives an argument of "T" type, where "T" is any type that implements the "Draw" trait. Because of this, it is allowed to invoke the "draw" function on that argument.

So, whenever the compiler encounters an invocation of the "draw_text" function, it determines the type of the argument, and checks if such type implements the "Draw" trait. In case that trait is not implemented, a compilation error is generated. Otherwise, a concretized version of the "draw_text" function is generated, in which the "T" type is replaced by the type of the argument, and the invocation of the "draw" generic method in the body of the function is replaced by an invocation of the implementation of "draw" for the type of the argument.

This technique is named *"static dispatch"*. In computer science, *"dispatch"* means choosing which function to invoke when there are several functions with the same name. In this program there are two functions named "draw", and so a dispatch is required to choose between them. In this program, this choice is performed by the compiler, at compile time, and so this dispatch is "static".

Dynamic Dispatch

The previous program can be changed a little, by replacing the last seven lines with the following ones:

```
// SOLUTION 1/bis //
fn draw_text<T>(txt: &T) where T: Draw {
    txt.draw();
}
draw_text(&greeting);
print!(", ");
draw_text(&boxed_greeting);
```

This version has substantially the same behavior of the previous version. Now, the "draw_function" receives its argument by reference, and so an "&" character has been added in its signature, and other two "&" characters have been added where this function is invoked.

This solution is still a case of static dispatch. So, we see that static dispatch can work both with pass-by-value and with pass-by-reference.

The previous program can be changed further, by replacing the last seven lines with the following ones:

```
// SOLUTION 2 //
fn draw_text(txt: &Draw) {
    txt.draw();
}
draw_text(&greeting);
print!(", ");
draw_text(&boxed_greeting);
```

Also this program has the same external behavior than before, but this uses another kind of technique. Only the "draw_text" signature has been changed. The "T" generic parameter has been removed, the "where" clause has been removed, and the argument has type "&Draw" instead of "&T". So now, instead of a generic function, we have a concrete function, which gets as argument a reference to a trait.

That is something new. A trait is not a type. You cannot declare a variable or a function argument having a trait as type. But a reference to a trait is a valid type. However, it is not an ordinary reference.

In the first place, if it were an ordinary reference, it would be forbidden to pass a reference to "Text" or a reference to "BoxedText" as an argument of a function expecting a reference to "Draw"; instead, it is allowed. Consider this:

```
trait Tr {}
impl Tr for bool {}
let _a: &Tr = &true;
```

Here, the "bool" type implements the "Tr" trait, and so "&true", that is a reference to a value having type "bool", can be used to initialize "_a", that is a reference to "Tr".

Instead, this is not valid:

```
trait Tr {}
let _a: &Tr = &true;
```

Here, the "bool" type does not implement the "Tr" trait, and so "&true", which is a reference to a value having type "bool", cannot be used to initialize a reference to "Tr".

In general, any reference to a "T" type can be used to initialize a reference to a trait implemented by "T". Passing an argument to a function is a kind of initialization, and so any reference to a "T" type can be passed as a function argument where a reference to a trait implemented by "T" is expected.

In the second place, if "&Draw" were an ordinary pointer, and "txt" were of such type, the expression "txt.draw()" would invoke the same function, independently of the object referred to by the "txt" name. Instead we need a dispatch, which is we need that when "draw_text" receives a "Text", the "draw" method associated with the "Text" type is invoked, and when "draw_text" receives a "BoxedText", the "draw" method associated with the "BoxedText" type is invoked. And this is exactly what actually happens.

So, "&Draw" is not an ordinary pointer, but a pointer capable of choosing the right method to invoke, according to the type of the referred object. This is a kind of dispatch, but it happens at runtime, and so it is a "dynamic dispatch".

Dynamic dispatch is handled in C++ by using the "virtual" keyword, albeit with a slightly different mechanism.

Implementation of References to Traits

Get back to the program showing the solutions to the dispatch problem, and replace the last seven lines (from the one starting with "// SOLUTION") with the following code:

```
use std::mem::size_of_val;
print!("{} {} {}, {} {} {}, ",
    size_of_val(&greeting),
    size_of_val(&&greeting),
    size_of_val(&&&greeting),
    size_of_val(&boxed_greeting),
    size_of_val(&&boxed_greeting),
    size_of_val(&&&boxed_greeting));
fn draw_text(txt: &Draw) {
    print!("{} {} {} ",
        size_of_val(txt),
        size_of_val(&txt),
        size_of_val(&&txt));
    txt.draw();
}
draw_text(&greeting);
print!(", ");
draw_text(&boxed_greeting);
```

The resulting program, in a 64-bit target, will print: "24 8 8, 32 8 8, 24 16 8 Hello, 32 16 8 [Hi]".

Remember that the "size_of_val" standard library generic function gets a reference to an object of any type, and returns the size in bytes of that object.

First, the "greeting" variable is processed. Its type is the "Text" struct, which contains only a "String" object. We already discovered that "String" objects occupy 24 bytes in the stack, plus a variable buffer in the heap. Such buffer is not taken into account by the "size_of_val" function. The "size_of_val" function requires a reference, and so the expression "size_of_val(greeting)" would be illegal.

Then the size of a reference to a "Text" is printed, and then the size of a reference to a reference to a "Text". They are ordinary references, and so they occupy 8 bytes.

Then, the "boxed_greeting" variable is processed in the same way. This struct contains a "Text" and two "char" objects. Each "char" occupies 4 bytes, and so it is 24 + 4 + 4 = 32 bytes. Its references are normal references too.

Then the expression "&greeting", having type "&Text", is passed as an argument to the "draw_text" function, where it is used to initialize the argument "txt", having type "&Draw".

The "txt" argument is a kind of reference, and so it is possible to evaluate the expression "size_of_val(txt)". It will return the size of the referred object. But which type has the object referenced to by an object of type "&Draw"? Of course, it is not "Draw", because "Draw" is not a type. Actually, this cannot be said at compile time. It depends on the object referenced at runtime by the expression used to initialize the "txt" argument. The first time that the "draw_text" function is invoked, the "txt" argument receives a reference to a "Text" object, and so 24 is printed.

If you jump forward in the output, going after the comma, you see that the second time that the "draw_text" function is invoked, the "txt" argument receives a reference to a "BoxedText" object, and so 32 is printed.

Going back to the invocation using "greeting", we see that the value of the expression "size_of_val(&txt)" is 16. That is strange. This expression is the size of an object having type "&Draw", initialized by an object having type "&Text". So we use a normal 8-byte reference to initialize a 16-byte reference to a trait. Why is a reference to a trait so large? The mechanism of dynamic dispatch lies in how a reference to a trait is initialized.

Actually any reference to a trait has two fields. The first one is a copy of the reference used to initialize it, and the second one is a pointer used to choose the proper version of the "draw" function, or any other function needing dynamic dispatch. It is named a "virtual table pointer". This name comes from C++.

At last, the size of a reference to a reference to a trait is printed. This is a normal reference, occupying 8 bytes.

The same numbers are printed for the references to the "boxed_greeting" variable.

Static vs. Dynamic Dispatch

So you can use static or dynamic dispatch. Which should you use?

Like any instance of static-vs-dynamic dilemma, where "static" means "compile-time", and "dynamic" means "run-time", static requires a somewhat longer compilation time, and generates somewhat faster code, but if not enough information is available to the compiler, the dynamic solution is the only possible one.

Assume that, for the example program showed before the solutions to the dispatch problem, there is the following requirement. The user is asked to enter a string, and if that string is "b", a boxed text should be printed, and for any other input a non-boxed text should be printed.

Using the static dispatch, the final part of the program becomes:

```
// SOLUTION 1/ter //
fn draw_text<T>(txt: T) where T: Draw {
    txt.draw();
}
let mut input = String::new();
std::io::stdin().read_line(&mut input).unwrap();
if input.trim() == "b" {
    draw_text(boxed_greeting);
} else {
    draw_text(greeting);
}
```

While using the dynamic dispatch, you have:

```
// SOLUTION 2/bis //
fn draw_text(txt: &Draw) {
    txt.draw();
}
let mut input = String::new();
std::io::stdin().read_line(&mut input).unwrap();
let dr: &Draw = if input.trim() == "b" {
    &boxed_greeting
} else {
    &greeting
};
draw_text(dr);
```

The static dispatch requires you to write several function invocations, while the dynamic dispatch allows you to save in the "dr" variable the object chosen by the user, and then write just one function invocation for it.

In addition, static dispatch uses generic functions, and this technique may create code bloat, and so it may end up being slower.

CHAPTER 20

Standard Library Collections

In this chapter, you will learn:

- How to measure the time spent running portions of Rust code

- How performance reasons suggest the use of several kinds of collections

- Which is the best collection for various kinds of operations: sequential scan, insertion and removal of items at both ends, removal of the largest item, search, search by key, keeping items sorted

Collections

Arrays, vectors, structs, tuple-structs, tuples, and enums are data types whose objects may contain several other objects. However, for structs, tuple-structs, tuples, and enums, for each contained object a specific clause must be specified both in the type declaration and in the object construction, and so they are not usable to contain hundreds of objects. Instead, arrays and vectors are data types that may contain many objects, even if they are defined and instantiated with simple formulas. The objects of such kinds are named "collections".

Arrays and vectors are optimal collections in many cases: they use memory efficiently, they are fast to scan, they use CPU caches efficiently, and they allow fast direct access through an integer offset (or index). Yet, for some operations, they are definitely inefficient, and so in such cases it is appropriate to use other kinds of collections. And the Rust standard library provides various kinds of them: VecDeque<T>, LinkedList<T>, BinaryHeap<T>, BTreeSet<T>, BTreeMap<K,V>, HashSet<T>, and HashMap<K,V>.

© Carlo Milanesi 2018
C. Milanesi, *Beginning Rust*, https://doi.org/10.1007/978-1-4842-3468-6_20

Speaking of collections, arrays are a separate case, because they are entirely stack-allocated, and they have a size defined at compile time. All the other collections, including vectors, contain a variable number of items, and they store a fixed-length header in the stack, while the data, if there is some, is allocated in the heap. We will name them "dynamically-sized collections".

Measuring Execution Time

Because the choice of a collection depends much on its performance, here we take a detour, where we see how we can measure with precision the time spent by different portions of Rust code.

Performance is important for all software developers. However, those who program in a high-level language typically reason about how many milliseconds or how many seconds are spent by a command, while those who program in a low-level language, like Rust, often reason about how many microseconds or even nanoseconds are spent by a single function.

In the Rust standard library, there are functions that can measure precisely the time elapsed between two source code points:

```
use std::time::Instant;
fn elapsed_ms(t1: Instant, t2: Instant) -> f64 {
    let t = t2 - t1;
    t.as_secs() as f64 * 1000.
        + t.subsec_nanos() as f64 / 1e6
}

let time0 = Instant::now();
for i in 0..10_000 {
    println!("{}", i);
}
let time1 = Instant::now();
println!("{}", elapsed_ms(time0, time1));
```

This program first will print all the integer numbers from 0 to 9999, and then it will print the number of milliseconds spent to print such numbers.

Of course, such time depends on the power of the computer used, on the operating system, on the terminal emulator program, but also on the optimization level used by the Rust compiler.

Indeed, at the beginning of the book we saw that to compile a Rust program it was enough to write the "rustc" command, followed by the name of the source file, with no need of any other argument. Yet, such a command does not activate the compiler optimizations, and so it generates machine code that is good for debugging, but not as efficient as it could be.

If you are interested in performance, you should activate the compiler optimizations. These are activated using the command-line option "-O" (it's a letter, not a zero). If such option is omitted, every optimization is disabled.

Therefore, in this chapter it is assumed that the examples are compiled by the following command line:

```
rustc -O main.rs
```

If you get back to the previous example, you will notice that first the "elapsed_ms" function has been defined. It receives two arguments having "Instant" type, which represent time instants, and it returns the number of milliseconds elapsed from the first instant to the second one.

In all of this chapter, it is assumed that every program begins with such a function definition, which for brevity will not be repeated in the examples.

To measure a time, you should invoke the "now" function of the "Instant" type. This type is part of the Rust standard library. Every invocation of "now" returns the current time instant. Then, if you invoke the "elapsed_ms" function and pass to it two instants, you get the time span between them in milliseconds and millisecond fractions.

Performing Arbitrary Insertions and Removals

Now let's get back to the operations on the collections.

The following program is very efficient:

```
const SIZE: usize = 100_000_000;
let t0 = Instant::now();
let mut v = Vec::<usize>::with_capacity(SIZE);
let t1 = Instant::now();
```

```
for i in 0..SIZE {
    v.push(i);
}
let t2 = Instant::now();
for _ in 0..SIZE {
    v.pop();
}
let t3 = Instant::now();
print!("{} {} {}", elapsed_ms(t0, t1),
    elapsed_ms(t1, t2), elapsed_ms(t2, t3));
```

Remember to add the declaration of the "elapsed_ms" function, and to compile specifying the option "-O".

This program will print three numbers that depend on the computer, on the operating system, and possibly even on the version of the compiler.

A possible result is: "0.002667 454.516057 87.302678".

That means that to create a vector that allocates room for one hundred million "usize" objects, which in a 64-bit system occupy 800 MB, less than three microseconds are spent; to put one hundred million values in such space, without ever allocating memory, less than half a second is spent, and to remove all such numbers, one at a time, proceeding from the last one, less than one-tenth of a second is spent.

Instead, the following program is very *inefficient*:

```
const SIZE: usize = 100_000;
let t0 = Instant::now();
let mut v = Vec::<usize>::with_capacity(SIZE);
let t1 = Instant::now();
for i in 0..SIZE {
    v.insert(0, i);
}
let t2 = Instant::now();
for _ in 0..SIZE {
    v.remove(0);
}
let t3 = Instant::now();
print!("{} {} {}", elapsed_ms(t0, t1),
    elapsed_ms(t1, t2), elapsed_ms(t2, t3));
```

It could print: "0.00178 2038.879344 2029.447851".

First of all, notice that this time only one hundred thousand items are processed, which is one-thousandth of those processed by the previous example.

To create the 800KB-large vector, less than two microseconds are spent, but to insert one hundred thousand items from the beginning of the vector, more than 2 seconds are spent, and as many seconds are spent to remove them by proceeding from the first one. So, such an insertion operation appears to be more than four thousand times slower than that of the previous example, and such a deletion operation appears to be more than twenty thousand times slower than that of the previous example.

The reason of such times is easy to explain.

To add an item at the end of a vector having enough capacity, all you need to do is to check that there is enough space, to copy the item into the vector buffer, and to increment the item count. That, for a usize, in the computer used to measure those times, takes less than five nanoseconds, including the time to move the iterator to the next item.

To remove an item from the end of a non-empty vector, all you need to do is to check that the vector is not empty, and to decrement the item count. That takes less than one nanosecond.

Instead, to insert an item at the beginning of a vector, first you need to translate by one place all the items already in the vector, to free the first place for the new item. At the start of the loop, such translation is fast, but as the item count grows, the time spent to insert an item at the beginning of the vector grows as much.

Similarly, to remove the first item, you must translate all the items but the first one, which will be overwritten by the second item.

Using the notation of the theory of computational complexity, we can say that the insertion and removal of an item at the end of a vector have a $O(K)$ complexity, which is *constant complexity*, while the insertion and the removal of an item at the beginning of a vector already containing N items have $O(N)$ complexity, which is *linear complexity*.

If the insertions and the removals are not really at the beginning, but in an intermediate position, the performance will be better, but still much slower than insertion and removal at the end.

Queues

If you need to insert and remove items only at the beginning of a vector, it is enough to redesign the vector in inverted order, so that such operations will be applied at the end.

Instead, if you need to insert or remove items both at the beginning and at the end, the vector type is not the optimal collection. A typical case is that of a queue, in which items are inserted at the end and are extracted from the beginning (or vice versa):

```
const SIZE: usize = 40_000;
let t0 = Instant::now();
let mut v = Vec::<usize>::new();
for i in 0..SIZE {
    v.push(i);
    v.push(SIZE + i);
    v.remove(0);
    v.push(SIZE * 2 + i);
    v.remove(0);
}
let t1 = Instant::now();
while v.len() > 0 {
    v.remove(0);
}
let t2 = Instant::now();
print!("{} {}", elapsed_ms(t0, t1), elapsed_ms(t1, t2));
```

This could print: "561.189636 276.056133".

The first timed code portion creates an empty vector, and then, for forty thousand times, it inserts three numbers at the end of the vector, and it extracts two items from the beginning. The second code portion extracts from the beginning all the remaining items. The first portion spends about half a second, and the second portion about a quarter of a second. Actually, almost all the time is spent for the extractions, because insertions are extremely fast.

We could try to insert always at the beginning and extract at the end:

```
const SIZE: usize = 40_000;
let t0 = Instant::now();
let mut v = Vec::<usize>::new();
```

```
for i in 0..SIZE {
    v.insert(0, i);
    v.insert(0, SIZE + i);
    v.pop();
    v.insert(0, SIZE * 2 + i);
    v.pop();
}
let t1 = Instant::now();
while v.len() > 0 {
    v.pop();
}
let t2 = Instant::now();
print!("{} {}", elapsed_ms(t0, t1), elapsed_ms(t1, t2));
```

This could print: "790.365012 0.000112".

Now the insertions are slow, and the removals spend virtually zero time. Indeed, the second portion, containing only removals, spends a few nanoseconds.

However, the sum of the two times hasn't improved much.

Now, instead of the "Vec" type, let's use the "VecDeque" type:

```
const SIZE: usize = 40_000;
let t0 = Instant::now();
let mut vd = std::collections::VecDeque::<usize>::new();
for i in 0..SIZE {
    vd.push_back(i);
    vd.push_back(SIZE + i);
    vd.pop_front();
    vd.push_back(SIZE * 2 + i);
    vd.pop_front();
}
let t1 = Instant::now();
while vd.len() > 0 {
    vd.pop_front();
}
let t2 = Instant::now();
print!("{} {}", elapsed_ms(t0, t1), elapsed_ms(t1, t2));
```

This could print: "0.40793 0.050257".

The difference from the previous times is abysmal. Indeed, the whole program spends less than half a millisecond, compared with the around 800 milliseconds spent by the version using a vector.

Notice that while the "Vec" type is automatically imported in the current namespace, the "VecDeque" type, like the types of the other collections, must be explicitly qualified.

The "VecDeque" name is a shorthand for "vector-like double-ended queue". The "queue" word means "sequential collection into which items are inserted at one end and from which items are extracted at the other end". The fact of being "double-ended" means that the items can be inserted at both ends and extracted from both ends, with no penalty. Finally, the fact of being "vector-like" means that it can be accessed by an integer offset, similarly to arrays and vectors.

To insert or remove items at the end of a vector, you can use the simple words "push" and "pop", without specifying the point of insertion or extraction, since it is understood that such point is the end, which is the only point where such operations are mostly efficient. Instead, because queues handle equally well both ends, the recommended functions to insert items are "push_front" and "push_back", respectively, to insert at the beginning and at the end, while the recommended functions to remove items are "pop_front" and "pop_back", respectively to remove from the beginning and from the end. Also the "VecDeque" type supports the "insert" and "remove" functions, but such functions are not recommended because, similarly to vectors, they can be inefficient.

Given that queues are so efficient, why shouldn't we use that always, instead of vectors?

The reason is that for the most frequent operations on vectors, which are iteration and direct access, vectors are faster by a constant factor.

```
const SIZE: usize = 40_000;
let mut v = Vec::<usize>::new();
let mut vd = std::collections::VecDeque::<usize>::new();
let t0 = Instant::now();
for i in 0..SIZE {
    v.push(i);
}
let t1 = Instant::now();
for i in 0..SIZE {
    vd.push_back(i);
}
```

```
let mut count = 0;
let t2 = Instant::now();
for i in v.iter() {
    count += i;
}
let t3 = Instant::now();
for i in vd.iter() {
    count += i;
}
let t4 = Instant::now();
print!("{} {} {} {} {}", count,
    elapsed_ms(t0, t1), elapsed_ms(t1, t2),
    elapsed_ms(t2, t3), elapsed_ms(t3, t4));
```

This could print: "1599960000 0.230073 0.203979 0.013144 0.035295".

This means that to insert each item at the end of a collection, the Vec and the VecDeque collection types have almost the same performance, with a small advantage for "VecDeque", but for scanning the whole collection, "Vec" is more than twice as fast.

Linked Lists

For some applications, there is the need to frequently insert and remove items in intermediate positions. In such cases, both vectors and queues perform such operations inefficiently, and so, if you have such a need, you can resort to another kind of collection, LinkedList.

However, if you need to do a bulk operation on a collection, like adding or removing or moving many items, it is faster to use a Vec or a VecDeque, and create a new temporary collection, and then replace the original collection with the temporary one.

The usage of a LinkedList should be confined to the rare cases in which insertions and deletions in intermediate positions are about as frequent as read accesses.

Binary Heaps

There can be another way to access a collection, the so-called "priority queue". It happens when only two functions are used: one to insert an item and one to extract it, but every item has a priority value, and the function to extract an item must get the item with the highest value among the items contained in the collection. Using vectors, you could obtain that behavior with this code:

```
fn add(v: &mut Vec<i32>, a: i32) {
    v.push(a);
    v.sort();
}
let a = [48, 18, 20, 35, 17, 13, 39,
    12, 42, 33, 29, 27, 50, 16];
let mut v = Vec::<i32>::new();
for i in 0..a.len() / 2 {
    add(&mut v, a[i * 2]);
    add(&mut v, a[i * 2 + 1]);
    print!("{} ", v.pop().unwrap());
}
while ! v.is_empty() {
    print!("{} ", v.pop().unwrap());
}
```

This will print: "48 35 20 39 42 33 50 29 27 18 17 16 13 12".

The "a" array is used as a number provider. Its 14 numbers are processed, two each iteration, in the 7 iterations of the first loop. At each iteration, two numbers of the array are passed to the add function, which inserts the items into the vector. Then, the last item is extracted from the vector and printed. The last statement of the program extracts and prints repeatedly the last items of the vector, until the vector becomes empty.

Each time a value is added to the vector, the vector is sorted again, so that the values are always in ascending order. This guarantees that the extracted value is always the largest among those contained in the collection.

The same result can be obtained, still using a vector, if the vector is sorted just before any extraction:

```
fn extract(v: &mut Vec<i32>) -> Option<i32> {
    v.sort();
    v.pop()
}
let a = [48, 18, 20, 35, 17, 13, 39,
    12, 42, 33, 29, 27, 50, 16];
let mut v = Vec::<i32>::new();
for i in 0..a.len() / 2 {
    v.push(a[i * 2]);
    v.push(a[i * 2 + 1]);
    print!("{} ", extract(&mut v).unwrap());
}
while ! v.is_empty() {
    print!("{} ", extract(&mut v).unwrap());
}
```

Both versions have the drawback of invoking quite often the "sort" function, which has a significant cost.

The following version is equivalent and much faster:

```
let a = [48, 18, 20, 35, 17, 13, 39,
    12, 42, 33, 29, 27, 50, 16];
let mut v = std::collections::BinaryHeap::<i32>::new();
for i in 0..a.len() / 2 {
    v.push(a[i * 2]);
    v.push(a[i * 2 + 1]);
    print!("{} ", v.pop().unwrap());
}
while ! v.is_empty() {
    print!("{} ", v.pop().unwrap());
}
```

As you can see, binary heaps are used by invoking the "push" and "pop" functions, similarly to vectors, but while in these last collections the "pop" function extracts the last inserted item among those still contained in the collection, in binary heaps the "pop" function extracts the item having the largest value among those still contained in the collection.

Regarding the implementation, here we can say that both when an item is added and when an item is removed, some items are moved, so that the last item is always the largest; instead, the other items are not necessarily sorted.

Ordered Sets and Unordered Sets

Another way to use a collection is to insert an item only if it is not already contained in the collection. That realizes the concept of mathematical set. Indeed, in mathematics it has no sense to say that an item is contained several times in a set.

A way to implement this kind of insertion using a vector would be to scan the whole vector at every insertion, and insert the item only if it is not found. Of course, such an algorithm would be inefficient.

There are several techniques to create a collection that inserts efficiently an item only if it is not already contained, which is a collection that implements the concept of a set without duplicates.

The most efficient technique to store arbitrary objects uses a kind of data structure named "hashtable", and so, such a type of collection is named "HashSet".

However, such a collection has the drawback that its items are not sorted. If you need sorted items, you can use a collection using a data structure named "B-tree", and therefore it is named BTreeSet:

```
let arr = [6, 8, 2, 8, 4, 9, 6, 1, 8, 0];
let mut v = Vec::<_>::new();
let mut hs = std::collections::HashSet::<_>::new();
let mut bs = std::collections::BTreeSet::<_>::new();
for i in arr.iter() {
    v.push(i);
    hs.insert(i);
    bs.insert(i);
}
```

```
print!("Vec:");
for i in v.iter() { print!(" {}", i); }
println!(". {:?}", v);
print!("HashSet :");
for i in hs.iter() { print!(" {}", i); }
println!(". {:?}", hs);
print!("BTreeSet:");
for i in bs.iter() { print!(" {}", i); }
println!(". {:?}", bs);
```

This could print:

```
Vec: 6 8 2 8 4 9 6 1 8 0. [6, 8, 2, 8, 4, 9, 6, 1, 8, 0]
HashSet : 8 2 9 6 4 0 1. {8, 2, 9, 6, 4, 0, 1}
BTreeSet: 0 1 2 4 6 8 9. {0, 1, 2, 4, 6, 8, 9}
```

As you can see, the Vec v collection contains all the 10 inserted items, in insertion order; instead, the Hashset hs collection and the BTreeSet bs collection contains only 7 items, as there is only one of the two 6s and only one of the three 8s. Moreover, the bs collection is sorted, while the hs collection is in random order. A different run can generate a different order.

Regarding performance:

```
const SIZE: i32 = 40_000;
fn ns_per_op(t1: Instant, t2: Instant) -> f64 {
    elapsed_ms(t1, t2) / SIZE as f64 * 1_000_000.
}
let mut v = Vec::<_>::new();
let mut hs = std::collections::HashSet::<_>::new();
let mut bs = std::collections::BTreeSet::<_>::new();
let t0 = Instant::now();
for i in 0..SIZE { v.push(i); }
let t1 = Instant::now();
for i in 0..SIZE { hs.insert(i); }
let t2 = Instant::now();
for i in 0..SIZE { bs.insert(i); }
let t3 = Instant::now();
for i in 0..SIZE { if ! v.contains(&i) { return; } }
```

```
let t4 = Instant::now();
v.swap(10_000, 20_000);
v.sort();
let t5 = Instant::now();
for i in 0..SIZE {
    if v.binary_search(&i).is_err() { return; }
}
let t6 = Instant::now();
for i in 0..SIZE { if ! hs.contains(&i) { return; } }
let t7 = Instant::now();
for i in 0..SIZE { if ! bs.contains(&i) { return; } }
let t8 = Instant::now();
println!("Pushes in Vec: {}", ns_per_op(t0, t1));
println!("Insertions in HashSet: {}", ns_per_op(t1, t2));
println!("Insertions in BTreeSet: {}", ns_per_op(t2, t3));
println!("Linear search in Vec: {}", ns_per_op(t3, t4));
println!("Sort of Vec: {}", ns_per_op(t4, t5));
println!("Binary search in Vec: {}", ns_per_op(t5, t6));
println!("Search in HashSet: {}", ns_per_op(t6, t7));
println!("Search in BTreeSet: {}", ns_per_op(t7, t8));
```

This could print:

```
Pushes in Vec: 6.4021
Insertions in HashSet: 139.214
Insertions in BTreeSet: 127.3047
Linear search in Vec: 17389.3111
Sort of Vec: 3.1132
Binary search in Vec: 47.7641
Search in HashSet: 36.5041
Search in BTreeSet: 56.2444
```

To insert a number at the end of a Vec, 6 nanoseconds are taken, while to insert it into a HashSet or BTreeSet it takes around 20 times as long.

To search sequentially that forty-thousand-items vector for an existing number, more than 17000 nanoseconds are taken. Then, the vector is sorted (actually it was already sorted, and so two items are swapped beforehand, to make timing more realistic). To search that sorted vector using the binary search algorithm, an item is found in less than 50 nanoseconds on average. It comes out that, if insertions are much rarer than searches, it is more efficient to sort the array after every insertion and then use binary search.

To search the HashSet for a number, about 40 nanoseconds are taken; and to search the BTreeSet for a number, about 60 nanoseconds are taken.

All this happens in a particular platform, with a particular type of item, with a particular number of items, and with a particular sequence of operations. If you change something of these, the algorithm that used to be slower can become the fastest.

The best way to optimize a data structure whose performance is critical is the following one. First declare a trait having all the operations that your data structure will offer to the rest of the application. Then you create the simplest possible implementation of such trait and use that trait and its methods in the rest of the program. Then you measure if the performance of such methods is good enough. If it is good enough, there is no need to optimize it. Otherwise, you keep changing the implementation of the trait, and you measure the performance of the application until you find a satisfying implementation.

Ordered Dictionaries and Unordered Dictionaries

In addition to the collections containing simple objects, accessible by their location, another commonly used kind of collection is the "dictionary", which is a collection accessible by a search key.

Dictionaries can be considered sets of key-value pairs, with the peculiarity that the look-up is not performed using the whole pair, but only the key. As a consequence, a dictionary cannot contain two pairs having the same key, even if their values are different.

In this case also, there are several possible algorithms, and the two main ones are provided by the Rust standard library with the names HashMap and BTreeMap. The first one, similar to HashSet, is somewhat faster but does not keep the items sorted; the second one is slower, but it keeps the items sorted by their key.

```
let arr = [(640, 'T'), (917, 'C'),
    (412, 'S'), (670, 'T'), (917, 'L')];
let mut v = Vec::<_>::new();
let mut hs = std::collections::HashMap::<_, _>::new();
let mut bs = std::collections::BTreeMap::<_, _>::new();
```

```
for &(key, value) in arr.iter() {
    v.push((key, value));
    hs.insert(key, value);
    bs.insert(key, value);
}
print!("Vec:");
for &(key, value) in v.iter() {
    print!(" {}: {},", key, value);
}
println!("\n    {:?}", v);
print!("HashMap:");
for (key, value) in hs.iter() {
    print!(" {}: {},", key, value);
}
println!("\n    {:?}", hs);
print!("BTreeMap:");
for (key, value) in bs.iter() {
    print!(" {}: {},", key, value);
}
println!("\n    {:?}", bs);
```

This could print:

```
Vec: 640: T, 917: C, 412: S, 670: T, 917: L,
    [(640, 'T'), (917, 'C'), (412, 'S'), (670, 'T'), (917, 'L')]
HashMap: 917: L, 412: S, 640: T, 670: T,
    {917: 'L', 412: 'S', 640: 'T', 670: 'T'}
BTreeMap: 412: S, 640: T, 670: T, 917: L,
    {412: 'S', 640: 'T', 670: 'T', 917: 'L'}
```

First, notice how the debugging print of such collections is similar to the print obtained by iterating over those collections and printing each key-value pair.

Then, notice that among the items contained in the array, the 'T' value appears twice, in the first and fourth pairs, and the 917 key appears twice, in the second and fifth pairs. When such items are inserted into the vector, obviously they are kept, but when they are inserted into the dictionaries, while duplicate values are allowed, duplicate keys are not allowed. Therefore, when the pair (917, 'L') is inserted, it replaces the pair (917, 'C') already contained in the dictionary.

Last, notice that in the vector the items are in insertion order, in the BTreeMap collection they are in key order, and in the HashMap collection they are in random order.

Their performance is similar to that of the corresponding HashSet and BTreeSet collections.

Collections in C++ and in Rust

Those who know the C++ standard library will find useful the following table that puts in correspondence C++ collections with Rust collections.

For some C++ collections there is no corresponding Rust collection. In such cases, the most similar collection is indicated, preceded by a tilde (~), to indicate an approximate correspondence. Such an indication should be particularly useful to those who have some C++ code to convert into Rust code.

C++	Rust
array<T>	[T]
vector<T>	Vec<T>
deque<T>	VecDeque<T>
forward_list<T>	~ LinkedList<T>
list<T>	LinkedList<T>
stack<T>	~ Vec<T>
queue<T>	~ VecDeque<T>
priority_queue<T>	BinaryHeap<T>
set<T>	BTreeSet<T>
multiset<T>	~ BTreeMap<T,u32>
map<K,V>	BTreeMap<K,V>
multimap<K,V>	~ BTreeMap<K,(V,u32)>
unordered_set<T>	HashSet<T>
unordered_multiset<T>	~ HashMap<T,u32>
unordered_map<K,V>	HashMap<K,V>
unordered_multimap<K,V>	~ HashMap<K,(V,u32)>

CHAPTER 21

Drops, Moves, and Copies

In this chapter, you will learn:

- Why deterministic and implicit destruction of objects is a big plus of Rust

- The concept of ownership of objects

- Why custom destructors may be useful, and how to create them

- The three kinds of assignment semantics: share semantics, copy semantics, and move semantics

- Why implicit share semantics is bad for software correctness

- Why move semantics may have better performance than copy semantics

- Why some types need copy semantics and others do not, and how to specify that

- Why some types need to be non-cloneable, and how to specify that

Deterministic Destruction

So far, we saw several ways to allocate objects, both in the stack and in the heap:

- Temporary expressions, allocated in the stack;

- Variables (including arrays), allocated in the stack;

- Function and closure arguments, allocated in the stack;

- Box objects, with the reference allocated in the stack, and the referenced object allocated in the heap;

- Dynamic strings and collections (including vectors), with the header allocated in the stack, and the data allocated in the heap.

© Carlo Milanesi 2018
C. Milanesi, *Beginning Rust*, https://doi.org/10.1007/978-1-4842-3468-6_21

The *actual* instant when such objects are allocated is hard to predict, because it depends on compiler optimizations. So, let's consider the *conceptual* instant of such allocations.

Conceptually, every stack allocation happens when the corresponding expression first appears in code. So:

- Temporary expressions, variables, and arrays are allocated when they appear in code;

- Function and closure arguments are allocated when the function/ closure is invoked;

- Box-es, dynamic strings, and collections headers are allocated when they appear in code.

Every heap allocation happens when there is a need for such data. So:

- Box-ed objects are allocated by the `Box::new` function;

- Dynamic strings chars are allocated when some chars are added to the string;

- Collections contents are allocated when some data is added to the collection.

All this is not different from most programming languages.

And when does deallocation of a data item happen?

Conceptually, in Rust, it happens automatically when such data item is not more accessible anymore. So:

- Temporary expressions are deallocated when the statement containing them ends (that is, at the next semicolon or when the current scope ends);

- Variables (including arrays) are deallocated when the scope containing their declaration ends;

- Function and closure arguments are deallocated when their function/closure block ends;

- Box-ed objects are deallocated when the scope containing their declaration ends;

- Chars contained in dynamic strings are deallocated when they are removed from the string, or anyway when the string is deallocated;

- Items contained in collections are deallocated when they are removed from the collection, or anyway when the collection is deallocated.

This is a concept that differentiates Rust from most programming languages. In any language that has temporary objects or stack-allocated objects, the objects of such kinds are deallocated automatically. But heap-allocated object deallocation differs for different languages.

In some languages, like Pascal, C, and C++, heap objects are usually deallocated only explicitly, by invoking functions like "free" or "delete". In other languages, like Java, JavaScript, C#, and Python, heap objects are not immediately deallocated when they are not reachable anymore, but there is a routine, run periodically, which finds unreachable heap objects and deallocates them. This mechanism is named "garbage collection" because it resembles the urban cleaning system: it periodically cleans the town, when some garbage has piled up.

So, in C++ and similar languages, heap deallocation is both *deterministic and explicit*. It is deterministic, because it happens in well-defined positions of source code; and it is explicit, because it requires that the programmer writes a specific deallocation statement. To be deterministic is good, because it has better performance and it allows the programmer to control better what is going on in the computer. But to be explicit is bad, because if deallocations are performed wrongly, nasty bugs result.

Instead, in Java and similar languages, heap deallocation is both *non-deterministic and implicit*. It is non-deterministic because it happens in unknown instants of execution; and it is implicit because it does not require specific deallocation statements. To be non-deterministic is bad, but to be implicit is good.

Differing from both techniques, in Rust, usually, heap deallocation is both *deterministic and implicit*, and this is a great advantage of Rust over the other languages.

This is possible because of the following mechanism, based on the concept of "ownership".

Ownership

Let's introduce the term **"to own"**. In computer science, for an identifier or an object A, "to own" an object B, means that A is responsible for deallocating B, and that means two things:

- *Only* A can deallocate B.

- When A becomes unreachable, A *must* deallocate B.

In Rust, there is no explicit deallocation mechanism, so this definition can be reworded as "A owns B means that B is deallocated when and only when A becomes unreachable".

```
let mut a = 3;
a = 4;
let b = vec![11, 22, 33, 44, 55];
```

In this program, the variable a owns an object initially containing the value 3, because when a gets out of its scope, and so it becomes unreachable, that object initially having value 3 is deallocated. We can also say that "a is the owner of an object, whose initial value is 3". Though, we shouldn't say that "a owns 3", because 3 is a value, not an object; only objects can be owned. In memory, there can be many objects having value 3, and a owns just one of them. In the second statement of the previous program, the value of such object is changed to 4; but its ownership hasn't changed: a still owns it.

In the last statement, b is initialized to a vector of five items. Such vector has a header and a data buffer; the header is implemented as a struct containing three members: a pointer to the data buffer, and two numbers; the data buffer contains the five items, and possibly some additional space. Here we can say that "b owns the header of a vector, and the pointer contained in the header of the vector owns the data buffer". Indeed, when b gets out of its scope, the vector header is deallocated; and when that vector header is deallocated, its contained pointer becomes unreachable; and when such vector represents a non-empty vector, also the buffer containing the vector items is deallocated.

Not every reference owns an object, though.

```
let a = 3;
{
    let a_ref = &a;
}
print!("{}, a);
```

Here, the a_ref variable owns a reference, but that reference does not own anything. Indeed, at the end of the nested block, the a_ref variable gets out of its scope, and so the reference is deallocated, but the referenced object, which is the number having value 3, shouldn't be immediately deallocated, because it must be printed at the last statement.

To ensure that every object is automatically deallocated when referenced no more, Rust has the simple rule that, in every instant of execution, every object must have exactly one "owner", no more, no less. When that owner is deallocated, the object itself is deallocated. If there were several owners, the object could be deallocated several times, and this is not allowed. If there were no owners, the object could never be deallocated, and this is a bug named "memory leak".

Destructors

We saw that object creation has two steps: allocation of the memory space needed by the object, and initialization of such space with a value. For complex objects, initialization is so complex that usually a function is used for that. Such functions are named "constructors", as they "construct" new objects.

We just saw that when an object is deallocated, something rather complex could happen. If that object refers to other objects in the heap, a cascade of deallocations could happen. So, even the "destruction" of objects may need to be performed by a function, named "destructor".

Usually destructors are part of the language or of the standard library, but sometimes you may need to perform some cleanup code when an object is deallocated, and so you need to write a destructor.

```rust
struct CommunicationChannel {
    address: String,
    port: u16,
}
impl Drop for CommunicationChannel {
    fn drop(&mut self) {
        println!("Closing port {}:{}",
            self.address, self.port);
    }
}
```

```rust
impl CommunicationChannel {
    fn create(address: &str, port: u16)
        -> CommunicationChannel
    {
        println!("Opening port {}:{}", address, port);
        CommunicationChannel {
            address: address.to_string(),
            port: port,
        }
    }
    fn send(&self, msg: &str) {
        println!("Sent to {}:{} the message '{}'",
            self.address, self.port, msg);
    }
}
let channel = CommunicationChannel::create(
    "usb4", 879);
channel.send("Message 1");
{
    let channel = CommunicationChannel::create(
        "eth1", 12000);
    channel.send("Message 2");
}
channel.send("Message 3");
```

This program will print:

```
Opening port usb4:879
Sent to usb4:879 the message 'Message 1'
Opening port eth1:12000
Sent to eth1:12000 the message 'Message 2'
Closing port eth1:12000
Sent to usb4:879 the message 'Message 3'
Closing port usb4:879
```

The second statement implements the trait Drop for the newly declared type CommunicationChannel. Such trait, defined by the language, has the peculiar property that its only method, named drop, is automatically invoked exactly when the object is deallocated, and therefore it is a "destructor". In general, to create a destructor for a type, it is enough to implement the Drop trait for such a type. As any other trait not defined in your program, you cannot implement it for types defined outside of your program.

The third statement is a block that defines two methods for our struct: the create constructor and the send operation.

At last, there is the application code. A communication channel is created, and such a creation prints the first line of output. A message is sent, and that operation prints the second line. Then there is a nested block, in which another communication channel is created, printing the third line, and a message is sent through such channel, printing fourth line.

The channel created in the nested block is associated to a variable having the same name of an existing variable, and that causes this variable to shadow the other. We could just as well use a different name for the second variable.

So far, there is nothing new. But now, the nested block ends. That causes the inner variable to be destroyed, and so its drop method is invoked, and that prints the fifth line.

Now, after the nested block has ended, the first variable is visible again. Another message is sent to it, causing to print the last-but-one line. At last, the first variable is destroyed, and that prints the last line.

In Rust, memory is already released by the language and the standard library, and therefore there is no need to invoke functions similar to the free function of C language, or the delete operator of C++ language. But other resources are not automatically released. Therefore destructors are most useful to release resources like file handles, communication handles, GUI windows, graphical resources, and synchronization primitives. If you use a library to handle such resources, that library should already contain a proper implementation of Drop for any type that handles a resource.

Another use of destructors is to understand better how memory is managed.

```
struct S ( i32 );
impl Drop for S {
    fn drop(&mut self) {
        println!("Dropped {}", self.0);
    }
}
```

```
let _a = S (1);
let _b = S (2);
let _c = S (3);
{
    let _d = S (4);
    let _e = S (5);
    let _f = S (6);
    println!("INNER");
}
println!("OUTER");
```

This will print:

```
INNER
Dropped 6
Dropped 5
Dropped 4
OUTER
Dropped 3
Dropped 2
Dropped 1
```

Notice that objects are destroyed in exactly the opposite order than their construction order, and just when they get out of their scope.

```
struct S ( i32 );
impl Drop for S {
    fn drop(&mut self) {
        println!("Dropped {}", self.0);
    }
}
let _ = S (1);
let _ = S (2);
let _ = S (3);
{
    let _ = S (4);
    let _ = S (5);
```

```
    let _ = S (6);
    println!("INNER");
}
println!("OUTER");
```

This will print:

```
Dropped 1
Dropped 2
Dropped 3
Dropped 4
Dropped 5
Dropped 6
INNER
OUTER
```

In this program, there are no variables, just variable placeholders, and so all the objects are temporary. Temporary objects are destroyed at the end of their statements, that is, when a semicolon in encountered.

This program is equivalent to the following one:

```
struct S ( i32 );
impl Drop for S {
    fn drop(&mut self) {
        println!("Dropped {}", self.0);
    }
}
S (1);
S (2);
S (3);
{
    S (4);
    S (5);
    S (6);
    println!("INNER");
}
println!("OUTER");
```

Assignment Semantics

What does the following program do?

```
let v1 = vec![11, 22, 33];
let v2 = v1;
```

Conceptually, first, the header of v1 is allocated in the stack. Then, as such vector has content, a buffer for such content is allocated in the heap, and the values are copied onto it. Then the header is initialized so that it references the newly allocated heap buffer.

Then the header of v2 is allocated in the stack. Then, there is the initialization of v2 using v1. But, how is that implemented?

In general there are at least three ways to implement such operation:

- **Share semantics**. The header of v1 is copied onto the header of v2, and nothing else happens. Subsequently, both v1 and v2 can be used, and they both refer to the same heap buffer; therefore, they refer to the same contents, not to two equal but distinct contents. This semantics is implemented by garbage-collecting languages, like Java.

- **Copy semantics**. Another heap buffer is allocated. It is as large as the heap buffer used by v1, and the contents of the preexisting buffer is copied onto the new buffer. Then the header of v2 is initialized so that it references the newly allocated buffer. Therefore, the two variables refer to two distinct buffers that initially have equal contents. This is implemented, by default, by C++.

- **Move semantics**. The header of v1 is copied onto the header of v2, and nothing else happens. Subsequently, v2 can be used, and it refers to the heap buffer that was allocated for v1, but v1 *cannot be used anymore*. This is implemented, by default, by Rust.

```
let v1 = vec![11, 22, 33];
let v2 = v1;
print!("{}", v1.len());
```

This code generates the compilation error use of moved value: `v1` at the last line. When the value of v1 is assigned to v2, the variable v1 ceases to exist. Trying to use it, even only to get its length, is disallowed by the compiler.

Let's see why Rust does not implement share semantics. First, if variables are mutable, such semantics would be somewhat confusing. With share semantics, after an item is changed through a variable, that item appears to be changed also when it is accessed through the other variable. And it wouldn't be intuitive, and possibly a source of bugs. Therefore, share semantics would be acceptable only for read-only data.

But there is a bigger problem, regarding deallocation. If share semantics was used, both v1 and v2 would own the single data buffer, and so when they are deallocated, the same heap buffer would be deallocated twice. A buffer cannot be allocated twice without causing memory corruption and consequently program malfunction. To solve this problem, the languages that use share semantics do not deallocate memory at the end of the scope of the variable using such memory, but resort to garbage collection.

Instead, both copy semantics and move semantics are correct. Indeed, the Rust rule regarding deallocation is that any object must have exactly one owner. When copy semantics is used, the original vector buffer keeps its single owner, which is the vector header referenced by v1, and the newly created vector buffer gets its single owner, which is the vector header referenced by v2. On the other hand, when move semantics is used, the single vector buffer changes owner: before the assignment, its owner is the vector header referenced by v1, and after the assignment, its owner is the vector header referenced by v2. Before the assignment, the v2 header does not exist yet, and after the assignment the v2 header does not exist anymore.

And why does Rust not implement copy semantics?

Actually, in some cases copy semantics is more appropriate, but in other cases it is move semantics to be more appropriate. Even C++, since 2011, allows both copy semantics and move semantics.

```cpp
#include <iostream>
#include <vector>
int main() {
    auto v1 = std::vector<int> { 11, 22, 33 };
    const auto v2 = v1;
    const auto v3 = move(v1);
    std::cout << v1.size() << " "
        << v2.size() << " " << v3.size();
}
```

This C++ program will print: 0 3 3. The vector v1 is first copied to the vector v2 and then moved to the vector v3. The C++ move standard function empties the vector but does not make it undefined. Therefore, at the end, v2 has a copy of the three items, v3 has just the original three items that were created for v1, and v1 is empty.

And also Rust allows both copy semantics and move semantics.

```rust
let v1 = vec![11, 22, 33];
let v2 = v1.clone();
let v3 = v1;
// ILLEGAL: print!("{} ", v1.len());
print!("{} {}", v2.len(), v3.len());
```

This will print 3 3.

This Rust program is similar to the C++ program above, but here it is forbidden to access v1, at the last-but-one line, because it is moved. While in C++ the default semantics is a copy, and it is needed to invoke the "move" standard function to make a move, in Rust the default semantics is a move, and it is needed to invoke the "clone" standard function to make a copy.

In addition, while the v1 moved vector in C++ is still accessible, but emptied, in Rust such a variable is not accessible at all anymore.

Copying vs. Moving Performance

The choice of Rust to favor move semantics is about performance. For an object that owns a heap buffer, like a vector, it is faster to *move* it than to *copy* it, because a move of the vector is just a copy of the header, while a copy of the vector requires allocating and initializing a potentially large heap buffer, which eventually will be deallocated. In general, the design choices of Rust are to allow any operation, but to use smaller syntaxes for the safest and more efficient operations.

In addition, in C++, moved objects are not meant to be used anymore, but, to keep the language backward-compatible with legacy code base, moved objects are still accessible, and there is the chance that a programmer erroneously uses such objects. In addition, to empty a moved vector has a (small) cost, and when a vector is destructed it should be checked if it is empty, and also that has a (small) cost. Rust has been designed to avoid using moved objects, and so there is no chance of erroneously using a moved vector, and the compiler can produce better code because it knows when a vector is moved.

We can measure such performance impact using the following code, which is not so simple, because otherwise the compiler optimizer would remove any work from the loop.

The following Rust program uses copy semantics.

```rust
use std::time::Instant;
fn elapsed_ms(t1: Instant, t2: Instant) -> f64 {
    let t = t2 - t1;
    t.as_secs() as f64 * 1000. + t.subsec_nanos() as f64 / 1e6
}
const N_ITER: usize = 100_000_000;
let start_time = Instant::now();
for i in 0..N_ITER {
    let v1 = vec![11, 22];
    let mut v2 = v1.clone(); // Copy semantics is used
    v2.push(i);
    if v2[1] + v2[2] == v2[0] {
        print!("Error");
    }
}
let finish_time = Instant::now();
print!("{} ns per iteration\n",
        elapsed_ms(start_time, finish_time) * 1e6 / N_ITER as f64);
```

And the following one is a C++ program equivalent to it.

```cpp
#include <iostream>
#include <vector>
#include <ctime>
int main() {
    const int n_iter = 100000000;
    auto start_time = clock();
    for (int i = 0; i < n_iter; ++i) {
        auto v1 = std::vector<int> { 11, 22 };
        auto v2 = v1; // Copy semantics is used
        v2.push_back(i);
        if (v2[1] + v2[2] == v2[0]) { std::cout << "Error"; }
    }
```

```
    auto finish_time = clock();
    std::cout << (finish_time - start_time) * 1.e9
        / CLOCKS_PER_SEC / n_iter << " ns per iteration\n";
}
```

The following Rust program uses move semantics instead. It differs from the previous Rust program only by the second line of the loop.

```
use std::time::Instant;
fn elapsed_ms(t1: Instant, t2: Instant) -> f64 {
    let t = t2 - t1;
    t.as_secs() as f64 * 1000. + t.subsec_nanos() as f64 / 1e6
}
const N_ITER: usize = 100_000_000;
let start_time = Instant::now();
for i in 0..N_ITER {
    let v1 = vec![11, 22];
    let mut v2 = v1; // Move semantics is used
    v2.push(i);
    if v2[1] + v2[2] == v2[0] {
        print!("Error");
    }
}
let finish_time = Instant::now();
print!("{} ns per iteration\n",
        elapsed_ms(start_time, finish_time) * 1e6 / N_ITER as f64);
```

And the following is a C++ program equivalent to it.

```
#include <iostream>
#include <vector>
#include <ctime>
int main() {
    const int n_iter = 100000000;
    auto start_time = clock();
    for (int i = 0; i < n_iter; ++i) {
        auto v1 = std::vector<int> { 11, 22 };
        auto v2 = move(v1); // Move semantics is used
```

```
        v2.push_back(i);
        if (v2[1] + v2[2] == v2[0]) { std::cout << "Error"; }
    }
    auto finish_time = clock();
    std::cout << (finish_time - start_time) * 1.e9
        / CLOCKS_PER_SEC / n_iter << " ns per iteration\n";
}
```

Here are the approximate times obtained in a specific computer by one pair of compilers, with optimization turned on:

	Rust	C++
Copy semantics	157	87
Move semantics	67	67

Both in Rust and in C++, move semantics is faster than copy semantics. By the way, the two languages have the same performance when move semantics is used, while C++ is much better than Rust when copy semantics is used.

If, instead of a small vector, the object to move or copy is a large vector, or a linked tree of objects, the difference between moving and copying would be much bigger.

Moving and Destroying Objects

All these concepts apply not only to vectors, but also to any object that has a reference to a heap buffer, like a String or a Box.

This a Rust program:

```
let s1 = "abcd".to_string();
let s2 = s1.clone();
let s3 = s1;
// ILLEGAL: print!("{} ", s1.len());
print!("{} {}", s2.len(), s3.len());
```

and this a similar C++ program:

```
#include <iostream>
#include <string>
int main() {
    auto s1 = std::string { "abcd" };
    const auto s2 = s1;
    const auto s3 = move(s1);
    std::cout << s1.size() << " "
        << s2.size() << " " << s3.size();
}
```

The Rust program will print 4 4, and any attempt to access s1 at the end of the program will cause a compilation error. The C++ program will print 0 4 4, because the moved string s1 has become empty.

And this Rust program:

```
let i1 = Box::new(12345i16);
let i2 = i1.clone();
let i3 = i1;
// ILLEGAL: print!("{} ", i1);
print!("{} {}", i2, i3);
```

is similar to this C++ program:

```
#include <iostream>
#include <memory>
int main() {
    auto i1 = std::unique_ptr<short> {
        new short(12345)
    };
    const auto i2 = std::unique_ptr<short> {
        new short(*i1)
    };
    const auto i3 = move(i1);
    std::cout << (bool)i1 << " " << (bool)i2 << " "
        << (bool)i3 << " " << *i2 << " " << *i3;
}
```

The Rust program will print 12345 12345, and any attempt to access i1 at the end of the program will cause a compilation error. The C++ program will print 0 1 1 12345 12345. In the last statement, first, it is checked which unique pointers are null; only i1 is null, because it was moved to i3. Then, the values referenced by i2 and i3 are printed.

Objects are not moved only when they are used to initialize a variable, but also when assigning a variable having already a value, like this:

```
let v1 = vec![false; 3];
let mut v2 = vec![false; 2];
v2 = v1;
v1;
```

and also when passing a value to a function argument, like this:

```
fn f(v2: Vec<bool>) {}
let v1 = vec![false; 3];
f(v1);
v1;
```

and also when the assigned object at the moment does not refer to an actual heap, like this:

```
let v1 = vec![false; 0];
let mut v2 = vec![false; 0];
v2 = v1;
v1;
```

Compiling any of the previous three programs, the last statement causes the use of a moved value compilation error.

In particular, in the last program, v1 is *moved* to v2, even if they are both empty, and so no heap is used. Why? Because the rule of moves is applied by the compiler, and so it must be independent of the actual content of an object at runtime.

But also compiling the following program causes an error at the last line. How come?

```
struct S {}
let s1 = S {};
let s2 = s1;
s1;
```

Here the compiler can be sure that such objects won't contain references to the heap, but still it complains about moves. Why does Rust not use copy semantics for this type that will never have references to the heap?

Here is the rationale for this. The user-defined type S now has no references to memory, but after future maintenance of the software, one reference to the heap may easily be added, as a field of S or as a field of a field of S, and so on. So, if we now implement copy semantics for S, when the program source is changed so that a `String` or a `Box` or a collection is added, directly or indirectly, to S, a lot of errors would be caused by this semantic change. So, as a rule, it's better to keep move semantics.

Need for Copy Semantics

So, we have seen that for many types of objects, including vectors, dynamic strings, boxes, and structs, move semantics is used. Yet, the following program is valid.

```
let i1 = 123;
let _i2 = i1;
let s1 = "abc";
let _s2 = s1;
let r1 = &i1;
let _r2 = r1;
print!("{} {} {}", i1, s1, r1);
```

It will print: "`123 abc 123`". How come?

Well, for primitive numbers, static strings, and references, Rust does not use move semantics. For these data types, Rust uses copy semantics.

Why? We saw previously that if an object can own one or more heap objects, its type should implement move semantics; but if it cannot own any heap memory, it can implement copy semantics just as well. Move semantics is a nuisance for primitive types, and it is improbable that they will ever be changed to own some heap objects. So, for them, copy semantics is safe, efficient, and more convenient.

So, some Rust types implement copy semantics, and others implement move semantics. In particular, numbers, Booleans, static strings, arrays, tuples, and references to any type implement copy semantics. Instead, dynamic strings, boxes, any collection (including vectors), enums, structs, and tuple-structs implement, by default, move semantics.

Cloning Objects

However, regarding the copying of objects, there is another important distinction to apply. All the types that implement copy semantics can be copied quite easily, with an assignment; but also objects that implement move semantics can be copied, using the `clone` standard function. We already saw that a `clone` function can be applied to dynamic strings, boxes, and vectors. However, for some kind of types, a `clone` function shouldn't be applicable, because no kind of copying is appropriate. Think about a file handle, a GUI window handle, or a mutex handle. If you copy one of them, and then you destroy one of the copies, the underlying resource gets released, and the other copies of the handle have an inconsistent handle.

So, regarding the ability to be copied, there are three kinds of objects:

- Objects that do not own anything, and are easy and cheap to copy.

- Objects that own some heap objects, but do not own external resources, and so can be copied, but with a significant runtime cost.

- Objects that own an external resource, like a file handle, or a GUI window handle, and so they should never be copied.

The types of the first kind of objects can implement copy semantics, and they should, because it is more convenient. Let's call them "copyable objects".

The types of the second kind of objects can implement copy semantics, but they should implement move semantics instead, to avoid the runtime cost of unneeded duplications. Moreover, they should provide a method to explicitly duplicate them. Let's call them "cloneable but non-copyable objects".

The types of the third kind of objects should implement move semantics, too, but they shouldn't provide a method to explicitly duplicate them, because they own a resource that cannot be duplicated by Rust code, and such resource should have just one owner. Let's call them "non-cloneable objects".

Of course, any object that can be automatically copied can also be explicitly copied, and so any copyable object is also a cloneable object.

To summarize, some objects are non-cloneable (like file handles), and other are cloneables (explicitly). Some cloneable objects are also (implicitly) copyable (like numbers), while others are non-copyable (like collections).

To distinguish among these three categories, the Rust standard library contains two specific traits: Copy and Clone. Any type implementing the Copy trait is copyable; any type implementing the Clone trait is cloneable.

So, the three kinds described above are characterized in this way:

- The objects, like primitive numbers, that implement both Copy and Clone, are "copyable" (and also "cloneable"). They implement copy semantics, and they can also be cloned explicitly.

- The objects, like collections, that implement Clone, but don't implement Copy, are "cloneable but non-copyable". They implement move semantics, but they can be cloned explicitly.

- The objects, like file handles, that implement neither Copy nor Clone, are "non-cloneable" (and also "non-copyable"). They implement move semantics, and they cannot be cloned.

- No object can implement Copy but not Clone. This means that no object is "copyable but not cloneable", because such object would be copied implicitly but not explicitly, and this is pointless.

Here is an example of all these cases:

```
let a1 = 123;
let b1 = a1.clone();
let c1 = b1;
print!("{} {} {}", a1, b1, c1);

let a2 = Vec::<bool>::new();
let b2 = a2.clone();
let c2 = b2;
print!(" {:?}", a2);
// ILLEGAL: print!("{:?}", b2);
print!(" {:?}", c2);

let a3 = std::fs::File::open(".").unwrap();
// ILLEGAL: let b3 = a3.clone();
let c3 = a3;
// ILLEGAL: print!("{:?}", a3);
print!(" {:?}", c3);
```

This program prints: "123 123 123 [] [] File", and then some information regarding your current directory. It can be compiled only because the three illegal statements have been commented out.

First, a1 is declared as a primitive number. Such type is copyable, and so it can be both explicitly cloned to b1 and implicitly copied to c1. So, there are three distinct objects having the same value, and we can print them all.

Then, a2 is declared as a collection, and specifically a vector of Booleans. Such type is cloneable but not copyable, and so it can be explicitly cloned to b2, but the assignment of b2 to c2 is a move, which leaves b2 as undefined, and so, after that assignment, we can print a2 and c2, but trying to compile the statement that prints b2 would generate an error with message: use of moved value: `b2`.

At last, a3 is declared as a resource handle, and specifically a file handle. Such type is not cloneable, and so trying to compile the statement that clones a3 would generate an error with message: no method named `clone` found for type `std::fs::File` in the current scope. It is allowed to assign a3 to c3, but it is a move, and so we can print some debug information of a3, but trying to compile the statement that prints a3 would generate an error with message: use of moved value: `a3`.

Making Types Cloneable or Copyable

As said before, enums, structs and tuple structs, by default, do not implement either the Copy trait or the Clone trait, and so they are non-cloneable. Though, you may implement the single Clone trait for each of them, of both the Clone trait and the Copy trait.

The following program is illegal:

```
struct S {}
let s = S {};
s.clone();
```

But is it enough to implement Clone, to make it valid.

```
struct S {}
impl Clone for S {
    fn clone(&self) -> Self { Self {} }
}
let s = S {};
s.clone();
```

Notice that to implement Clone, it is required to define the clone method, that must return a value whose type must be equal to the type of its argument. Also the value should be equal to the value of its argument, but that is not checked.

Implementing Clone does not automatically implement Copy, and so the following program is illegal:

```rust
struct S {}
impl Clone for S {
    fn clone(&self) -> Self { Self {} }
}
let s = S {};
s.clone();
let _s2 = s;
s;
```

But is it enough to implement also Copy, to make it valid.

```rust
struct S {}
impl Clone for S {
    fn clone(&self) -> Self { Self {} }
}
impl Copy for S {}
let s = S {};
s.clone();
let _s2 = s;
s;
```

Notice that an implementation of Copy can be empty; it is enough to declare that Copy is implemented, to activate the copy semantics.

The following program is illegal, though:

```rust
struct S {}
impl Copy for S {}
```

The error message explains why: "the trait bound `main::S: std::clone::Clone` is not satisfied". The Copy trait can be implemented only if the Clone trait is also implemented.

But also the following program is illegal:

```
struct S { x: Vec<i32> }
impl Copy for S {}
impl Clone for S {
    fn clone(&self) -> Self { *self }
}
```

The error message says: "the trait `Copy` may not be implemented for this type", indicating the type Vec<i32>.

The program tries to implement the Copy trait for a struct containing a vector. Rust allows you to implement the copy trait only for types that contain only copyable objects, because copying an object means to copy all its members. Here, Vec does not implement the Copy trait, and so S cannot implement it.

Instead, the following program is valid:

```
struct S { x: Vec<i32> }
impl Clone for S {
    fn clone(&self) -> Self {
        S { x: self.x.clone() }
    }
}
let mut s1 = S { x: vec![12] };
let s2 = s1.clone();
s1.x[0] += 1;
print!("{} {}", s1.x[0], s2.x[0]);
```

It will print: "13 12".

Here, the S struct is not copyable, but it is cloneable, as it implements the Clone trait. Therefore, a duplicate of s1 can be assigned to s2. After that, s1 is modified, and the print statement shows that they are different.

CHAPTER 22

Borrowing and Lifetimes

In this chapter, you will learn:

- The concepts of "borrowing" and "lifetime"

- Which are the typical programming errors regarding borrowing, that plague system software

- How Rust strict syntax can prevent such typical errors, using a borrow checker

- How inserting a block can restrict the scope of borrowing

- Why functions returning references need lifetime specifiers

- How to use lifetime specifiers for functions, and what they mean

- What is the task of the borrow checker

Ownership and Borrowing

We already saw that when you assign a variable "a" to a variable "b", there are two cases: either their type is copyable, that is, it implements the "Copy" trait (and it surely implements the "Clone" trait, too); or their type is not copyable, that is it does not implement the "Copy" trait (and it may implement the Clone trait or it may not).

In the first case, *copy semantics* is used. That means that, in that assignment, while "a" keeps the ownership of its object, a new object is created, initially equal to the object represented by "a", and "b" gets the ownership of this new object. When "a" and "b" get out of their scope, their owned objects are destroyed (aka "dropped").

Instead, in the second case, *move semantics* is used. That means that, in that assignment, "a" hands over the ownership of its object to "b", no object is created, and "a" is no longer accessible. When "b" gets out of its scope, its owned object is destroyed. When "a" gets out of its scope, nothing happens.

337

© Carlo Milanesi 2018
C. Milanesi, *Beginning Rust*, https://doi.org/10.1007/978-1-4842-3468-6_22

All this guarantees the proper management of memory, *as long as no references are used*.

But look at this valid code:

```
let n = 12;
let ref_to_n = &n;
```

After the first statement, the "n" variable owns a number.

After the second statement, the "ref_to_n" variable owns a reference, and that reference refers to the same number referenced by "n". Is this an ownership or not?

It cannot be an ownership, because that number is already owned by "n", and if it would be owned also by this reference, it would be destroyed twice. So, references like this one never own an object.

The "n" and "*ref_to_n" expressions refer to the same object, but only the "n" variable owns it. The "ref_to_n" variable can access that object, but it does not own it. Such a concept is named **"borrowing"**. We say that "ref_to_n" "borrows" the same number owned by "n". Such borrowing begins when the reference begins to refer to that object, and ends when the reference is destroyed.

Regarding mutability, there are two kinds of borrowing:

```
let mut n = 12;
let ref1_to_n = &mut n;
let ref2_to_n = &n;
```

In this program, the "ref1_to_n" variable borrows *mutably* the number owned by "n", while the "ref2_to_n" variable borrows *immutably* that object. The first one is a *mutable borrowing*, while the second one is an *immutable borrowing*. Of course you can take a mutable borrowing only from a mutable variable.

Object Lifetimes

Notice that the concept of "scope" is applied to compile-time variables, not to runtime objects. The relative concept regarding runtime objects is named **"lifetime"**. In Rust, the lifetime of an object is the sequence of instruction executions between the instruction execution that creates it and the instruction execution that destroys it. During this time interval, that object is said "to live" or "to be alive".

Of course, there is a relation between scope and lifetime, but they are not the same concept. For example:

```
let a;
a = 12;
print!("{}", a);
```

In this program, the scope of the "a" variable begins at the first line, while the lifetime of the object owned by "a" begins at the second line. In general, the scope of a variable begins when that variable is declared, and the lifetime of an object begins when that object receives a value.

Even the end of the scope of a variable does not always coincide with the point where the lifetime of its owned object ends.

```
let mut a = "Hello".to_string();
let mut b = a;
print!("{}, ", b);
a = "world".to_string();
print!("{}!", a);
b = a;
```

This will print: "Hello, world!".

At the first statement, the "a" variable is declared and initialized. Therefore, the scope of "a" begins, and the object owned by "a" is created, and so its lifetime begins.

At the second statement, the "b" variable is declared and initialized by moving the "a" variable. Therefore, the scope of "b" begins, and the scope of "a" is suspended, because it is moved, and so it is accessible no more. The object owned by "b" is not created, because it is the same object created at the previous statement.

At the third statement, "b" (and its owned object) is accessed. It would be illegal to access "a" in this statement.

At the fourth statement, the "a" variable is assigned a new value, by creating a new string. Here, "a" resumes its scope, which had not ended yet. A new object is created, and so its lifetime begins here. The "a" variable was "moved", and so it didn't own any object. So this statement is similar to an initialization.

At the fifth statement, "a" (and its owned object) is accessed.

At the sixth statement, "a" is moved again to "b", and so its scope is suspended again. Instead, "b" was active and remains active. The object owned by "b" is replaced by the object moved from "a", and so the previous object is destroyed here, and it ends its lifetime. If the type of that object implemented the "Drop" trait, its "drop" method would be invoked at this statement on the object previously owned by "b".

At the end of the program, first "b" and then "a" exit their scope. The "b" variable owned an object (containing the "world" string), and so this object is now destroyed, therefore ending its lifetime. Instead, the "a" variable was "moved", and so it didn't own anything, and so nothing else is destroyed.

Errors Regarding Borrowing

Programs written in C and C++ are plagued by errors that Rust avoids by design. One is the "use after move" error, seen in the previous chapter. Another one is exemplified by the following program:

```
let ref_to_n;
{
    let n = 12;
    ref_to_n = &n;
    print!("{} ", *ref_to_n);
}
print!("{}", *ref_to_n);
```

First, the "ref_to_n" variable is declared, but not initialized. Then, in an inner block, the "n" mutable variable is declared and initialized, and so it allocates a number in the stack, whose value is 12.

Then, the former variable is initialized with a reference to the "n" variable, and so it borrows that object.

Then, the object referred to by the "ref_to_n" variable, whose value is 12, is printed.

Then, the inner block ends, and so the inner variable "n" ends its scope, and so its object is destroyed.

Then, the object referred to by the "ref_to_n" variable is printed again. But such an object was the one owned by the "n" variable and now doesn't exist anymore! Fortunately, the Rust compiler rejects this code, emitting the error message "`n` does not live long enough" at the brace that closes the block. That message means that the "n" variable is dying, but there are still some references to the object it owns, and so it should live longer; it should live at least as long as all the borrowers of the object it owns.

By the way, the corresponding C and C++ program is this:

```c
#include <stdio.h>
int main() {
    int* ref_to_n;
    {
        int n = 12;
        ref_to_n = &n;
        printf("%d ", *ref_to_n);
    }
    printf("%d", *ref_to_n);

    return 0;
}
```

Such program is accepted by C and C++ compilers. The resulting program prints "12", and then behaves in an unpredictable way (although usually it prints another number).

Let's name "use after drop" this kind of programming errors.

But there is another kind of errors avoided by Rust, exemplified by the following program:

```rust
let mut v = vec![12];
let ref_to_first = &v[0];
v.push(13);
print!("{}", ref_to_first);
```

The corresponding program in C language is:

```c
#include <stdio.h>
#include <stdlib.h>
int main() {
    int* v = malloc(1 * sizeof (int));
    v[0] = 12;
    const int* ref_to_first = &v[0];
    v = realloc(v, 2 * sizeof (int));
    v[1] = 13;
    printf("%d", *ref_to_first);
    free(v);
}
```

and in C++ it is:

```
#include <iostream>
#include <vector>
int main() {
    std::vector<int> v { 12 };
    const int& ref_to_first = v[0];
    v.push_back(13);
    std::cout << ref_to_first;
}
```

Needless to say, the latter two programs are accepted by the respective compilers, even if their behavior is undefined. Instead, the Rust compiler rejects the first program, emitting the error message "cannot borrow `v` as mutable because it is also borrowed as immutable". Let's see what's wrong with this program.

First, the "v" mutable variable is declared and initialized with a vector object containing only the number 12.

Then, the "ref_to_first" variable is declared and initialized with a reference to the first item of "v". So, it is a reference to the object containing the number 12.

Then, another number is added to the vector, whose value is "13". But such an insertion could cause a reallocation in another place of the buffer containing the items of the vector. Even in such a case, the "ref_to_first" variable would continue to refer to the old, no more valid, memory location.

At last, the old, possibly wrong, memory location is read and its value is printed, with unpredictable results.

This error has been caused by the fact that inserting items to or removing items from a vector "invalidates" all the references to that vector. In general, this error belongs to a broader category of errors, in which a data structure is accessible through several paths, or aliases, and when the data structure is changed using one alias, it cannot be properly used by another alias.

Let's name "use after change by an alias" this kind of programming errors.

How to Prevent "Use After Drop" Errors

The technique used by Rust to prevent using an already dropped object is simple.

Just consider that the objects directly referred to by variables, following the criterion of stack allocation, are dropped in the reverse order of declaration of the variables, not in the reverse order of initialization.

```rust
struct X(char);
impl Drop for X {
    fn drop(&mut self) {
        print!("{}", self.0);
    }
}
let _a = X('a');
let _b;
let _c = X('c');
_b = X('b');
```

This program will print "cba". The three objects are constructed in the order "acb", but the three variables that own them are allocated in the order "abc", and so the deallocations and drops follow its opposite order.

To avoid using dropped objects, all the variables that need to borrow an object owned by another variable must be declared *after* that variable.

Examine this code:

```rust
let n = 12;
let mut _r;
let m = 13;
_r = &m;
_r = &n;
```

This code generates the error message: "`m` does not live long enough". This is because "_r" borrows from both "m" and "n", albeit it does not refer to both at the same time, and it is declared before "m". To have a correct program, you should remove the fourth line, or swap the second and third lines.

```rust
let n = 12;
let m = 13;
```

```
let mut _r;
_r = &m;
_r = &n;
```

This is valid, because when the objects owned by "n" and "m" are dropped, there are no more references to them.

How to Prevent "Use After Change by an Alias" Errors

The rules to avoid using an object that is changed through another variable are somewhat more complex.

First of all, it is required to consider any statement that reads an object, and does not write it, like a *temporary immutable* borrowing of that object, and any statement that changes an object, like a *temporary mutable* borrowing of that object. Such borrowings start and end within that statement.

Then, it is required to remember that, any time a reference to an object is taken and assigned to a variable, a borrowing begins; and that borrowing ends at the end of the scope of such variable.

Here is an example:

```
let a = 12;
let mut b = 13;
print!("{} ", a);
{
    let c = &a;
    let d = &mut b;
    print!("{} {} ", c, d);
}
b += 1;
print!("{}", b);
```

This will print: "12 12 13 14".

Both at the third and last lines, an immutable borrowing begins and ends. At the fifth line, an immutable borrowing begins, and at the sixth line, a mutable borrowing begins; they both end at the closed brace at the eighth line. At the ninth line, a mutable borrowing begins and ends.

Then, the rule is simply that any object, in any point of the code, cannot have at the same time a mutable borrowing and some other borrowing.

Put in other words, it can have:

- no borrowing

- or a single mutable borrowing

- or a single immutable borrowing

- or several immutable borrowings

But it cannot have:

- several mutable borrowings

- nor a single mutable borrowing and one or more immutable borrowings

Listing the Possible Cases of Multiple Borrowings

Here are all six of the allowed cases.

First case:

```
let a = 12;
let _b = &a;
let _c = &a;
```

There are two immutable borrowings, which both hold until the end.

Second case:

```
let mut a = 12;
let _b = &a;
print!("{}", a);
```

There is an immutable borrowing followed by a temporary immutable borrowing, when both immutable borrowings hold.

Third case:

```
let mut a = 12;
a = 13;
let _b = &a;
```

There is a temporary mutable borrowing followed by an immutable borrowing, when the first borrowing is already finished.

Fourth case:

```
let mut a = 12;
a = 13;
let _b = &mut a;
```

There is a temporary mutable borrowing followed by a mutable borrowing, when the first borrowing is already finished.

Fifth case:

```
let mut a = 12;
print!("{}", a);
let _b = &a;
```

There is a temporary immutable borrowing followed by an immutable borrowing, when the first borrowing is already finished.

Sixth case:

```
let mut a = 12;
print!("{}", a);
let _b = &mut a;
```

There is a temporary immutable borrowing followed by a mutable borrowing, when the first borrowing is already finished.

Here are all the six illegal cases.

First case:

```
let mut a = 12;
let _b = &mut a;
let _c = &a;
```

There is a mutable borrowing and an immutable borrowing, which both would hold until the end. The compiler emits the error message: "cannot borrow `a` as immutable because it is also borrowed as mutable".

Second case:

```
let mut a = 12;
let _b = &a;
let _c = &mut a;
```

There is an immutable borrowing and a mutable borrowing, which both would hold until the end. The compiler emits the error message: "cannot borrow `a` as mutable because it is also borrowed as immutable".

Third case:

```
let mut a = 12;
let _b = &mut a;
let _c = &mut a;
```

There are two mutable borrowings, which both would hold till the end. The compiler emits the error message: "cannot borrow `a` as mutable more than once at a time".

Fourth case:

```
let mut a = 12;
let _b = &a;
a = 13;
```

There is an immutable borrowing followed by a temporary mutable borrowing. The compiler emits the error message: "cannot assign to `a` because it is borrowed".

Fifth case:

```
let mut a = 12;
let _b = &mut a;
a = 13;
```

There is a mutable borrowing followed by a temporary mutable borrowing. The compiler emits the error message: "cannot assign to `a` because it is borrowed".

Sixth case:

```
let mut a = 12;
let _b = &mut a;
print!("{}", a);
```

There is a mutable borrowing followed by a temporary immutable borrowing. The compiler emits the error message: "cannot borrow `a` as immutable because it is also borrowed as mutable".

To put it clear, let's repeat the same rules in another way. The only operations allowed on a not-currently-borrowed object are the following ones:

1. It can be borrowed several times only immutably, and then it can be only read by the owner and by any borrower.

2. It can be mutably borrowed only once, and then it can be read or changed only through such a borrower.

Using a Block to Restrict Borrowing Scope

When a borrowing of an object ends, that object becomes available to other borrowings. We already saw that temporary borrowings last for a single statement, but any kind of borrowing can be limited using a block.

```
let mut a = 12;
{
    let b = &mut a;
    *b += 1;
}
let c = &mut a;
*c += 2;
```

This is allowed, because the borrowing that begins at the third line ends at the fifth line, and so at the seventh line "a" is available for another borrowing.

This is quite typical when invoking a function. The previous code is equivalent to the following one, in which the block has been transformed in a function definition and an invocation to it:

```
let mut a = 12;
fn f(b: &mut i32) {
    *b += 1;
}
f(&mut a);
let c = &mut a;
*c += 2;
```

When the "f" function is invoked, a mutable borrowing begins on the object owned by "a". But when the function ends, for whatever reason, such borrowing ends, and so that object can be borrowed by "c", or by another function invocation.

These rules were adopted by Rust to ensure automatic deterministic memory deallocation, and to avoid invalid references; though, curiously, these rules were already well-known in computer science for other reasons. "Allow only one writer or several readers" is the rule to avoid the so-called "data races" in concurrent programming. So, this rule allows also Rust to have data-race-free concurrent programming.

In addition, avoiding data races has a good impact also on the performance of single-threaded programs, because it eases CPU cache coherence.

The Need of Lifetime Specifiers for Returned References

Now look at this code:

```
let v1 = vec![11u8, 22];
let result;
{
    let v2 = vec![33u8];
    result = {
        let _x1: &Vec<u8> = &v1;
        let _x2: &Vec<u8> = &v2;
        _x1
    }
}
print!("{:?}", *result);
```

It will print: "[11, 22]".

There are two vectors, owned by the variables "v1" and "v2". Then, these vectors are borrowed by two references, owned by the variables "_x1" and "_x2". So, after the seventh line, "_x1" is borrowing the vector owned by "v1", and "_x2" is borrowing the vector owned by "v2". This is allowed, because "_x1" is declared after "v1", and "_x2" is declared after "v2", and so these references live less than the objects they borrow.

At the eighth line, there is the simple expression "_x1". As it is the last expression of a block, the value of such expression becomes the value of the block itself, and so such value is used to initialize the "result" variable. Such value is a reference to the vector owned by "v1", and so also the "result" variable borrows that vector. Also this is allowed, because "result" is declared after "v1", and so it can borrow the object owned by "v1".

Now, make a tiny change: replace "1" with "2" in the eighth line.

```
let v1 = vec![11u8, 22];
let result;
{
    let v2 = vec![33u8];
    result = {
        let _x1: &Vec<u8> = &v1;
        let _x2: &Vec<u8> = &v2;
        _x2
    }
}
print!("{:?}", *result);
```

This will generate the compilation error: "`v2` does not live long enough". This happens because now "result" gets its value from the "_x2" expression, and as "_x2" borrows the vector owned by "v2", also "result" borrows that vector. But "result" is declared before "v2", and so it cannot borrow its object.

All this reasoning is just a review of what we have already seen about borrowing, but it shows how borrowing can get complicated in only a few lines. By the way, the portion of the Rust compiler dedicated to such reasoning is named **"borrow checker"**. We just saw that the borrow checker has hard work to do.

Now, let's try to transform the two previous programs, by encapsulating in a function the code in the innermost block. The first program becomes:

```
let v1 = vec![11u8, 22];
let result;
{
    let v2 = vec![33u8];
    fn func(_x1: &Vec<u8>, _x2: &Vec<u8>) -> &Vec<u8> {
        _x1
    }
```

```
    result = func(&v1, &v2);
}
print!("{:?}", *result);
```

And the second program becomes:

```
let v1 = vec![11u8, 22];
let result;
{
    let v2 = vec![33u8];
    fn func(_x1: &Vec<u8>, _x2: &Vec<u8>) -> &Vec<u8> {
        _x2
    }
    result = func(&v1, &v2);
}
print!("{:?}", *result);
```

The only difference between them is the body of the "func" function.

According to our rules so far, the first program should be valid, and the second one illegal. But both versions of the "func" function are valid *per se*. It's just the borrow checker that would find them incompatible with their specific usage.

As we already saw about generic function parameter bounds using traits, it is a bad thing to consider valid or invalid a function invocation according to the *contents of the body* of such a function. The main reason is that an error message would be understandable only by those who know the code inside the body of the function. One other reason is that, if the body of any invoked function can make valid or invalid the code where the function is invoked, to be sure that the "main" function is valid, the borrow checker should analyze all the functions of the program. Such a whole-program analysis would be overwhelmingly complex.

So, similarly to generic functions, also functions returning a reference must isolate the borrow-checking at the function signature threshold. There is the need to borrow-check any function considering only its signature, its body, and the signatures of any invoked functions, without considering the bodies of the invoked functions.

Therefore, both previous programs emit the compilation error: "missing lifetime specifier". A **"lifetime specifier"** is a decoration of a function signature that allows the borrow checker to check separately the body of that function, and any invocation of that function.

Usage and Meaning of Lifetime Specifiers

To talk about function invocations and lifetimes, here is a simple example function.

```
fn func(v1: Vec<u32>, v2: &Vec<bool>) {
    let s = "Hello".to_string();
}
```

Inside any Rust function, you can refer only to:

1. objects owned by function arguments (like the vector owned by "v1");

2. objects owned by local variables (like the dynamic string owned by "s");

3. temporary objects (like the dynamic string expression "Hello".to_string());

4. static objects (like the string literal "Hello");

5. objects that are borrowed by function arguments, and that are owned by some variable that preexists the current function invocation (like the vector borrowed by "v2").

When a function returns a reference, such a reference cannot refer to an object owned by an argument of that function (case 1), or owned by a local variable of that function (case 2), or a temporary object (case 3), because when the function returns, every local variable, every function argument, and every temporary object is destroyed. So, such a reference would be dangling.

Instead, a reference returned by a function can refer either to a static object (case 4), or to an object borrowed by a function argument (case 5).

Here is an example of the first one of these two last cases (although this code is not really allowed by Rust):

```
fn func() -> &str {
    "Hello"
}
```

And here is an example of the other case:

```
fn func(v: &Vec<u8>) -> &u8 {
    &v[3]
}
```

So, the borrow checker is interested only in the references contained in the return value, and such references can be of two kinds: referring to static objects, or borrowing one object received as an argument. To accomplish its job without analyzing the body of the function, the borrow checker needs to know which returned references refer to static objects, and which borrows one object received as argument; and in the second case, if there are several objects received as an argument, which of them is borrowed by any non-static returned reference.

Let's see a function signature, without lifetime specifiers, and therefore illegal:

```
trait Tr {
    fn f(flag: bool, b: &i32, c: (char, &i32)) -> (&i32, f64, &i32);
}
```

This function signature has two references among its arguments, and also two references inside its return value type. Each of the last two references could refer to a static object, or it could borrow the object already borrowed by the "b" argument, or it could borrow the object already borrowed by the second field of the "c" argument.

Here is the syntax to specify a possible case:

```
trait Tr {
    fn f<'a>(flag: bool, b: &'a i32, c: (char, &'a i32))
        -> (&'a i32, f64, &'static i32);
}
```

Just after the name of the function, a parameter list has been added, like the one used for generic functions. But instead of a type parameter, there is a lifetime specifier.

The "<'a>" clause is just a declaration. It means: <<In this function signature, a lifetime specifier is used; its name is "a">>. The name "a" is arbitrary. It simply means that in all the occurrences it appears, such occurrences *match*. It is similar to the type parameters of generic functions, so there is the need to distinguish lifetime specifiers from type parameters. The prefixed single quote makes such a distinction. In addition, while by convention type parameters begin with an uppercase letter, lifetime specifiers are single lowercase letters, like "a", "b", or "c".

Then, this signature contains three other occurrences of the "'a" lifetime specifier, in the type of the "b" argument, in the second field of the type of the "c" argument, and in the first field of the return value type. Instead, the third field of the return value type is annotated by the "'static" lifetime specifier.

The use of such "a" lifetime specifier means: "the first field of the return value borrows the same object already borrowed by the b argument and by the second field of the c argument, and so it must live less than such object".

Instead the use of the "static" lifetime specifier means: "the third field of the return value refers to a static object, and so it can live any time, even as long as the whole process".

Of course this was just one possible lifetime annotation. Here is another one:

```
trait Tr {
    fn f<'a>(flag: bool, b: &'a i32, c: (char, &i32))
        -> (&'static i32, f64, &'a i32);
}
```

In this case, the first field of the return value has a static lifetime, meaning that it is not constrained to live less than some other object. Instead, the third field has the same lifetime specifier than the "b" argument, meaning that it should live less than it, as it borrows the same object. The reference in the type of the "c" argument is not annotated, as the object it refers is not borrowed by any reference in the return value.

Here is still another possible lifetime annotation:

```
trait Tr {
    fn f<'a, 'b, T1, T2>(flag: bool, b: &'a T1, c: (char, &'b i32))
        -> (&'b i32, f64, &'a T2);
}
```

This generic function has two lifetime parameters and also two type parameters. The lifetime parameter "a" specifies that the third field of the return value borrows the object already borrowed by the "b" argument, while the lifetime parameter "b" specifies that the first field of the return value borrows the object already borrowed by the second field of the "c" argument. Moreover, the function has the two type parameters "T1" and "T2" used as usual, here without trait bounds.

Checking the Validity of Lifetime Specifiers

We said that the borrow checker, when compiling any function, has two jobs:

- Check that the signature of that function is valid, by itself and with respect to its body.

- Check that the body of that function is valid, taking into account the signatures of any function invoked in the body.

In this section, we'll see the first one of such jobs.

If in the function return value there are no references, the borrow checker has nothing to check.

Otherwise, for every reference contained in the return value type, it must check that it has a proper lifetime specifier.

Such a specifier can be "'static". In such a case, such a reference must refer to a static object.

```
static FOUR: u8 = 4;
fn f() -> (bool, &'static u8, &'static str, &'static f64) {
    (true, &FOUR, "Hello", &3.14)
}
print!("{} {} {} {}",
    f().0, *f().1, f().2, *f().3);
```

It will print: "true 4 Hello 3.14". This is valid because all the three references returned are actually static objects.

Instead, this program

```
fn f(n: &u8) -> &'static u8 {
    n
}
print!("{}", *f(&12));
```

will generate the compilation error: "lifetime of reference outlives lifetime of borrowed content...". This is illegal because the returned value is not a reference to a static object; it is actually the same value received as parameter, and so such a return value borrows the same object as the one referenced by the function argument.

The other lifetime specifier allowed is one defined in the parameter list, just after the name of the function.

```
fn f<'a, 'b>(x: &'a i32, y: &'b i32) -> (&'b i32, bool, &'a i32) {
    (y, true, x)
}
let i = 12;
let j = 13;
let r = f(&i, &j);
print!("{} {} {}", *r.0, r.1, *r.2);
```

It will print: "13 true 12". This is valid because the reference returned as the first field of the tuple is the value of the "y" expression, and the y argument has the same lifetime specifier of the first field of the return value; it is "b" for both of them. And the same correspondence holds for the third field of the return value and the "x" argument; they both have an "a" lifetime specification.

Instead, this program

```
fn f<'a, 'b>(x: &'a i32, y: &'b i32) -> (&'b i32, bool, &'a i32) {
    (x, true, y)
}
let i = 12;
let j = 13;
let r = f(&i, &j);
print!("{} {} {}", *r.0, r.1, *r.2);
```

will generate two compilation errors, both with the error message: "lifetime mismatch". Actually both the first and the third fields of the return value have a lifetime specified in the argument list that is different from the one specified in the return value type.

Notice that it is possible to use one lifetime specifier for several return values fields:

```
fn f<'a>(x: &'a i32, y: &'a i32) -> (&'a i32, bool, &'a i32) {
    (x, true, y)
}
let i = 12;
let j = 13;
let r = f(&i, &j);
print!("{} {} {}", *r.0, r.1, *r.2);
```

Here, the "b" lifetime specifier has been replaced by "a". However, this solution has a different meaning than the previous one.

In the previous solution, the two references contained in the argument list had independent lifetimes; instead, in this last solution, they share the same lifetime.

The job of the borrow checker is not always so easy. Let's consider a more complex function body:

```
fn f<'a>(n: i32, x: &'a Vec<u8>, y: &Vec<u8>) -> &'a u8 {
    if n == 0 { return &x[0]; }
    if n < 0 { &x[1] } else { &x[2] }
}
```

This function is valid. In the body there are three possible expressions that return the value of the function, and all of them borrow the same object borrowed by the "x" argument. Such an argument has the same lifetime of the return value, and so the borrow checker is satisfied.

Instead, in this function,

```
fn f<'a>(n: i32, x: &'a Vec<u8>, y: &Vec<u8>) -> &'a u8 {
    if n == 0 { return &x[0]; }
    if n < 0 { &x[1] } else { &y[2] }
}
```

one of the possible return values, the value of the expression "&y[2]", borrows the object borrowed by "y", and such an argument has no lifetime specifier, and so this code is illegal.

Even this code is illegal:

```
fn f<'a>(x: &'a Vec<u8>, y: &Vec<u8>) -> &'a u8 {
    if true { &x[0] } else { &y[0] }
}
```

When performing data-flow analysis, the compiler could detect that "y" is never borrowed by the return value of this function; but the borrow checker insists that "&y[0]" is a possible return value, and so it spots this code as invalid.

Using the Lifetime Specifiers of Invoked Functions

As we said at the beginning of the previous section, one of the two jobs of the borrow checker is to check, when compiling a function, that the body of that function is valid, taking into account the signatures of any function invoked in the body.

As an example, get back to the two last programs of the section "The Need of Lifetime Specifiers for Returned References". We said that, according to our rules of borrowing, the first program should be valid, and the second one illegal; though, we got the "missing lifetime specifier" for both programs. The following ones are those two programs, with the addition of the appropriate lifetime specifiers.

This is the first one:

```
let v1 = vec![11u8, 22];
let result;
{
    let v2 = vec![33u8];
    fn func<'a>(_x1: &'a Vec<u8>, _x2: &Vec<u8>) -> &'a Vec<u8> {
        _x1
    }
    result = func(&v1, &v2);
}
print!("{:?}", *result);
```

And this is the second one:

```
let v1 = vec![11u8, 22];
let result;
{
    let v2 = vec![33u8];
    fn func<'a>(_x1: &Vec<u8>, _x2: &'a Vec<u8>) -> &'a Vec<u8> {
        _x2
    }
    result = func(&v1, &v2);
}
print!("{:?}", *result);
```

The first program is valid, and it will print "[11, 22]", while for the second program the compiler will print "`v2` does not live long enough". Both have exactly the same behavior of the original programs, which didn't use functions.

The reason why the two "func" functions have been written in these ways has been explained in the previous section.

Now let's see how the "main" function in the first program works. When "func" is invoked, the live variables are "v1", "result", and "v2", declared in that order, with "v1" and "v2" already initialized. The signature of "func" says that the result value has the same lifetime specifier of the first argument, and that means that the value assigned to "result" must live no longer than "v1". And this holds actually, because "result" has been declared after "v1", and so it will be destroyed before it.

And finally, let's see why the "main" function in the second program is illegal. Here, the signature of "func" says that the result value has the same lifetime specifier of the second argument, and that means that the value assigned to "result" must live no longer than "v2". But this doesn't hold actually, because "result" has been declared before "v2", and so it will be destroyed after it.

And now let's explain why, in the last example of the previous section, using only one lifetime specifier is not as good as using two lifetime specifiers for the "f" function.

This program is valid:

```
fn f<'a, 'b>(x: &'a i32, y: &'b i32) -> (&'a i32, bool, &'b i32) {
    (x, true, y)
}
let i1 = 12;
let i2;
let j1 = 13;
let j2;
let r = f(&i1, &j1);
i2 = r.0;
j2 = r.2;
print!("{} {} {}", *i2, r.1, *j2);
```

It will print "12 true 13".

Instead, this program, in which the "b" lifetime parameter in the first line has been replaced by "a", is illegal:

```
fn f<'a>(x: &'a i32, y: &'a i32) -> (&'a i32, bool, &'a i32) {
    (x, true, y)
}
let i1 = 12;
let i2;
let j1 = 13;
let j2;
let r = f(&i1, &j1);
i2 = r.0;
j2 = r.2;
print!("{} {} {}", *i2, r.1, *j2);
```

It generates the compilation error: "`j1` does not live long enough".

In both versions, the f function receives references to the numbers "i1" and "j1", the returned tuple is stored first in the "r" variable and then its first and third values are used to initialize the "i2" and "j2" variables, respectively.

In the first version of the program, the first argument and the first field of return value have the same lifetime specifier, and that causes that "i2" must live less than "i1". Similarly, "j2" must live less than "j1". Actually, the order of the declaration of such variables satisfies such requirements.

In the second version of the program there is just one lifetime specifier, according to which both "i2" and "j2" must live less than "i1" and "j1". Actually, "i2" is declared before "j1" and does not satisfy such requirements.

CHAPTER 23

More About Lifetimes

In this chapter, you will learn:

- How to avoid having to write lifetime specifiers for simple free functions and methods, as they are inferred
- Why lifetime specifiers are needed also for structs, tuple-structs, and enums containing references
- How to write lifetime specifiers for structs, tuple-structs, and enums
- Why structs containing references to generic parameters need lifetime bounds

Lifetime Elision

In the previous chapter, we saw that every function signature must specify, for each returned reference, whether that reference has a static lifetime or otherwise to which function arguments its lifetime is associated.

This required annotation may be a nuisance and sometimes can be avoided.

```
trait Tr {
    fn f(x: &u8) -> &u8;
}
```

This code is allowed. The return value is a reference with an unspecified lifetime, but it is not static, and so the implicit lifetime specifier must be the same of one of the arguments. But there is only one function argument, and so its lifetime specifier would

© Carlo Milanesi 2018
C. Milanesi, *Beginning Rust*, https://doi.org/10.1007/978-1-4842-3468-6_23

be necessarily equal to that of such argument. In other words, the previous declaration of f is equivalent to the following one:

```
trait Tr {
    fn f<'a>(x: &'a u8) -> &'a u8;
}
```

Even the following declaration is valid:

```
trait Tr {
    fn f(b: bool, x: (u32, &u8)) -> &u8;
}
```

This is because in the arguments there is just one reference, and so it must be the one whose referred object is borrowed by the return value.

Even the following code is valid:

```
trait Tr {
    fn f(x: &u8) -> (&u8, &f64, bool, &Vec<String>);
}
```

In this case there are several references in the return value, but still only one reference in the arguments.

You can also omit the lifetime specifier for some returned references only, and specify it for others:

```
trait Tr {
    fn f<'a>(x: &'a u8) -> (&u8, &'a f64, bool, &'static Vec<String>);
}
```

Here the return value contains three references: the first has unspecified lifetime, the second has "a" lifetime, and the third (that is the fourth field of the tuple), has "static" lifetime. However, there is still only one reference in the arguments, and so the first returned reference has an implied "a" lifetime.

Such an allowed omission of the lifetime specifier is named **"lifetime elision"**. To simplify the syntax, the lifetime specifier can be *elided* when there is only one possible non-static value, and that happens when among the function arguments there is exactly one reference.

Lifetime Elision with Object-Oriented Programming

Consider this:

```
trait Tr {
    fn f(&self, y: &u8) -> (&u8, &f64, bool, &Vec<String>);
}
```

Here, the "f" function has two references in its arguments, and so the previous rule does not apply. However, when a method returns some references, in most cases such references borrow the current object, which is referred to by "&self". So, to simplify the syntax, the previous code is considered equivalent to the following one:

```
trait Tr {
    fn f<'a>(&'a self, y: &u8) -> (&'a u8, &'a f64, bool, &'a Vec<String>);
}
```

Yet, you can override such behavior for selected references. In case, say, you meant that the second returned reference had a lifetime associated to the "y" argument, you had to write:

```
trait Tr {
    fn f<'a>(&self, y: &'a u8) -> (&u8, &'a f64, bool, &Vec<String>);
}
```

Here, the object referred to by the second field of the returned tuple must live no longer than the object referred to by "y", while the objects referred to by the first and fourth fields must live no longer than the object referred to by "self".

Of course, the same rule applies also for a "&mut self" argument.

The Need of Lifetime Specifiers for Structs

In the previous chapter, we saw that this is valid:

```
let x: i32 = 12;
let _y: &i32 = &x;
```

because, although "_y" holds a reference to "x", it lives less than "x".

Instead, this is illegal:

```rust
let _y: &i32;
let x: i32 = 12;
_y = &x;
```

because "_y" holds a reference to "x", but it lives longer than "x".

We also saw that function signatures have to be suitably annotated to perform the lifetime check of borrowings considering only one function body at a time.

A similar issue occurs when a struct contains some references.

This code appears to be legal (but it isn't):

```rust
struct S {
    _b: bool,
    _ri: &i32,
}
let x: i32 = 12;
let _y: S = S { _b: true, _ri: &x };
```

while this one is clearly illegal:

```rust
struct S {
    _b: bool,
    _ri: &i32,
}
let _y: S;
let x: i32 = 12;
_y = S { _b: true, _ri: &x };
```

The latter code is illegal because "_y", through the "_ri" field of "S", holds a reference to "x", but it lives longer than "x".

This case was quite simple, but a real-world program (already containing the "main" function) could be:

```rust
// In some library code:
struct S {
    _b: bool,
    _ri: &i32,
}
```

```
fn create_s(ri: &i32) -> S {
    S { _b: true, _ri: ri }
}

// In application code:
fn main() {
    let _y: S;
    let x: i32 = 12;
    _y = create_s(&x);
}
```

This application code is invalid, because, by invoking "create_s", a reference to "x" gets stored inside the "_y" object, and "_y" lives longer than "x".

But how can the application programmer know that the "create_s" function stores into the returned object the reference it gets as an argument, without watching the function body? Let's see the following valid program, which has the same application code of the previous program:

```
// In some library code:
struct S {
    _b: bool,
    _ri: &'static i32,
}
fn create_s(ri: &i32) -> S {
    static ZERO: i32 = 0;
    static ONE: i32 = 1;
    S {
        _b: true,
        _ri: if *ri > 0 { &ONE } else { &ZERO },
    }
}

// In application code:
fn main() {
    let _y: S;
    let x: i32 = 12;
    _y = create_s(&x);
}
```

In this code, the "`create_s`" function uses the "`ri`" argument just to decide how to initialize the "`_ri`" field of the structure to create. The value of such an argument is not stored in the structure. In any case, the "`_ri`" field will surely contain a reference to a static value, which can be "`ZERO`" or "`ONE`", which will never be destroyed.

This "`create_s`" function has the same signature as that of the previous example; but the previous example was invalid, as the argument was stored in a field of the struct, while this example is valid, as the argument is discarded after having been used.

So, without lifetime specifiers, the application programmer would be forced to read the body of the "`create_s`" library function to know if that function stores the reference it gets as an argument into the returned object or not. And this is bad.

For the application programmer (and to the compiler) to avoid the need to analyze the body of the "`create_s`" function to discover if the lifetimes of the objects used in the "`main`" function are correct, there is a need for further lifetime annotations.

So, even structs, similarly to functions, must explicitly specify the lifetimes of every reference contained in their fields.

This explains why even the former, apparently valid snippet, in fact generates the "`missing lifetime specifier`" compilation error.

Possible Lifetime Specifiers for Structs

Actually, for the lifetime of a reference field of a struct, the Rust compiler allows only two possibilities:

- Such a field is allowed to refer only to static objects.

- Such a field is allowed to refer to static objects or to objects that, albeit non-static, preexist the whole struct object, and live longer than it.

The first case is just the one considered by the last example program. In it there was the line:

```
struct S { _b: bool, _ri: &'static i32 }
```

Such a struct actually contains a reference, but it is a `static` reference that cannot be assigned the value of any borrowed reference. So there is never a lifetime issue in such case, as long as only static references are assigned to the "`_ri`" field.

Instead, applying the second case, the following valid program is obtained:

```
// In some library code:
struct S<'a> { _b: bool, _ri: &'a i32 }
fn create_s<'b>(ri: &'b i32) -> S<'b> {
    S { _b: true, _ri: ri }
}

// In application code:
fn main() {
    let x: i32 = 12;
    let _y: S;
    _y = create_s(&x);
}
```

Here the "x" variable is borrowed in a more persistent way by the "create_s" function. Indeed, it is stored in the "_ri" field of the returned struct-object; and such object is used to initialize the "_y" variable in the "main" function. Therefore, the "_y" variable must live less than the "x" variable, and it does so. If the declaration of "_y" was moved before the declaration of "x", the usual "`x` does not live long enough" error would appear.

To know that "_x" could be stored inside the struct, it is not required to examine the body of the "create_s" function nor the field list of the "S" struct; it is enough to examine the signature of the "create_s" function and the signature of "S", that is, the portion of its declaration before the open brace.

By examining the signature of the "create_s" function, it appears that it gets a reference as argument, it returns a value of "S" type, and such argument and return value have the same lifetime specifier, "b". That means that such a returned struct must live less than the borrowed "i32" object.

By examining the signature of the "S" struct, it appears that it is parameterized by a lifetime specifier, and that means that some of its fields are non-static references.

So, we found that the "create_s" function gets a reference as an argument and returns an object parameterized by the same lifetime specifier. And this implies that such an object could borrow the object referenced by the argument, by storing into itself that object.

The compiler must separately check the consistency of the struct declaration. The clause "struct S<'a>" means that "S" borrows some objects, and the clause "_ri: &'a i32" inside the struct body means that the "_ri" field is a reference that borrows an object.

Therefore, each reference field in a struct can have only two legal syntaxes: "field: &'static type" or "field: &'lifetime type", where "lifetime" is also a parameter of the struct itself. If there are no reference fields or only static reference fields, the struct can have no lifetime parameter.

So, there are several possible syntax errors caught by the compiler.

```
struct _S1 { _f: &i32 }
struct _S2<'a> { _f: &i32 }
struct _S3 { _f: &'a i32 }
struct _S4<'a> { _f: &'static i32 }
struct _S5 { _f: &'static i32 }
struct _S6<'a> { _f: &'a i32 }
```

The first four statements are illegal. The declarations of "_S1" and "_S2" are illegal because the "_f" field is a reference field with no lifetime specifier. The declaration of "_S3" is illegal because the "'a" lifetime specifier is not declared as a parameter of "S". And the declaration of "_S4" is illegal because the parameter "'a" is never used inside the body of the struct.

Instead, the last two struct declarations are valid. "_S5" contains a reference to static objects, while "_S6" contains a reference to an object that anyway must live longer than the struct itself.

Other Uses of Lifetime Specifiers

We saw that when defining a struct type containing references, lifetime specifiers are required. But also tuple-structs and enums are types that may contain references, and so also for them lifetime specifiers are required for any contained reference.

```
struct TS<'a>(&'a u8);
enum E<'a, 'b> {
    _A(&'a u8),
    _B,
    _C(bool, &'b f64, char),
    _D(&'static str),
}
```

```
let byte = 34;
let _ts = TS(&byte);
let _e = E::_A(&byte);
```

This code is valid, but if any lifetime specifier is removed, the usual "missing lifetime specifier" error is generated.

By the way, notice the definition of the "E::_D" field. That is a reference to a static string slice. But we saw such things since the beginning of this book; they are the *string literals*.

To make things simpler, we never mixed lifetime specifiers with mutable references. Actually, it is allowed, albeit quite unusual:

```
fn f<'a>(b: &'a mut u8) -> &'a u8 {
    *b += 1;
    b
}
let mut byte = 12u8;
let byte_ref = f(&mut byte);
print!("{}", *byte_ref);
```

This will print: "13". A reference to the byte is passed to "f", which increments it and then returns back a reference to it. It is unusual because when a mutable argument is passed to a function, usually there is no need to return a reference that borrows it.

We already saw in the previous chapter that a function can be parameterized both by a lifetime specifier and by a type parameter, and they can be used for the same function argument. So this is valid:

```
fn f<'a, T>(b: &'a T) -> &'a T { b }
let pi = 3.14;
let pi_ref = f(&pi);
print!("{}", *pi_ref);
```

It will print: "3.14".

Yet, this is illegal:

```
struct S<'a, T> { b: &'a T }
```

The compiler emits "the parameter type `T` may not live long enough". The reason for this is that the generic type T could be concretized by a type containing a reference, and such a reference could cause lifetime errors. To prevent them, the compiler forbids such syntax. Actually there are two cases:

- the type represented by "T" will not contain references, or it will contain only references to static objects;

- the type represented by "T" could contain references to non-static objects, whose lifetime must be specified;

The first case is specified in this way:

```
struct S<'a, T: 'static> { b: &'a T }
let s = S { b: &true };
print!("{}", *s.b);
```

It will print: "true".

The second case is specified in this way:

```
struct S<'a, T: 'a> { b: &'a T }
let s1 = S { b: &true };
let s2 = S { b: &s1 };
print!("{} {}", *s1.b, *s2.b.b);
```

It will print: "true true".

In the first line, the "T" type parameter is bounded to the "a" lifetime specifier, meaning that such type, whatever it will be, could contain a reference that borrows the same object already annotated by such lifetime specifier, that is, the whole struct-object itself.

In the second line, the "S" struct is instantiated specifying implicitly "bool" as its "T" type parameter. Actually, this type does not contain any references, and so for this line also a static bounding would have been enough, as shown by the previous example program.

But in the third line, the "S" struct is instantiated specifying implicitly "S<bool>" as its "T" type parameter. Actually, this type does contain a non-static reference, and so for this line a static bounding wouldn't have been enough.

Index

A

Arithmetic operation
    floating-point arithmetic, 11–12
    integer numbers, 9–11
Arrays, 97
    copying, 59–60
    creation, 48
    elements, 48
    empty arrays and vectors, 57–58
    executable program, 49
    expressions, 48
    multidimensional, 52–53
    mutable, 50–51
    single variable, 47
    specified size, 51–52
Assignment arithmetic operators, 31
Assignments, 28–29
Assignment Semantics, 322–324

B

Bare-metal systems, 136
Base-ten notation, 62
Binary heaps, 304, 306
Binary search algorithm, 309
Boolean values, 25–27
Borrowing
    block to restrict, 348–349
    errors, 340–342
    listing, 345–348
    object lifetimes, 338–339
    and ownership, 337–338
    "use after change by an alias"
        errors, 344–345
    "use after drop" errors, 343–344
BTreeMap, 309

C

Changable strings
    concatenating strings, 180–182
    creating, 179–180
    dynamic strings, 176
    implementation, 177–179
    static strings, 173–175
Class methods, 277
Clone trait, 333–335
Cloning objects, 331–333
Closures, 168
    cmp function, 169
    desc function, 168
    examples, 170–171
    use directive, 169
Command-line arguments, 223–224
Command-line script, 7
Comments, 8
Compiler, 2
Conditioned loops (while), 38–39
Constant complexity, 299
Constructors, 282
Copy trait, 333–335

Get the eBook for only $5!

Why limit yourself?

With most of our titles available in both PDF and ePUB format, you can access your content wherever and however you wish—on your PC, phone, tablet, or reader.

Since you've purchased this print book, we are happy to offer you the eBook for just $5.

To learn more, go to http://www.apress.com/companion or contact support@apress.com.

Apress®

Lightning Source UK Ltd.
Milton Keynes UK
UKHW030127051021
391659UK00005B/351

9 781484 234679